# BASIC INTERESTS

# BASIC INTERESTS

THE IMPORTANCE OF GROUPS IN
POLITICS AND IN POLITICAL SCIENCE

*Frank R. Baumgartner*

*and*

*Beth L. Leech*

PRINCETON UNIVERSITY PRESS    PRINCETON, NEW JERSEY

*Library of Congress Cataloging-in-Publication Data*
Baumgartner, Frank R., 1958–
Basic interests : the importance of groups in politics
and in political science / Frank R. Baumgartner and Beth L. Leech.
p.   cm.
Includes bibliographical references (p.   ) and index.
ISBN 0-691-05914-4 (CL : alk. paper). — ISBN 0-691-05915-2 (PB : alk. paper)
1. Pressure groups—United States.   2. Lobbying—United States.
I. Leech, Beth L., 1961–   .  II. Title.
JK1118.B29   1998
322.4—dc21      9742952

This book has been composed in Caledonia

http://pup.princeton.edu

Printed in the United States of America

1   3   5   7   9   10   8   6   4   2

(Pbk.)
1   3   5   7   9   10   8   6   4   2

In Memory of Jack L. Walker, Jr.

# Contents

# *Illustrations*

## TABLES

## FIGURE

_____ *Preface* _____

THE IDEAS presented in this book grew out of the influence of Jack Walker. Jack viewed the importance of interest groups broadly, feeling that they were central to many elements of political representation, social mobilization, and the emergence of issues onto the nation's political agenda. Jack had an integrating mind. He was more interested in demonstrating the links and commonalities among different elements of the political system than in illustrating the peculiarities of any given political institution. He saw the activities of organized interests as among the fundamental means by which the most basic elements of the political process unfolded. Accordingly, these activities had implications in many areas of political science. Jack's work, dealing with agenda-setting, normative theory, group mobilization, and lobbying, and even his earlier work on race relations and the diffusion of innovations, was linked by a common intellectual concern for the processes of social mobilization and political change.

Many people in the profession have been influenced by various parts of Jack's work, but few more so than his colleagues, students, and collaborators. Frank Baumgartner was among Jack's last students, working closely with him on the research stemming from his two large surveys of interest groups in Washington in the 1980s. He was one of a group that worked to bring Jack's manuscript to publication in 1991. This book stems in many ways from that earlier experience. Colin Day and Malcolm Litchfield first suggested that Baumgartner write an "extended essay" about the state of the field as an outgrowth of some of the ideas developed in Jack's posthumously published book. Eventually that idea was too interesting to pass up. Amid years of rumination, lots of reading, and work on a few other research projects, Baumgartner found an excellent collaborator, Beth Leech, and this is the book that has resulted. We both would like to express our appreciation to Malcolm Litchfield of Princeton University Press for showing continued interest in the project.

The book stems indirectly from Jack's work because of the intellectual debt that the authors owe to him. The political science profession lost a lot when Jack Walker passed away. He had a way of explaining the importance of new ideas, and several of his articles have generated large research programs. His work pointed toward the centrality of groups in the political process, even as groups became less than central in political science. Certainly we are not able to argue with the force that Jack could bring to such an argument, and certainly his arguments would have been different from those that we make here. However, we believe, as Jack did, that the discipline will benefit from a renewed emphasis on the study of organized interests in politics.

As is fitting in a project so much inspired by Jack's work, this book has developed into a true collaboration between a faculty member and a graduate student. Beth Leech began her graduate career after Jack Walker's death, but her studies and her research have been deeply influenced by his work. Beyond this project, the idea for Leech's dissertation research began with the possibility of creating a third wave to the Walker surveys of the 1980s. The project that resulted was different from those surveys but strongly influenced by Jack's findings regarding the ways political circumstances affect interest-group actions. Leech's dissertation is based on a large survey of groups in Washington, much as Walker's last project was. Mail surveys take a long time, so while that survey was in the field, the two of us have worked together, pouring over every paragraph of the pages that follow, hoping to finish this book before all the surveys were returned and Leech needed to return to that project on a full-time basis. (Naturally, we failed. Books take even longer to write than surveys take to come back in the mail.) Not many students have the opportunity to work closely with their professors, but even fewer professors have the opportunity to see a graduate student develop into a real colleague even before leaving campus. In this case, we both feel lucky.

During the years that we have been working on this manuscript, we have been fortunate to get useful comments from a number of colleagues and support from several sources. Leech was supported during the writing of this manuscript by a National Science Foundation graduate fellowship and the Department of Political Science at Texas A&M University. We received helpful comments over the past few years either on this manuscript or on a series of conference papers that led to it from Joel Aberbach, Scott Ainsworth, Jeff Berry, Jon Bond, John Brehm, Nicole Canzoneri, Gretchen Casper, Al Cigler, Lee Cronk, George Edwards, Scott Gates, Virginia Gray, Mark Hansen, Paul Johnson, Dave King, Ken Kollman, Glen Krutz, David Lowery, Burdett Loomis, Dan Lowenstein, Andrew McFarland, Gary McKissick, Mark Peterson, Mike Rosenstiehl, Robert Salisbury, Kay Schlozman, and Melissa Thompson. Jim Anderson, Bill Browne, and Jeff Talbert, and several anonymous reviewers commented on the entire manuscript. Ten students in an honors section of a course on interest groups read the entire manuscript as well and provided a range of useful comments, pointing out, for example, in that special way that students have, which sections were just too boring. Bryan Jones not only gave Baumgartner no grief over the time this project took away from their collaborative work, but offered his usual set of positive suggestions.

We are happy to acknowledge institutional support from the Department of Political Science and the Center for Presidential Studies at Texas A&M

University. Thanks to Charles A. Johnson and George C. Edwards III for facilitating this work in a variety of ways. John Jackson, chair of the Political Science Department at the University of Michigan, also merits thanks for helping to arrange for Baumgartner to come for an extended summer stay in 1996, during which time he drafted considerable parts of the manuscript. In a work so much inspired by the work and spirit of Jack Walker, it seemed only right to do some of the writing in Haven Hall. The book is, naturally enough, dedicated to the memory of Big Jack. His influence will be clear enough to many readers.

# _Introduction_

THROUGHOUT the twentieth century, political scientists, journalists, politicians, and popular commentators have recognized the central role that interest groups play in all areas of politics. Many have bemoaned the roles of groups as advocates and defenders of special privileges; some have celebrated their diversity; virtually all have recognized that organized interests in politics are a decidedly mixed blessing. Most who have looked seriously at the group system have agreed with James Madison, who argued in _The Federalist Papers_ that groups are a necessary evil best controlled rather than eliminated. Groups at once represent the freedom to join with others to make demands on political leaders and the threat that those already endowed with important resources will mobilize more effectively than others, thus reinforcing any disparities in political power. Eliminating the threat of increased inequality by somehow controlling the "mischiefs of faction" would also eliminate the freedom to mobilize for social change. These ambivalent views of interest groups have not changed much over the centuries. At times, scholars have focused on the potentials of the group system to foster democratic representation through the mobilization of citizens into political life; at other times, commentators have dwelled on the excesses associated with the power of lobbies.

## INTEREST GROUPS IN POLITICS AND IN POLITICAL SCIENCE

Just as our collective views of the roles of groups in government have been the subject of ambivalence, so too have our views of the roles of groups in political science. Groups have been seen as the single most important element in understanding the nation's political system, and they have been seen as inconsequential. Entire generations of scholars have developed their understanding of the political system with the "group struggle" at its core; other generations have discounted the roles of groups in politics. Forty years ago, the group approach to politics was so dominant that it virtually defined the contemporary approach to political science. Built up largely as a reaction against the constitutional legalism that had come before it, the observation of politics through the activities of organized interests provided a way to see how the system "really worked" and revolutionized the discipline. In a way, the approach suffered from its own success: As everything came to be explained through group struggle, nothing could be so explained. In another way, the group approach fell victim to methodological trends emphasizing the analysis of the individual rather than aggregates. Whatever the reasons (and we will review them in some detail in this book), groups were once seen to be central to any understanding of politics, but today they are seen as small parts of a picture whose focus is elsewhere. Textbooks, graduate seminars, and reviews of American politics today generally reserve scant space for interest groups. The widely acknowledged importance of groups in politics is not reflected in the teaching or research agendas of political scientists.

In this book, we discuss the importance of groups to an understanding of politics. We take a relatively long-term perspective on the literature, beginning with those elements that made the group approach to politics so intellectually attractive to scholars of generations past. We discuss the rise and decline of this approach, and we review the state of the interest-group literature today. Whereas previous generations of political scientists shared a consensus that groups offered an important lens through which to view the workings of a nation's political system, scholars today are more likely to see the roles of interest groups only as small and relatively marginal parts of literatures based mostly on the institutions of government. Elections, Congress, the presidency, and the judiciary are the primary objects of analysis, with group activities as minor parts of these broader literatures. How did the study of groups shift from a central focus to a peripheral one? The answer has little to do with changes in the interest-group system itself and much to do with changes in the ways interest groups have been studied.

Whereas scholars who studied interest groups once aspired to build complete understandings of how groups affect the political system, narrower studies have become the norm in more recent decades. As scholars attacked a series of problems associated with the internal dynamics of membership recruitment, collective action dilemmas, and internal group maintenance, they made considerable progress in those areas. To the extent that scholars abandoned the study of group influence, they avoided a research topic that had proven difficult to subject to objective and quantitative analysis. In the search for analytic tractability, however, interest-group scholars have increasingly defined themselves into a position of diminished importance to the rest of the discipline. Our understandings of the difficulties of mobilization may have improved as we have focused on this new research question, but our collective understandings of the roles of groups in the policy process have not. In studies of groups' external political activities, even a recent multiplication of research efforts has led to few strong conclusions, as successive studies have suffered from such problems of comparability that few collective conclusions can be drawn. Each of the individual studies may be well designed, but they are often so narrowly defined that their results can hardly be generalized. As these trends have developed within interest-group studies, the broader discipline has reacted by paying less and less attention to the work. Paradoxically, research on interest groups seems to add up to less than the sum of its parts. Individual studies are often excellent, but the cumulative impact of the literature does not correspond to the wealth of well-done projects.

We argue in this book that interest-group studies have defined themselves into a position of elegant irrelevance. For reasons that we will review in detail, scholars rightfully abandoned the all-encompassing aspirations of previous generations of group scholars. However, in their search for clear findings, a generation of scholars has been drawn to issues more often because of their amenability to certain research approaches than because of their importance to politics. Most of these problems are questions of opportunity cost and represent a collective dilemma for the literature as a whole rather than the shortcomings of any individual researchers. As we will review in detail in chapter 1, research on the roles of interest groups in politics has progressed substantially in the past two generations. Our understandings of the roles of groups in 1998 are much more complete, accurate, and well documented than they were in 1948. Areas of substantial advance have been built up on many important topics relating to groups, but there are also many gaps in our collective knowledge. We hope in this book to draw some lessons from the areas of advance and to compare those areas with areas where less progress has been made. Finally, we hope to use these comparisons to provide some suggestions for further progress. Inevitably, our tone will strike some as negative because we focus on the areas where we think the literature can improve. Interest-group scholars have much to be proud of. However, our goal here is not to applaud past accomplishments but to push scholars toward the creation of a more influential research program in the future.

In many ways, the literature on interest groups, so dependent on the collective-action dilemma for its analytical power, faces a collective-action dilemma of its own. How can it be organized to encourage the creation of a substantially cumulative and broad literature when incentives are strong to conduct tightly argued and narrow projects that may not be easily related to the corpus of previous or subsequent literature in the field? With few incentives to organize the types of large and complex projects that might take years to conduct and could have broad long-term impacts, and with few widely shared analytical questions, progress is made more difficult. In this way, individually well-done studies can proliferate, but the literature as a whole can stagnate.

Douglas Arnold has pointed out the importance of the social nature of the research enterprise. Scholars may think they work in isolation, but they do not: "The allocation of scholarly labor takes place in a delightfully free market; each social scientist studies whatever he or she chooses. But all must live with the consequences of everyone else's decisions. . . . Thus, although scholars can marvel at a system that gives each of them the freedom to manage their own lives, they cannot be indifferent to how others manage theirs" (1982, 91). In the area of interest-group studies, this delightful freedom to choose research topics has led to the massive flow of scholarly resources into the study of some topics and to the exclusion of others. Correspondingly, some areas have been the subject of significant theoretical advance, in particular the general area of group mobilization, where work has centered around the puzzles of the collective-action dilemma and its consequences. At the same time, the study of external lobbying activities, to take a single prominent example, has been the subject of only a handful of large-scale national research projects in the past twenty years. In this area, the literature is typified by case studies rather than large projects. We will review these literatures in detail in subsequent chapters, but the simple point for now is a paradox: Each scholar has the freedom to choose whatever research questions seem interesting to him or her, but the field as a whole will progress only if the individual projects address important issues and if their results are comparable. In this way, the cumulative impact of a literature may differ from the sum of the results of the individual studies that make it up.

If scientific advance is largely a product of collective efforts but individual scholars are free to select any research topic that interests them, then advance is largely dependent on a shared understanding of the important research dilemmas and of the most useful methods for attacking them. This system of self-guidance can easily break down, as we believe it has in interest-group studies since the 1970s. As this has occurred, the topic has moved from a position of absolute centrality, at the very core of political science, to a self-imposed marginality. Not only are interest-group studies small in scope and increasingly ignored by scholars in other areas, but those working on other topics do not systematically incorporate the roles of organized interests into their models of these other institutions. Only a redirection of our collective research efforts could move the study of organized interests back to a position of prominence within political science. Without a good understanding of the roles of interest groups, our understandings of the functioning of our political system cannot possibly be complete. The entire field of political science, therefore, stands to benefit from more progress in the area of interest-group activities.

The analysis presented here is based on a broad and critical reading of hundreds of books and articles published on the topic of organized interests in politics throughout the century. No review of this literature could be complete: the boundaries of the interest-group literature are difficult to define with precision, as works veer off into economics, sociology, history, political psychology, journalism, and other fields. However, within the constraints imposed by these limits, we attempt to review the major trends in the theoretical and empirical work on interest groups in American national politics, especially since 1945. We touch on hundreds of individual works, though we focus particularly on no single one. Our primary focus is on national politics of the United States, but we make some reference to some influential studies done in the states and in other Western democracies. In several cases, we refer the reader to excellent published reviews, in particular for earlier works.

## AN ANALYTIC REVIEW OF THE LITERATURE

Our goals in this book are many. At the simplest level, we hope to review hundreds of books and articles, many of which are not commonly read anymore because they were written decades ago, and to provide a useful summary of the progress of the literature on groups over the past two generations. The literature is ripe for such a review because of a growing number of studies and because many younger students of politics are not familiar with some of the classics of the 1940s and 1950s, even though these books form the basis for subsequent works in many ways. As new literature has proliferated and as the older books have gone out of print, course syllabi and bibliographies have inevitably shown the effects of this pressure. At one level, therefore, we hope to provide a useful review and particularly to point scholars to the most prominent studies on a variety of topics over several decades of scholarship. This explains the broad range of topics we cover in our chapters; we hope to provide a summary of a range of fields for those interested in knowing what types of work has been done and what types of questions remain unaddressed.

Our second goal is to go beyond the mere presentation and summary of hundreds of studies and to analyze the literature. That is, we want to know which areas of the literature have been more successful than others and for what reasons. In this analysis, we are careful to distinguish between criticisms of individual studies and analyses of the strengths and weaknesses in whole bodies of literature. Our intent is neither to point to authors who have done good studies and to single them out for praise nor to engage in similar behavior toward those whose projects have been less successful. Rather, we hope to point to broad schools and approaches and to evaluate which questions have been effectively put to rest, which have not been sufficiently analyzed to reach strong conclusions, and which have been the subjects of contradictory or inconclusive findings. On the basis of these comparisons, then, a number of suggestions for fruitful research designs flow as a natural consequence.

Our third goal is to provide suggestions for the design of effective research projects. Some might argue that there is no need for a literature review to make suggestions about how to organize research projects. Individual studies, taken on their own, can be well done no matter where they fit into the broader literature. That is true. In many ways, a good research project is a good research project. However, it is worthwhile to step back occasionally and evaluate the overall impact of different types of research projects on a literature as a whole. In our last chapter, we lay out a range of suggestions of the types of studies that would be most useful in the literature as it stands today. We hope to demonstrate the value of certain types of designs over others, not in general and not in all areas of political science, but specifically in the case of research on interest groups in the United States as it stands in the late 1990s. Progress in a literature does not inevitably follow the accumulation of more studies over time; at the least, this progress may be more or less efficient. Occasionally scholars should consider exactly where their literature stands and what can be done to make further progress in the most efficient manner possible. Many scholars are active in doing important empirical work on organized interests in politics; we hope more will be so in the future. Given this investment in scholarly effort, it is worth considering how that effort can best be focused.

The literature on interest groups in politics is similar to many others in the social sciences in that scores of scholars simultaneously work on various parts of a single puzzle or related sets of puzzles. Many readers with greater knowledge of other areas of political science might well be reminded of familiar patterns of advance and confusion in these other literatures as they read through our review of the literature on groups. We hope to encourage such reflections and analyses generally.

In the chapters to come, we review the state of the literature on interest groups in American politics, discussing strengths and weaknesses and suggesting ways in which the literature could be made more effective. Chapter 1 notes the general state of the literature and uses other scholars' reviews to divide the literature into areas of advance, avoidance, and confusion. It notes the areas of substantial progress over the past two generations but also the persistence of significant barriers to firm conclusions on important questions even in those areas that have been the object of much attention. Chapter 2 reviews a number of potential reasons for these difficulties, focusing on a series of definitional ambiguities. Scholars do not use common definitions, even of such terms as *interest group*, *lobbying*, or *membership*. Chapter 3 moves on to discuss the development and the demise of the group approach to politics, with emphasis on the literature of the 1950s and 1960s. This chapter shows how groups once were the center of political science and why they no longer are. This, in turn, helps explain how the interest-group literature of the 1970s and 1980s developed as it did. In chapter 4, we review the development of a new literature on interest groups that focuses on the collective-action dilemma. This literature is based on a set of new techniques and on the hope that a narrower and more quantitative approach to the study of groups will allow the field to avoid many of the problems that had haunted it in the generation before. The first four chapters, then, present both an assessment of where the literature stands today and an explanation of how it developed as it did.

We continue our review of the state of the literature in chapters 5 through 8. Chapter 5 discusses the scope and bias of the interest-group system, both in Washington and with reference to participation among the mass public. Chapter 6 discusses how bias in the group system differs across time, from area to area, and from issue to issue. Chapter 7 reviews the findings of the numerous small-scale studies of lobbying and influence in Washington; and chapter 8 reviews the large-scale surveys of the Washington activities of interest groups. We pay special attention to the research designs used in the works reviewed in chapters 7 and 8, and show how the most commonly used designs have systematically left gaps in what we know about what groups do to influence the government.

We argue in chapter 9 for the organization of a smaller number of larger research projects designed to collect a range of evidence needed to address important questions of group behavior in diverse contexts. Our focus in this last chapter will be to draw the collective lessons from our review. We argue, on the basis of our review comparing areas of advance with areas of confusion, that the collective impact of the literature on groups would be much greater if scholars were to organize their projects in different ways. We review a range of studies here that illustrate the approaches most likely to bring the study of groups back to a position of influence within political science.

Throughout the book, we note the range of progress and difficulties apparent in the literature on organized interests, and we focus on the diversity of theoretical and methodological approaches being used. Is there likely to be a single theory of interest-group behavior in American politics? Of course not. Groups engage in a great range of activities, from organizational maintenance to lobbying strategies. No logic requires that a single approach be useful for these disparate questions, but neither does logic require that these approaches be mutually contradictory. It should be possible to relate what we learn about one aspect of groups with what we know about other aspects; at least, scholars should strive to make these connections. Within broad areas of interest-group research, and in particular within the area of group efforts to affect government decisions, greater coherence is not only needed, but is possible. The literature today appears to be made up of hundreds of microtheories, each developing an understanding of a precise and limited element of group behavior and each based on evidence collected specifically for it and often not comparable with that collected in other cases.

Without a set of connections between these microtheories, the literature could continue to grow for decades without accumulating any broad collective conclusions.

## A NOTE ON TERMINOLOGY

We use the term *interest group* quite broadly. When we refer to "interest groups," "groups," or "organized interests," we mean not only membership organizations but also advocacy organizations that do not accept members, businesses, and any other organization or institution that makes policy-related appeals to the government. Unless we specify otherwise, we usually do not mean to include general demographic categories such as women or blacks or workers as interest groups (although the National Organization for Women, the NAACP, and the AFL-CIO would be included). Some scholars prefer *organized interests* to *interest groups*; here we generally stick with the more traditional term, though we have no strong preference. We mean to analyze the roles of organized interests in politics and how these have been studied by other political scientists. Sometimes others have used the term *interest group*; sometimes *organized interest*; sometimes other terms. As may be fitting in a study on this topic, we are pluralists on this score.

# BASIC INTERESTS

# CHAPTER 1

# Progress and Confusion

SCHOLARS working in the area of organized interests in politics have made tremendous strides in the past two generations. Comparing the state of our knowledge in 1998 with that in 1948, for example, makes clear that our collective understanding of the roles of groups in politics has become considerably more complete, sophisticated, and accurate. We know more about the nature of political mobilization, about the political activities of organized interests, and about the contours of the group system, to mention a few areas of advance. Probably the most prominent example of progress is how far we have come in understanding the biases in mobilization that benefit certain types of groups, especially occupational ones, and discourage other types of potential groups from forming. Groups were once thought to spring naturally from society in response to disturbances, with little reference to any factors that might facilitate this process in some segments of society or inhibit it in others. David Truman's 1951 *Governmental Process* was rightly criticized for paying little attention to these issues, but his work represented the state of the art at the time. Today, two generations later, these issues are well recognized. The biases of mobilization contribute to a bias in the Washington interest-group community that has been amply and repeatedly documented over the past several decades. No understanding of the group system would even be attempted today that did not pay serious attention to these obstacles, but these were glossed over in the most prominent study of the topic in the early postwar period.

In this and other areas, scholars have made substantial progress in elaborating more complete, sophisticated, and nuanced views of the roles of groups in the political system. At the same time, however, serious gaps in our knowledge remain. While dramatic progress has been made in some areas of research on interest groups, other topics have either been ignored or have been the subject of inconclusive studies. We are not the first observers to note this unevenness. In this chapter, in fact, we rely heavily on the works of previous scholars who have reviewed the state of the interest-group literature in order to summarize our collective progress. We first look at areas that have proved quite fruitful, then turn to other areas of the literature that have either been avoided or have been investigated by many scholars while producing few conclusive results. The chapter concludes by drawing the lessons from these patterns of progress and confusion.

## THE STATE OF THE LITERATURE

Virtually all those who have attempted to summarize the state of the literature in interest-group studies have noted certain areas where an accumulation of studies has led to real and important progress. A few of the most
prominent areas of advance have included studies of the biases of mobilization; the collective-action dilemma; the occupational basis of most interest
groups; the choice of direct and indirect lobbying tactics; the importance of
long-term lobbying relations; the roles of groups in promoting new understandings of issues over the long run; the links between new social movements and the interest-group system; the effects of contextual factors such as
laws, government subsidies, institutions, and patrons of group activities on
group mobilization; and the roles of groups in elections, campaign finance,
and the courts. On the other hand, most reviewers have paid closer attention to a series of problems. Published reviews have noted a long series of
difficulties ranging from the choice of research topics to the theories and
methods used to investigate them. In this section, we review the range of
conclusions that other scholars have drawn in their efforts to state just what
we do and do not know about the nature, activities, and effects of interest
groups in American politics (for recent reviews, see Greenstone 1975; Salisbury 1975; Garson 1978; Knoke 1986; Schlozman and Tierney 1986; Walker
1991; Cigler 1991; Petracca 1992b; Heinz et al. 1993; Crotty, Schwartz, and
Green 1994; Smith 1995; Baumgartner and Leech 1996a; Berry 1997).

In his review of the distribution of scholarly resources in political science
in the early 1980s, Douglas Arnold singled out interest-group studies by
noting: "Interest groups also seem to have attracted relatively little scholarly
attention given their presumed importance. Here, surprisingly, the field is
theory rich and data poor. . . ." In spite of a wealth of available theories, he
continues, "there are relatively few empirical studies of how various groups
operate politically" (Arnold 1982, 97). Arnold attributes some of these problems to the difficulties and expense of data collection: Whereas scholars in
some areas can rely on the secondary analysis of large-scale data sets collected by others, interest-group studies require expensive, difficult, and
time-consuming field work or original data collection (101). In the years
since Arnold wrote, a vast outpouring of scholarly energy has transformed
the field. Hundreds of studies have collected data on interest groups and
their lobbying activities. The 1980s saw both a resurgence of large-scale
surveys of interest-group behavior (see Schlozman and Tierney 1986; Knoke
1990a; Walker 1991; Heinz et al. 1993; Gray and Lowery 1996) and a tremendous number of smaller-scale investigations of the lobbying efforts of
particular groups surrounding one or a few political decisions (see the works
reviewed in Smith 1995; his bibliography lists 257 entries, and he focuses
only on legislative lobbying). Since a lull during the 1960s and 1970s, a

resurgence has occurred in the study of interest groups, transforming the topic from one that was theory-rich but data-poor into one that is now rich on both counts. The 1980s constituted a period of rapid advance, at least in terms of the collection of vast amounts of new data on group activities.

Arnold was right to point out that scholars studying interest groups do not benefit from the large-scale and institutionally financed collection of data, as compared with other areas of political science, such as electoral behavior or international-conflict studies. Comparing how group scholars organize their research projects with how those in electoral behavior often do theirs is to compare an artisan working alone with a large corporation benefiting from a huge infrastructure. Even though we can note a great resurgence in data collection and empirical research into the roles of groups in politics, these projects have typically been of the scope that a single researcher could accomplish in a year with a modest budget. Exceptions include the studies by Walker, Knoke, Heinz and colleagues, Gray and Lowery, and a few others, as we will review in detail in chapter 8. Even Schlozman and Tierney's survey of groups was accomplished on a shoestring budget. One of the most prominent elements of empirical work on groups in the past few decades has been the modest scope of the projects.

Some of the largest collections of systematic data on groups come from the requirements of the Federal Election Campaign Act of 1971, as amended, or from congressional sources such as roll-call votes, interest-group rankings of members of Congress, and lists of witnesses at public hearings. These publicly available sources of information have led to massive literatures, to be reviewed in later chapters. This new and quantitative literature on groups shows that Arnold is right to point to the subsidization of research costs as an important determinant of scholarly agendas. The work that has stemmed from these studies has not been as coherent in its findings or as clear in its theoretical groundings as in other areas of political science because the data were not collected for a theoretical purpose, but rather constitute isolated bits of information without a set of complementary variables that would allow the systematic test of any particular theory. Contrast the collection of data on PAC contributions, to which the analyst must add a wide range of other bits of information, if possible, with the National Election Study, which is designed not to meet public demands of disclosure of a single piece of information but rather as a complete analytical tool in itself. In sum, interest-group scholars have not benefited from the collection of large, theoretically inspired data sets that would allow the field to base its research on a firm empirical foundation. Those data that have been collected, as in the areas of campaign contributions and roll-call votes, are simply not enough to test a complete theory of how groups behave. The burgeoning literature attempting to take advantage of these sources shows that scholars are willing to take advantage of publicly available sources of information and would likely make good use of more complete sets of information, were they available. In any case, Arnold is right to point to the importance of subsidies and infrastructure in determining the growth of a field. Interest-group researchers typically work alone with little institutional support.

How much further advanced are interest-group studies in the 1990s than they were when Arnold wrote? Unfortunately, the consensus seems to be that the addition of vast amounts of new observational data has not led to a comparable increase in our understandings of the roles and impacts of groups in politics. The large-scale surveys of groups have led to a number of important and consistent findings about the mobilization strategies, lobbying tactics, and Washington activities of interest groups. On the other hand, there have been only a half-dozen such projects in recent decades. The more numerous small studies often are conducted in such a way as to hinder if not preclude comparison of results from one study to those of the next. A mixture of theoretical problems, measurement difficulties, the prevalence of the case study as the research design of choice, and other analytic shortcomings has rendered the development of a cumulative body of evidence an elusive goal.

One of the strengths of the literature on groups has always been the artisanal structure of the field. Scores of scholars have produced a great range of studies on important topics, sometimes from innovative theoretical perspectives. We will note in some detail below how research on the roles of groups in politics benefits from a methodological and theoretical eclecticism. The great diversity of research approaches has led to a number of insights. At the same time that we recognize the value of this methodological pluralism, it is important to see the potential for inefficiencies. With few shared data sources and with a diversity of research and theoretical approaches, scholars working alone often organize research projects that make an interesting new point but that cannot be compared directly with studies done by others because of subtle differences in measurement, theoretical questions, and empirical context. Diversity of approach must be balanced with some degree of shared theoretical perspective in order to produce a literature endowed with coherence and comparability.

In reviews of the literature conducted since Arnold's, scholars have been more likely to note the resurgence in data collection on groups than to complain about the paucity of data. Concern now focuses on the disparity between the degree of effort being expended and the scientific payoffs. In a substantial review of the political science and sociology literatures on interest groups published in the mid-1980s, David Knoke points to the beginnings of the resurgence of data collection. He concludes his review of the state of the literature in these terms:

> This brief review of the past decade's major research on American associations and interest groups reveals a diverse specialty that has continued to uncover interesting findings about these forms of social organization. The volume of

factual knowledge at all levels of analysis has grown significantly. But association research as a field failed to achieve a sustained take-off into scientific maturity. Lacking consensus about the central issues and appropriate ways to study them, it remains a fragmented and unfocused enterprise at the margins of its parent disciplines. Sorely missing is an overarching paradigm that could crystallize attention and confer cachet upon the specialty. A fundamental theoretical goal must be to create coherence among the myriad empirical findings, particularly those bridging multiple levels of analysis from the individual, to the organizational, to the societal. (Knoke 1986, 17)

Knoke's assessment is echoed by virtually every political scientist who has attempted a significant review of this literature, as we will explain in some detail below. The literature may be divided into three areas: advance, avoidance, and confusion.

## AREAS OF ADVANCE

In his review of the state of the literature on interest-group studies, Allan Cigler divided the literature into two parts: "demand aggregation" and "group impact" (1991, 100). The first set of studies cover those topics concerning how groups mobilize, how group leaders relate to their memberships, and how they recruit their members or otherwise maintain themselves financially. The second category covers what groups do, and to what effect, in the political arena. Cigler notes that almost all the areas of strength and progress can be put in the first category rather than in the second: We collectively know a great deal now about how many groups there are, how the diversity and bias of the Washington group system has changed over time, who joins groups and why, and how groups maintain themselves financially than we do about what groups do once they exist. In a later review, Cigler writes:

I think it is fair to say that research on demand aggregation represents some of the most analytically and theoretically elegant scholarly work in all of political science. For example, the loosely integrated body of literature often referred to as incentive theory, ranging from formal models of the public choice theorists to the empirical tests of why and under what conditions individuals join groups, provides much insight into understanding collective action issues. (Cigler 1994, 32)

Among those who have reviewed the state of the literature, there seems a consensus that several areas deserve mention for significant advance. Within the broad area of what Cigler calls demand aggregation, we can note tremendous progress in elucidating the various processes of group mobilization, including work focusing on the individual's decision to join, the efforts of group leaders to attract members, and the impact of social and institutional environment in facilitating the mobilization of some types of groups more than others. Within the broad area of group impact, there has also been considerable progress in documenting the structures of the Washington group system, noting the techniques of influence and access, and noting the different structures of relations among groups within various policy domains, issue-networks, and policy subsystems. Comparative studies of the relations between groups and government have led to many important findings, as have longitudinal studies of the efforts of groups to maintain access and generate favorable public policies over time.

There is no shortage of areas of advance; in this section we mention a few of the most prominent. We begin with those associated with the topic of mobilization and then consider some of those related to lobbying. Our choice of topics here should not be taken to indicate that any studies not mentioned are somehow not substantial. We focus here on broad bodies of research, not individual studies; many excellent individual studies are not mentioned merely for lack of space. Our notation of areas of advance certainly does not imply that all the important questions in these areas have been laid to rest. In subsequent chapters we will note some ambiguities even in the broad areas where advances have been substantial. Likewise, in our review of areas of contradiction below, we do not seek to be exhaustive, but rather to point to some general patterns.

There is no doubt that the various questions associated with the collective-action dilemma have been the focus of significant new findings, both regarding the biases in the group system and the many ways in which groups work around these problems (see, e.g., Olson 1965; Wilson 1973 [1995]; Hardin 1982; Ostrom 1990; Chong 1991). Research into this topic has been multi-layered, with significant progress in developing general theory, in testing components of the theory at the level of the individual who may be a potential member of an organization, in noting the roles of group leaders in attempting to recruit members, and in noting the importance of structural, institutional, and contextual factors affecting the mobilization of different types of groups. We will review significant portions of these literatures in chapters 4, 5, and 6. For the moment, it is worth noting that scholars have made a lot of progress and that they have worked at many different levels simultaneously.

The motivations for individual participation in the group system and the impact of this participation on the citizenry has been the subject of considerable research (see, e.g., Verba and Nie 1972; Verba, Schlozman, and Brady 1995). Survey research on this topic has focused on two important questions: What types of people are more likely to become active in the group system, and what effect does participation in groups have on a person's other political activities? Scholars have repeatedly documented both the social class bias in group activities and the potential impact of participation in groups on an individual's subsequent political activities. We review this literature more substantially in chapter 5.

The various sources of financial support to which groups turn in their efforts to maintain themselves have become much better known over the decades. In contrast to early studies in the collective-action perspective, scholars rarely assume that mass memberships are the only, or necessarily even the most important, source of income for many interest groups (see Salisbury 1984; Walker 1991). The importance of occupations in structuring the group system has been largely confirmed, testimony to the importance of Olson's by-product theory of groups.

Scholars have developed much greater understandings of such topics as the roles of group entrepreneurs, of the importance of social movements, and of the roles of large institutional patrons of political action (see Salisbury 1969; Chong 1991; Walker 1991). Finally, the impacts of broad social, governmental, and environmental factors that foster the development of the group system have become much better understood (see, e.g., Salisbury 1984; Walker 1991; Gray and Lowery 1996). Groups do not develop in a social or legal vacuum; the contextual factors of American politics that promote the growth of some types of groups more than others is a topic that received little systematic attention two generations ago, but which is now the subject of some important studies.

A number of important studies have mapped out the structures of the national group system as a whole. Theories of group mobilization patterns have been developed, confirmed, and refined with the help of important empirical studies of the national group universe and the growth patterns of different types of groups (see, e.g., Schlozman and Tierney 1986; Walker 1991; Heinz et al. 1993). We review these studies more substantially in chapter 6; for now it is worth noting that their results have confirmed some elements of the theoretical work on the biases of mobilization—such as the advantage of business and of occupations generally—at the same time as they have led to further insights in other areas.

Studies of the Washington activities of groups have not only borne insights into the origins and maintenance of groups, but they have consistently documented a wide range of lobbying tactics and research activities that groups use in their attempts to affect policy outcomes (see, e.g., Milbrath 1963; Berry 1977; Schlozman and Tierney 1986; Walker 1991; Heinz et al. 1993). These studies have been supported by others focusing on the roles of groups within particular institutions of government, such as Congress (see Smith 1995), and in the courts, where the roles of groups have become an increasingly important part of the scholarly agenda (see for example Caldeira and Wright 1988, 1990; S. Olson 1990; Epstein and Rowland 1991).

Research into the policy activities of groups and the workings of Washington policy communities is one of the richest traditions in political science. Since the turn of the century, scholars have consistently paid attention to the structures and workings of various informal networks of policymakers. Research into policy subsystems, issue-networks, advocacy coalitions, and the like has expanded substantially over the past two generations. Our knowledge of the policy roles of groups has been expanded by substantial investigations of the activities of groups within single policy domains, such as Browne's studies of the agricultural policy domain (1988, 1990, 1995). Similar studies by Hansen (1991), laying out the development of close relations between agricultural interests and a supporting legislative coalition over seventy years, or by Bosso (1987) showing the impact of changes in the interest-group environment surrounding the use of pesticides over the postwar period, have paid important dividends. Massive studies into the structures of particular policy domains, such as those conducted by Laumann and Knoke (1987) or by Heinz and his colleagues (1993) have led to important improvements in how we understand the structures of Washington policy communities.

Many important policy studies have been done through a focus on a particular issue domain, but others have chosen to focus on a particular group or process. McFarland's study of the national experiment at negotiated compromise in settling environmental disputes in the energy field (1993) netted many new findings, such as the impact of internal constraints on groups' external lobbying positions. McFarland's (1984) and Rothenberg's (1992) studies of Common Cause have made that group familiar to everyone knowledgeable about the interest-group literature and have illustrated many important theories of how groups recruit members, how they induce them to remain, how groups decide on their legislative priorities, how they lobby, and to what effect.

Though our focus in this book is on American national politics, some of the most influential work on the roles of groups in policymaking has been in comparative politics, where the literature on corporatism, pluralism, and group-state relations has grown substantially since the 1970s (for a recent review, see Schmidt 1996). Scholarly concern with the relations between business, interest groups, and governments is likely only to grow as economic and trade pressures increasingly cause governments to work as the representatives of their national business communities in international disputes. Studies of the various forms that group-state relations may take, of the impact of the organization of national interest-group systems on governmental actions, and of the impacts of governmental organization on how groups themselves are organized, are likely to be of increasing concern to political scientists. Here, those interested in American politics may learn considerably from their colleagues studying similar ideas in other countries.

In contrast to their colleagues in American politics, those interested in the comparative study of groups in politics have almost always focused on the structures of relations between groups and government (for a few examples see Lijphart 1968; Schmitter 1974; Heclo 1974; Richardson and Jordon 1979; Lehmbruch and Schmitter 1982; Katzenstein 1985; Hall 1986; Baumgartner 1989; Wilsford 1991; Richardson 1993; Knoke et al. 1996; Schmidt 1996). Government structures, policies, and the international economic context affect not only how groups are organized, but how they relate to government officials, according to this large and growing literature. In comparative studies of groups, the focus is almost always on the relations between groups and government agencies. In American-only studies, groups often are studied in isolation.

All in all there are many areas of group behavior where our collective understandings in 1998 are substantially and unambiguously far advanced over what we knew in 1948. Two generations of scholarly research into the roles of groups in politics have paid some large dividends. This review of a select few areas of substantial advance points to several elements that the areas have in common. First, scholars work within a theoretical framework that, if it does not bind them all to the same perspective on what is important, it unites them at least with a common set of concerns. In that way, when one scholar adds a new insight, other scholars recognize its relevance for their work. This is most clear in the literature on mobilization. Second, many of the advances in the study of group lobbying behaviors have been noteworthy for their relatively large empirical scope. This is particularly the case with the Washington surveys of the 1980s and some of the most influential studies of particular policy domains. Finally, many important studies are especially careful in their attention to the context of group activities. Longitudinal studies of group activities within a particular policy domain have paid careful attention to the changing relationships between groups and their external context, especially government agencies. Comparative studies have typically treated the group-state relationship as the focus of attention, not the internal dynamics of the groups themselves. In these areas of progress, the points in common seem to be shared theoretical perspectives, a large empirical scope, and/or attention to context.

## AREAS OF AVOIDANCE

There are two basic reasons for the existence of large areas of unexplored territory in the study of organized interests. The first is simply that new research questions have been posed at such a rate that scholars have not yet organized research projects to solve them. The second is that some important puzzles have not been solved, and scholars have not figured out the best way to approach these issues. Gaps that stem from the first set of reasons are likely to be filled by the mere passage of time, but other areas will require new ways of thinking about the issue before progress can be made.

Gaps that result from the rapid accumulation of new research questions are a sign of a healthy and growing literature. What motivates private and public patrons of interest-group activity? What are the effects of this outside patronage on the freedom of action of interest-group leaders? What proportion of public-policy issues feature a one-sided versus a multi-sided constellation of interest groups? What proportion of these conflicts can be accounted for by the collective- versus selective-interest dichotomy implicit in the Olsonian perspective? How do the roles of interest groups differ when dealing with issues on and off of the national political agenda? How do groups redefine issues in order to achieve their lobbying goals? How do coalitions of groups decide on their legislative priorities for a given year? How are interests represented through the group system vicariously? How do contextual factors such as economic growth, direct and indirect government subsidies and regulations, and political conflict affect mobilization patterns of groups? What are the impacts of various group lobbying tactics, and in which circumstances are they most useful? How have new communications technologies affected these strategies? How can we reconcile the findings that groups spend much time monitoring their environment and working with their allies with an expectation that they would use limited resources to lobby the undecided? Recent research poses dozens if not hundreds of useful research questions to be addressed in the years to come. Certainly there are enough gaps in the literature for several generations of dissertation projects. Many of these are currently the subject of study; advances in these areas are likely as scholars continue their work.

Perhaps the single most remarkable feature of the literature on interest-group activities in Washington is the paucity of large-scale work. Some of the greatest advances in the past decade's research on groups have come from the few large-scale Washington surveys of groups that have been done. The works of Schlozman and Tierney, Walker, Heinz and colleagues, and Gray and Lowery have generated some of the most important insights into the roles and activities of groups in Washington and in the state capitals, and are certain to be cited for years to come. In spite of their prominence and impact, the examples that these authors set in conducting their large and respected projects have rarely been picked up by others. There remain, therefore, a great number of unaddressed empirical questions concerning such questions as the usefulness of common group tactics, the reactions of groups to changing technologies, and the impact on groups of changes in presidential administrations or partisan control of the Congress. In fact, given the paucity of large-scale survey work on the Washington interest-group community, our knowledge of any changes over time must be pieced together little by little from a variety of sources, as we will review in chapter 6. Nothing impedes this research agenda but a lack of willingness and effort.

Research into interest-group activities expands rapidly every year. New research projects promise to answer many of the questions mentioned here, and doubtless will continue to do so. Gaps in our collective knowledge will undoubtedly be filled more easily in some areas than in others, however. We turn now to consider some areas of interest group studies where even the investment of massive scholarly resources has shown little collective benefit.

## AREAS OF CONFUSION

Some issues in the study of interest groups have been avoided not out of a lack of time or effort but because of the inability of previous generations of scholars to generate positive conclusions despite the investment of tremendous energies. This is most clear in the area of power and influence. As we will review in chapter 3, the 1950s and 1960s were marked in both political science and sociology by vituperative and ultimately inconclusive debates about the distribution of power in society, with the literature on interest groups at the center of these debates. Because of these difficulties, and because of the multiple contradictions that previous generations created, a sensible reaction seemed to be to move on to other areas of research where conclusions could be better substantiated. One of the results of this has been that scholars have avoided some basic questions of political power, or have studied those questions in such circumscribed ways that their carefully designed studies can often not be generalized beyond the case on which their evidence is based. We will see in the next section that one of the most important ways in which scholars in the 1970s and 1980s attempted to be more scientific in the study of power and influence was to isolate particular cases for intensive analysis, but this approach has often led to its own set of contradictions rather than to clear conclusions.

Robert Salisbury (1994) has suggested that the problem here is not so much in the disagreements among scholars about how to measure power but rather in posing the question in the wrong way. The problems of the literature in the 1950s and 1960s may have been not so much the inability to measure influence, but rather a set of research questions that required this in the first place. As we will review in later chapters, the more recent and quantitative literature on groups has largely steered away from these matters. The literature on influence is an interesting example of avoidance based on a recognition that previous studies had mostly generated more smoke than fire, more debate than progress, more confusion than advance. Scholars may be right to avoid questions that cannot be answered, but then again it would be preferable to rephrase the questions so that they could be answered. Salisbury suggests that the literature has suffered from a view of influence as a game, where clear winners and losers can be identified. The political process, he points out, is continuous, with no clear resolution and no identifiable end point at which to sort out winners from losers. Looking at the question in the wrong way, Salisbury assures, "is likely to generate more misunderstanding than insight" (1994, 18). His solution? Greater attention to the context of group behavior, among other things. We will discuss in later chapters how this might work. In any case, some areas of research into interest groups have been avoided not because of a lack of time or interest, but because previous work has been inconclusive.

At least two broad areas of the literature related to the study of influence can be cited for a collectively inconclusive nature in spite of great numbers of well-conducted individual studies. These involve the effects of political action committees (PACs), and quantitative analyses of the impact of lobbying on congressional votes. As many scholars have noted, these two areas of research have generated a wealth of new empirical work since the 1970s, but there has been little corresponding increase in knowledge.

Allan Cigler points to the literature on PAC contributions as an area where massive efforts have generated few collective benefits. Since the Federal Election Commission began collecting data on the contributions of these organizations to candidates and legislators in the mid-1970s, scores of studies have been designed to show the impact of these contributions in elections or in Congress. Concerning electoral outcomes, such a range of important variables besides PAC contributions are typically excluded from the analysis that the literature is inconclusive. "The availability of funding data has not automatically produced good research or clear results. PAC money is analytically difficult to separate from all other sources of money in terms of its impact on elections, and money itself is only one of many political resources in a campaign" (Cigler 1991, 113). Similarly, the literature on PAC effects on legislative voting is tremendously confusing, supporting only the most general conclusions. Cigler summarizes the literature this way:

> What is the effect of PAC money? When one turns to the research literature on the relationship of PAC contributions to congressional voting, one finds that it "is filled with ambiguity and apparent contradiction" (Wright 1985, 401). Studies dealing with such issues as the B-1 Bomber (Chappell 1982), minimum wage legislation (Silberman and Durden 1976), the debt limit, windfall profits tax, wage and price controls (Kau and Rubin 1982), trucking deregulation (Frendreis and Waterman 1985), legislation of interest to doctors and auto dealers ([K.] Brown 1983), and gun-control legislation (Cleiber, King, and Mahood 1987), have concluded that special interest money does appear to make a substantial difference. Others find no simple, direct relationship between contribu-

tions and issues such as the Chrysler loan guarantee program (Evans 1986) or dairy price supports (Welch 1982). Two studies, each of which examines a large number of issues, make virtually no common generalizations (Ginsberg and Green 1986; Grenzke 1989). (Cigler 1991, 116)

Richard Smith reviews hundreds of articles on group activities in Congress and is scathing in his criticisms. Not only do we have tentative and conflicting conclusions in those areas of research where little work has been done but we have a similarly inconclusive set of findings even in the most well-trodden paths (Smith 1995, 122–23). Smith reinforces the comments of Cigler. First, he notes that the literature presents an unjustified but consistent divide between those studies focusing on PAC contributions and those focusing on other lobbying activities. Almost all admit that contributions and lobbying activities are linked, but few design their projects in a way to accommodate the potential spuriousness thus created. Smith notes the results of these research projects:

Consider first the scholarly work on the relationship between campaign contributions by interest groups and roll-call voting on the floors of the House and Senate. Over 35 studies have been published in recent years, and these studies have produced a literature filled with conflicting results. At one extreme are [the authors of eight studies] who report that interest group campaign contributions seem to be largely unrelated to the voting decisions of members of Congress.

At the other extreme are [the authors of seventeen studies] who report statistically significant relationships between interest group campaign contributions and the voting decisions of members of Congress. . . .

Between these two extremes are [the authors of twelve studies] who report more mixed results. . . .

These conflicting findings are present whether one looks at the House or at the Senate, whether one looks at single votes, at indexes of votes on single issues, or at indexes of votes across several different issues (typically ADA or COPE scores). Conflicting results also occur regardless of whether one examines the contributions of a single interest group or the combined contributions of several interest groups, whether one enters contributions in nominal dollars, as a percent of total contributions received, or as the ratio of contributions compared to another source of contributions ( . . . ), and whether one analyzes contributions in linear or logarithmic form. (Smith 1995, 92–93)

When a literature burgeons but does not produce a set of comprehensible findings, important conceptual issues apparently remain unresolved. PAC contributions are not the only area where such contradictions are common. Lobbying activities in general have seen a range of conflicting results. Those who have conducted large-scale surveys of interest-group behaviors have been remarkably consistent in their findings of what groups do, as we will discuss in chapter 8. However, those who have focused, as in the PAC literature, on one or a few cases at a time have generated a wealth of contradictions.

Groups are known to use a wide range of tactics and to focus sometimes on legislative allies and sometimes on fence-sitters or on opponents. Contradictions abound in this literature based on such questions as the type of issue being discussed, the degree of salience of the issue, the inclusion of controls in the statistical models employed, the validity and inclusiveness of the measurements used, the dynamic versus cross-sectional nature of the research design, and other factors. The literature is filled with such a diversity of theoretical and methodological approaches that we are left with a bewildering array of findings rather than a coherent set of results (see Baumgartner and Leech 1996a, 1996b). Richard Smith gives the same dim assessment of the literature on lobbying as he did of that on PAC contributions:

> Taken together, the recent theoretical developments about lobbying and persuasion and the empirical evidence about changes in the conduct of lobbying campaigns—especially the evidence about the emphasis on contacting undecided members of Congress—suggest that interest group lobbying should substantially affect the roll-call decisions of members of Congress, and should do so considerably more than conventional wisdom implies. But is this the case? Do the recent statistical studies of the relationship between lobbying and roll calls suggest a strong linkage? The answer is rather unclear. On first reading, the evidence from the statistical analyses is mixed, and suggests that the impact of lobbying depends on the presence or absence of a variety of conditions. A closer examination, however, suggests that there are methodological reasons to doubt all the statistical results, and hence the actual relationship between lobbying and voting remains obscure. (Smith 1995, 104)

PAC contributions and lobbying activities represent two areas where the publication of hundreds of studies in the past two decades has not generated the type of advance that one would hope, in contrast to the other areas of research on groups, such as that on collective action. Hugh Heclo wrote some time ago that the concept of the iron triangle was "not so much wrong as . . . disastrously incomplete" (1978, 88). Many of the works that make up the literatures discussed in this section may be evaluated in a similar manner: Each of them when taken individually is probably not so much wrong as it is profoundly disconnected from other studies on the same topic. This disconnection makes each study incomplete and potentially misleading, even if each is well done individually. Clearly, the mere accumulation of more studies over time does not inevitably lead to increases in knowledge.

There are at least three important lessons in the review of these two disappointing literatures. First is the impact of the availability of data sources.

The public availability of vast amounts of information concerning quantitative indicators of group activities such as campaign contributions seemed too good to pass up. Scores of political scientists went about correlating these figures with others in the hope of showing an important set of relationships. Many of these studies were individually well done, but in retrospect the literatures based on the exploitation of these data sources have been inconclusive. The mere availability of new data does not guarantee progress. Second, the inability of scholars to compare their disparate findings suggests that the impact of a literature may stem more from the interrelations among the studies that make it up than from the strengths of the individual studies themselves. Building in comparability is an important goal in any literature. Third, effort counts. To take publicly available information about a partial set of indicators and hope to add one or two pieces to the puzzle is a tempting research strategy. Unfortunately, it is no substitute for starting with a clear theoretical framework and going into the field to gather the information necessary to test the theory completely. Taken as a whole, the studies that make up the literatures reviewed in this section are remarkable for the modest efforts in research that they represent. (Two important exceptions to the generally inconclusive literature on PACs include Sorauf's 1992 review of campaign finance issues generally, and Gais's 1996 large-scale study of the unintended consequences of campaign finance reform efforts; these studies differ from others reviewed here in that they focus their attention much more clearly on a small range of questions and marshal a large amount of evidence based on many cases and several sources of data.)

## A LITERATURE THAT GROWS BUT DOES NOT ACCUMULATE

Comparing the state of knowledge in areas of interest-group scholarship where much progress has been made with those where less progress has been apparent allows us to note whether more work inevitably and inexorably leads to greater collective knowledge. It is tempting to think that knowledge will expand by the simple accretion of greater numbers of empirical projects over time. A review of the literature suggests that such optimism is unfounded. As the previous sections have demonstrated, there are important areas in the literature where investments have paid off in better understandings; there are areas where not enough work has yet been done to answer the important questions; and there are large areas where few strong conclusions have been reached in spite of a great number of studies. How can a literature grow without accumulating? We would point to three causes: Theoretical incoherence, lack of comparability across studies that often comes from ignoring the context of group behavior, and the scope of the research effort.

Many who have reviewed the literature on groups have pointed to the great diversity of theoretical approaches being used in explaining how there can be such confusion. Diversity can be a strength, but it can lead to incoherence as well. Without a clear set of theoretical questions, the literature on interest groups has balkanized into such a number of small and unrelated areas that its collective impact is low. One recent book that epitomizes the disappointing cumulative impact of recent work on groups is that edited by Mark Petracca (1992a). Noting the "avalanche of new empirical data on various aspects of the interest group system" (1992b, xviii), the editor expected to summarize a new set of findings. What he found, instead, was "no single question and most certainly no single approach that unites the study of interest groups. Neither is there a unifying theory nor even set of theories to guide interest group research" (Petracca 1992a, 348). Reviewing the same volume, Lawrence Rothenberg notes that the book accurately reflects the state of the art:

> One . . . leaves the book with an understanding that the study of interest groups still has considerable room for growth. Reflecting the general state of organizational research, exactly how associations fit into the political world remains somewhat mysterious. In particular, what groups provide to politicians, the impact of organizations on public policy, and the relationship between group influence and the perpetuation of the group system are still issues open to debate. . . . While *The Politics of Interests* provides partial answers to such questions, it also illustrates that much work remains to be done. (Rothenberg 1993, 1167)

If, after these decades of work, how groups relate to government can be said to remain "somewhat mysterious," it is worth wondering how all that effort could better have been spent. One way to look at this question is to compare areas of advance with areas of confusion along the dimensions of theoretical coherence, context, and scope.

The literature on the dilemmas of mobilization has progressed notably from an initial focus on the calculus of joining from the perspective of the potential member of the group (M. Olson 1965), to an increased awareness of the potential roles of group leaders in offering services to these potential members, thereby altering the membership calculation (Salisbury 1969; see also Moe 1980a, 1980b; Rothenberg 1988, 1992), to consideration of the broader social environment within which groups operate and which affects their abilities to recruit (see Walker 1983, 1991), to a population ecology perspective on group mobilization that puts more emphasis on environmental factors than on the internal factors that had once been the only factors considered in the literature (see Gray and Lowery 1996). With Gray and Lowery's perspective on how groups mobilize, not only are we much further advanced from the days of Truman, who mostly ignored these dilemmas, but indeed we are a long way from Olson's original focus on internal group dynamics. Theories of mobilization are an area of advance because the literature has progressively added new elements of theory and evidence at different levels. Though we do not yet observe a single unified theory in this area, we can see substantial progress in enunciating a perspective combining attention to individual behaviors, internal group dynamics, and the broader context of the group's social and political environment. The literature is vibrant and makes progress because many scholars work on different parts of the puzzle, but they all can see the relevance of the work of others. Progress is visible over the generations as successive theorists add new elements to the old.

Compare the cumulative nature of the literature on mobilization with the disjointed nature of the growing literature on lobbying. Working from many different theoretical perspectives, often taking advantage of small bits of publicly available data on one or a few cases of decision making, scholars often take refuge in the organization of very tightly organized case studies designed to address a limited theoretical question. To be sure, some large-scale work has been done. Considering the payoffs that have come from these few large studies, the continued willingness of scholars to organize small rather than large projects has been remarkable. As this proclivity for small projects is combined with a desire to address narrow theoretical questions based on case studies, this literature has grown without accumulating the record of progress that we can note in other areas of the study of groups.

The implications of the lack of a shared theoretical structure are much greater than scholars often realize. Many scholars hope to solve difficult problems of modeling group behavior by focusing on a limited theoretical question and using the tools of deductive analysis to isolate a set of behaviors to test a narrow theory. The hope, presumably, is that what the research projects suffer in generalizability will be offset by their internal coherence and by the internal coherence of other projects. To meet with success, this approach requires a level of comparability across research projects that is far from what we observe today. As scholars have increasingly followed the approach of limiting their research projects to narrow topics informed by a single and highly limited theoretical concern, the literature as a whole has shown less ability to generate a coherent picture of the political activities of groups. Each individual study may be well done, but it may use a slightly different set of indicators, a particular definition of key terms different from those used by others, or a precise model of external forces that makes it incomparable to other studies, even if these other studies would seem at first glance to be closely related. We will review this problem in some detail in chapter 2. Diversity of the type we observe there produces not an accumulation of results merging into an increasingly complete perspective but rather an incoherent cacophony of incomparable findings.

One potential route for improvement is the adoption of a more explicit deductive theoretical approach to the study of lobbying behaviors. This is, after all, what provided much of the impetus for improvements in the area of group mobilization. In an extensive review of the literature in economics relating to interest groups, William Mitchell and Michael Munger point to this problem in the political science literature. "In general, deductive theory has not provided the hypotheses and explanations offered by political science in studying interests. Accordingly, we have a vast and factually rich body of data but one that is analytically incoherent" (1991, 513). Their suggestion that economic models of groups may provide some of the theoretical structure that the literature needs fits with experience in the area of collective action, where the Olsonian dilemmas have indeed produced a range of important findings. Mancur Olson himself has described the problems of the literature on pluralism as stemming from its lack of deductive structure, making scientific progress impossible and guaranteeing the demise of the literature (1986, 166).

Many have noted the lack of a single structure, and many have proposed the adoption of a set of deductive approaches drawn from economics, as is implicit in Mitchell and Munger's review of the literature in that area. Interest-group research remains captivated by no single approach, however. On the contrary, as Cigler notes, "theoretical and methodological diversity is the hallmark of the interest group subfield" (1991, 125). David Knoke goes much further than Cigler, and makes clear that diversity has its costs:

> Research on associations expanded steadily during the decade. However, its surface diversity and richness mask the field's underlying anarchy. Put bluntly, association research remains a largely unintegrated set of disparate findings, in dire need of a compelling theory to force greater coherence upon the enterprise. Without a common agreement about central concepts, problems, explanations, and analytic tools, students of associations and interest groups seem destined to leave their subject in scientific immaturity. (Knoke 1986, 2)

A healthy diversity of theories, methods, and approaches to the study of group relations with government is sure to lead to an accumulation of important findings. However, a chaotic set of unrelated perspectives that do not produce comparable findings hinders the accumulation of knowledge. In looking at the development of the literature in the past generation, as we have begun in this chapter, we note that the literature suffers more from incoherence and chaos than it benefits from diversity. To be sure, not all areas of the literature are equally afflicted: Some show relative theoretical clarity and scientific progress. Other areas, however, have seen such a disjuncture between effort and progress that some serious questions should be posed. We pose such questions in the chapters to come and suggest some ways in which research projects can be organized to produce a literature whose constituent parts can be compared with each other.

There is not likely ever to be a single theoretical perspective to the study of groups in politics. Groups do many things, and depending on what elements of group activities they want to understand, scholars in the field will make use of a variety of theories. Progress will come from an increased willingness to be explicit in our theoretical perspectives, from clear statements of the limits of our chosen theoretical perspectives, from concerted efforts to build on the findings of others (even those working from slightly different theoretical perspectives), from constructing projects that are much larger in scope than is often the case today, and from ensuring the comparability of our research findings by paying more careful attention to the contexts of group behaviors. The accumulation of hundreds of small studies will not lead to a coherent literature if those studies cannot be compared with each other. In contrasting a few areas where progress has been apparent with some areas where more substantial problems remain, we find that attention to context, scope of the research effort, and theoretical relevance are the keys to accumulation.

# CHAPTER 2

# Barriers to Accumulation

SOME LITERATURES accumulate new knowledge and others merely grow larger. We saw in the previous chapter that some parts of the literature on interest groups have developed into relatively cumulative enterprises where scholars build on the works of others and collectively reach some important conclusions. In other areas, we noted a troubling tendency for the body of accumulated findings to grow larger and larger without generating a series of coherent and well-confirmed conclusions. One of the barriers to effective accumulation is the lack of a shared vocabulary. Interest-group studies benefit from the contributions of scholars in several disciplines operating from a great diversity of theoretical approaches. This diversity lends promise to the study of groups, but the lack of a shared vocabulary creates the risk that scholars might speak past each other. Scholars may hope that they are filling in small parts of a big picture, to be completed as others add to the collective work. Still, the troubling possibility remains that each may be toiling independently on a separate canvas never to be completed or even picked up by another. This chapter focuses on this lack of a shared vocabulary in order to show how the resulting confusion may constitute an important barrier to the accumulation of knowledge. These problems affect certain areas of interest-group research much more severely than others, of course, which helps explain the uneven patterns of progress pointed out in chapter 1.

For each topic discussed in this chapter, we describe how scholars working from different theoretical perspectives assign different meanings to the same terms, use different conventions on important elements of research design, and attach different levels of importance to different elements of their research projects. Each perspective, of course, offers a different set of findings. When it comes time to compare and perhaps to consolidate these diverse findings, we often find that subtle differences in vocabulary hinder the development of a body of evidence, arguments, and conclusions that would be directly comparable. The discussion in this chapter is kept relatively general; the themes introduced here are picked up in greater detail in later chapters.

## WHAT IS AN INTEREST?

Defining an interest and an interest group would seem a prerequisite for a fruitful research program in this area, but it has yet to be done. Robert Salisbury shows some displeasure with what he sees as a trend toward the adoption of increasingly narrow definitions of interests and interest groups in recent years. In one of the most influential articles on interest groups of the 1980s, he had to remind scholars that many organizations that we think of as interest groups are not membership organizations but are institutions such as cities, local governments, universities, corporations, and hospitals (Salisbury 1984). More recently, he noted that we gain little from an overly restrictive definition of interest groups:

> The intellectual domain of the student of interest groups cannot be restricted to voluntary associations. . . . [O]ur scope must include every active unit, from the isolated individual to the most complex coalition of organizations . . . that engages in interest-based activity relative to the process of making public policy. I recognize that this constitutes a supremely imperial conception of our field. So be it. What should we leave out? What organizations and/or active individuals fail to qualify? I see no need to restrict our jurisdiction in advance and much reason to be ready to incorporate more rather than less organizational variety. Indeed, it seems clear to me that our research heretofore has suffered more from omissions than from too expansive a notion of what to include. Let us not be reluctant to extend our reach in the future. (1994, 17)

Salisbury's remarks are designed to encourage grander and potentially more influential research projects. They reflect an increasing feeling that many studies have been defined so narrowly that they have lost much of their interest for the broader profession. Salisbury encourages the revival of a research tradition of long ago. In the early years of the century, scholars were much more likely to adopt extremely encompassing definitions. Sometimes, the groups in question were formal organizations that would today be called interest groups, but in many cases the definitions were more amorphous. An interest group might be an occupational or demographic category such as consumers or farmers—not necessarily membership organizations and not necessarily formal organizations at all. Bentley, for instance, defines a group as any subsection of society "acting, or tending toward action" (1908, 211). He argues: "There is no group without its interest. An interest . . . is the equivalent of a group. . . . The group and the interest are not separate." David Truman, for his part, defined an interest group as "any group that, on the basis of one or more shared attitudes, makes certain claims upon other groups in society" (1951, 33). Truman's distinction between latent interests, which might be mobilized if sufficiently threatened, and manifest groups, which have an actual organizational presence, implies that interests are real even if unmobilized. Such broad conceptions of interests remain common in the economics literature, where broad groups such as consumers and taxpayers are often included in models of political influence (see Buchanan and Tullock 1962; Tullock 1967, 1988; Niskanen 1971; Stigler 1971, 1972, 1974; Posner 1974; Peltzman 1976; Becker 1983, 1985; Mueller and Murrell 1986;

for a review see Mitchell and Munger 1991). Social psychologists and others interested in voting behavior often use similarly broad definitions, analyzing the behaviors of such "groups" as ethnic minorities, women, and the elderly (see, e.g., Paolino 1995). Interests, for many, are defined by one's social or demographic position.

A solid tradition in the literature attempts to define interests in objective terms: Working-class people have certain interests with respect to tax rates, job growth, and other issues; wealthy people have different interests with respect to these issues. Kay Lehman Schlozman and John Tierney discuss the use of objective definitions of interest, and note the prominence of economic motivations in these definitions. For interests that cannot be defined in economic terms, such as those involved in the abortion debate, the issue of capital punishment, or reforms in the electoral system, it is difficult to impute any interest on the basis of observable social characteristics, so the definition of interests must be subjective. They review a series of problems in defining exactly what we mean by an interest: The degree to which individuals are motivated by different and potentially conflicting objective and subjective interests; the importance of material versus nonmaterial incentives for creating interests; the concept of support for the public interest; and the problem of weighing differential intensities of interest, for example (see Schlozman and Tierney 1986, chap. 2).

Interests may be felt for a variety of reasons. Some feelings, however intense, may not be interests, but mere preferences unrelated to public policy. John Heinz, Edward Laumann, Robert Nelson, and Robert Salisbury give the following definition of interests:

> It is at the intersection of public policy and the wants and values of private actors that we discover interests. What we call the interests of the groups are not simply valued conditions or goals, such as material riches, moral well-being, or symbolic satisfaction. It is only as these are affected, potentially or in fact, by public policy, by the actions of authoritative public officials, that the valued ends are transformed into political interests that can be sought or opposed by interest groups. . . . This means that, in analyzing what interest groups do and with what effect, the very conception or definition of a group must be framed in terms of the public policy goals and objectives it seeks. If we are adequately to understand how groups function, it is necessary to study them in the context of policy. We cannot abstract groups from the substance of their interests without losing touch with what defines those groups. (Heinz et al. 1993, 24–25)

According to these authors, then, interests are only created when private values come into contact with government. The same values may not be interests if they have no relation with government action. The profit motive, religious beliefs, desire to achieve some public end, or views on any social issue, then, are not in themselves "interests," but become so only when those who share them make demands on government. As the scope of government has grown, therefore, many values have become interests, and many private organizations have become interest groups. According to Salisbury, Heinz, and colleagues, we cannot define the term *interest* without reference to government.

Scholars have used a variety of definitions of interests over the years. Each individual definition may make sense, but such a range of different definitions are used that the literature provides little guidance for the researcher attempting to reach a simple decision on what is an interest. Empirical research on groups has often used much more narrow definitions than might be expected, considering some of the conceptual work on interests just discussed. Schlozman and Tierney, like several other scholars, use a published directory of organizations active in Washington as their working definition of an interest group, even though their review at the conceptual level includes a much greater range of potential definitions of an interest.

## WHAT IS AN INTEREST GROUP?

If scholars have achieved no consensus on what an interest is, there should be no surprise that they do not agree on what an interest group is. Defining an interest group seems to be simpler than defining an interest because many people think they can recognize an interest group when it attempts to influence government. Still, a variety of definitions are used, and the differences among them are substantial.

David Knoke provides the sociologist's definition: "A minimal definition of an association is 'a formally organized named group, most of whose members—whether persons or organizations—are not financially recompensed for their participation.' . . . Whenever associations attempt to influence governmental decisions, they are acting as interest groups" (1986, 2). The sociologist hopes to distinguish associations and interest groups from such primary groups as the family, the corporation, and the bureaucracy. Sociologists typically define the field of voluntary associations separately from those of mass behavior or organizational dynamics, which explains the distinction in the first part of Knoke's definition. An association is different from a corporation or a bureaucracy because its members are not paid; it is different from a family because membership is voluntary. The second part of Knoke's definition defines when an association becomes an interest group: whenever it attempts to influence government, it is an interest group, just as for Heinz and colleagues. Whether Knoke would extend his definition of interest groups to other types of organizations that attempt to influence government decisions is unclear. In any case, sociologists typically begin with a definition of groups that takes the voluntary association as the base, then extend from there. As a result, they typically pay less attention to corporations, law firms, cities, and other organizations that are often involved in lobbying.

Economists and social psychologists interested in voting behavior often use extremely vague or highly abstract definitions of interest groups in their efforts to understand the workings of the electorate. Rebecca Morton gives an example of this type of analysis when she turns to the concept of groups in order to solve the paradox of voting. If each individual should know that the probability of affecting the outcome of an election is so small as to render irrational the act of voting, certain groups within the electorate may be large enough that their collective votes would matter. Therefore, perhaps, "the group provides a private benefit to the individual to induce voter turnout in the group's interest" (Morton 1991, 760). So the concept of groups may be useful in solving a puzzle in the economic analysis of voting: Incorporating the roles of groups "is a desirable approach to analyzing voting behavior" (774). But what is the concept of groups? For Morton, "it is assumed that individuals are divided into $m$ mutually exclusive groups in which members of each group have identical policy preferences within each group" (763; see also Morton 1987). The economist's definition of a group clearly has little in common with the sociologist's view, but it is a widely adopted definition in that field.

Like Morton, Carole Uhlaner turns to the roles of groups in her attempt to solve the puzzle of voting. Models of voting should note that individuals exist within a social structure, she notes. "There exist group affiliations and layers of intermediary elites between politicians and potential participators" (1989, 391; cf. Huckfeldt and Sprague 1992, 1995). What is Uhlaner's conception of a group?

> A polity contains the set of all voters and a set of all candidates. For purposes of this model, the voters are divided into groups. By "group" we mean loose connections of individuals who identify with each other when they relate themselves to political life and who retain this identity over some extended period of time (so group membership has stability). Such groups need not correspond to organized interest groups; formal structure is not necessary. On the other hand, the groups must have enough structure so that one could identify leaders as distinct from ordinary members. Many "reference groups" are groups in the sense used here. (Uhlaner 1989, 396)

John Turner uses a similar concept of group membership. These definitions of groups make clear that a group exists to the extent that people think it exists. No action is necessary; only thought: "A social group can be defined as two or more individuals who share a common social identification of themselves or, which is nearly the same thing, perceive themselves to be members of the same social category" (Turner 1982, 15).

For many economists, voting analysts, and social psychologists, then, a group is defined within the mind of the potential member of that group. To the extent that people believe they have shared identifications or shared interests, they are members of a group. To the extent that these shared interests lead to similar behavior in the political realm, such as voting, then these groups can be considered to be interest groups.

A definition of interest groups often used in the economics literature identifies groups by objective interests imputed by the researcher. Empirically based studies in the economics tradition typically focus on labor unions, business organizations, political action committees, and other formal organizations, whereas conceptual works typically use demographic or social groups as their definitions of interest groups (see Mitchell and Munger 1991 and the works reviewed there). As mentioned in the previous section, social psychologists often use definitions of groups related to a person's inclusion in some demographic category, generally requiring no formal membership. For journalists, interest groups are law firms, corporations, coalitions, public relations firms, and individual lobbyists active in the policy process.

Among political scientists, definitions vary widely. Those operating in the pressure-group tradition were more likely to use a restrictive definition of groups focusing on active governmental lobbying. For them, groups were corporations, industries, and hired lobbyists (see, for example, Crawford's 1939 book, *The Pressure Boys*). David Truman (1951), of course, made the distinction between active groups and latent interests, where latent interests exist in society but have yet to be mobilized into an organizational form. Pendleton Herring (1929) discussed those organizations with Washington representation, including private firms as well as membership groups. V. O. Key's (1964) definition was broad enough to include associations as well as economic interests such as firms, utility companies, and the like. In general, those writing before 1965 tended to use a definition that might be thought of as whomever one sees in Washington. A lobbyist might be a hired representative, the employee of a private corporation or public institution, or the representative of an organization with or without members. In this view, an organization could be considered an interest group when it had a lobbyist.

As political scientists became more concerned with the dynamics of organizational mobilization in the wake of Mancur Olson's 1965 *Logic of Collective Action*, they became more likely to use something closer to the sociologist's definition. Groups became synonymous with membership organizations. Here, the literature divided between those wanting to study the new questions of organizational maintenance and collective action, and those in the pressure group tradition who remained interested in lobbying per se. Jack Walker attempted to bridge this gap, but his work was greatly influenced by the state of the literature in the 1970s, when he designed his study. He describes his working definition: "My principal focus is limited to functioning associations in the United States that are open to membership and are concerned with some aspects of public policy at the national level" (Walker 1991, 4). This definition is very similar to that used by Knoke, above. Many types of organizations that others would think of as interest groups are excluded from this definition: Walker points out that it does not include corporations, public affairs and public relations firms, law firms and other lobbyists for hire; government institutions such as cities, states, and foreign governments; private and public institutions such as hospitals and universities, foundations, and philanthropic organizations; and many other entities that sometimes behave as lobbyists or otherwise become active in issues of public concern (Walker 1991, 5–6). Walker noted a number of important complications in the makeup of this universe of membership groups, such as the roles of institutions as members and the effects of large government and private patrons in shaping the interest-group system, but limiting his sample to membership groups had important implications for his ability to generalize about the interest-group system as a whole.

Salisbury reminded the profession that its increasing focus on membership organizations was distracting it from the important roles played by non-membership organizations in policy making. His 1984 article focused on the roles of institutions in lobbying. Within public administration, a long tradition has noted the importance of the "intergovernmental lobby" made up of cities, counties, states, and other governmental institutions as they attempt to influence the federal government (see for example Farkas 1971; Haider 1974; Commisa 1995).

In their large study Schlozman and Tierney (1986, 10) are careful to use the term "organized interests" because they want to include organizations such as corporations, hospitals, and others that do not have members, as well as membership organizations. Like Walker, they use a published directory to locate those interests active in Washington. Heinz and colleagues (1993) similarly are broad in their definition of interest groups, basing their interviews with Washington insiders on a combination of published lists, media reports, government hearings, and interviews with government officials about who was involved in various decisions. Hrebenar and Thomas, who have compiled four edited volumes outlining interest-group activities in each of the fifty states (1987, 1992, 1993a, 1993b), instruct their contributers to reserve the use of "interest group" to associations of individuals or organizations who attempt to influence public policy; they include businesses within this definition (1993a, 363). Virginia Gray and David Lowery use a broad definition of groups, including institutions, membership associations, and other types or organizations that were registered to lobby in their large-scale survey of interest communities in six states (1996).

No matter what the conceptual definition of interest groups that an author might want to use, those interested in large-scale investigations have consistently noted that there are few alternatives to consulting some sort of published list of groups. As the authors of each of the major surveys of interest groups conducted in the 1980s found out, establishing a definition of groups, and then getting a list of the full set from which to sample, is no easy task. Most empirical projects rely on published directories, legislative registrations, financial disclosure forms, testimony before congressional committees or in the rule-making process, or on some other published list. (See, e.g., Schlozman and Tierney 1986; Sabatier 1988; Hall and Wayman 1990; Knoke 1990a; Walker 1991; Jenkins-Smith, St. Clair, and Woods 1991; Baumgartner and Jones 1993; Golden 1995; Salisbury 1995; Gray and Lowery 1996; Hojnacki 1997. Cf. Browne 1995, who uses a reputational approach rather than published lists, and Heinz et al. 1993, who use a combination of approaches.)

All in all, one can note at least the following types of definitions used by various scholars interested in the roles of interest groups in politics:

social or demographic categories of the population
membership organizations
any set of individuals with similar beliefs, identifications, or interests
social movements
lobbyists registered in legislatures
political action committees
participants in rule-making or legislative hearings
institutions, including corporations and government agencies
coalitions of organizations and institutions
prominent individuals acting as political entrepreneurs or lobbyists

The diversity of definitions represents an underlying diversity of theoretical concerns. Different scholars are trying to explain different things about interest groups, and therefore define their tasks differently. Ambiguity of reactions toward interest groups and lobbyists is not a scholarly affectation: it is widely shared in the public and among politicians. Lawmakers have adopted a wide range of definitions in their efforts to regulate or control interest-group activities. Edgar Lane (1964) reviews the periodic efforts that legislators have made to control "the lobby problem" in the states and at the national level. Some definitions of lobbying equated the practice with bribery; others were so vague that almost all activities were included. The results of these ambiguities have been an ineffectual series of laws, either because they are hopelessly restrictive infringements on free speech or because they are so narrow that only a few rare behaviors are affected. Neither legislators nor scholars have devised an all-purpose definition of interest groups. This confusion explains not only a chaotic set of research findings but also a generally ineffectual set of laws.

Exactly how one defines an interest group can have important implications for one's findings. For example, a 1995 study of participation on federal rule making (Golden 1995) relied upon lists of those who intervened in a sample of rule-making procedures rather than sampling from a list of interests generally present in Washington. Golden's research showed a much greater range of participants than had typically been noted by others before her. How one defines an interest group is no mere detail. It can affect one's conclusions about the diversity of interests present in Washington as well as other important questions. Most seriously, however, the great variety of definitions used by different scholars makes it difficult to compare their results. When one scholar finds greater diversity of interests present in a policy area than another had found, is that because there is greater diversity or because the two scholars used different definitions or sampling frames? This problem is not limited only to the concepts of interests and interest groups. It extends much further into a series of basic concepts, including the concept of membership.

## WHAT IS MEMBERSHIP?

Just as the number of definitions of groups used in the literature is high, so too is the number of different conceptions of membership. For some, belonging to a particular social or ethnic class is enough; for others, a commitment of time and energy is necessary. Sometimes it requires only a psychological commitment or feeling of solidarity; in other cases, it means formal membership complete with dues and attendance at meetings; and in still other studies, it means only contributions of time or money. Dramatically different estimates of overall levels of membership in mass surveys naturally result from these different definitions, as has been repeatedly found in the literature in American and in comparative politics for the past forty years. Wide variation in estimates of public involvement result from variations in question wordings, question orders, and other elements of survey design. Some scholars have made estimates of American public involvement as low as 36 percent; others have given figures from 80 to 90 percent (compare, e.g., Wright and Hyman 1958; Babchuck and Booth 1969; Curtis 1971; Curtis, Grabb, and Baer 1992). Baumgartner and Walker (1988) review some of the difficulties in ascertaining membership in groups in a survey of the public (see also Schlozman, Verba, and Brady 1995). In the most recent and exhaustive study of its type, Verba, Schlozman, and Brady (1995) report higher levels of participation in groups than others before them, partly because they use a more expansive definition of group involvement. Increasingly, as groups make use of new fund-raising and mobilization techniques, they blur some common distinctions between members and nonmembers. Debates about the degree of public participation in the group system are often obscured by different definitions of interest groups and membership.

When discussing membership issues, scholars often adopt the perspective of the hypothetical citizens' group: members are predominantly individuals, and anyone may join for a nominal fee. Most groups, however, are not Common Cause. Even most environmental and public interest organizations limit their reliance on individual memberships by diversifying their sources of income. Christopher Bosso reports, for example, that the mean revenues coming from membership dues in a sample of large environmental organizations in the late 1980s was only 32 percent (1995, 107). Similarly, he reports that even among the major environmental organizations, only a few rely predominantly on funds from individuals to meet their annual revenue needs: grants from foundations and other sources of institutional support are increasingly important (108). With the rise of a variety of new fund-raising and political mobilization techniques, groups with access to large mailing and phone lists often reach well beyond their own memberships in their appeals for support or political action.

In adopting the perspective of the group relying on individuals for their membership support, scholars can address many important questions relating to how groups overcome the collective-action dilemma, the extent to which the group system is representative of the citizenry, and the impact of group involvement on individual feelings of political efficacy. Kenneth Goldstein (1995) reports, for example, that the single most powerful predictor of whether an individual will contact their representative in Congress is having been asked to do so by an organization. Clearly, individual members are important to groups, and groups have important impacts on individuals.

Individual members are the basis for much group activity, but most interest groups do not have only individuals as members, many groups have strict rules restricting the list of people who may join, and many interest groups have no members at all. A large part of the group universe is made up of organizations whose members are corporations, cities, hospitals, or some other type of organization. Others have strict limits on who may join, as is commonly the case among professional associations. These organizations often face quite different problems and opportunities for member development than those faced by the hypothetical citizens' group dependent on a large number of small dues-payments. The U.S. Chamber of Commerce, for example, has a complex membership structure allowing direct membership to individual people, corporations, state and local chapters, and other disparate units (see Walker 1991; Salisbury 1995). The Association of American Universities limits its membership only to the fifty or so largest research universities, thus distinguishing itself from other higher education organizations such as the National Association of State Universities and Land Grant Colleges. Neither group has any individuals as members. In any case, no single definition of membership could be applicable to all types of interest groups. As in the case of the term *interest groups* just described, it is clear that no single definition of "membership" is likely to fit in all cases, adding further difficulties to comparison across studies when scholars are not careful in comparing only apples to apples.

Why limit a study of interest groups to a study of membership organizations? The main reason would seem to be a desire to address the dilemmas of collective action presented by Olson or to resolve some of the questions of how membership groups survive and prosper. As with all such decisions, this focus comes with some costs as well as some benefits. For those interested in how groups interact with government, there is no reason to limit the focus only to groups open to members. If one hopes to focus on lobbying, influence, and the power of organizations in Washington, certainly one would not want to define interest groups in such a way as to exclude General Motors from discussions of automobile and tariff policies, or AT&T, Netscape Communications, and Microsoft from discussions of telecommunications policies. This is exactly what many scholars have done, however, because of their preoccupation with membership mobilization as the most important analytic question of the 1980s.

A second limitation of many studies of membership organizations has been the belated discovery that even most membership organizations do not rely primarily on the contribution of dues from their rank and file. Membership dues constitute only a fraction of the means of support for the typical interest group. Even those groups with few material incentives or selective benefits to offer rely on a small number of loyalists for the bulk of their support. Professional fund-raisers routinely speak in terms of a "pyramid of support," in which a small number of very large gifts are expected, along with smaller contributions from larger numbers of members. In his primer for nonprofit managers charged with fund-raising, Peter Edles includes a section entitled "Expect the most money from the least people." He notes that in the typical fund-raising campaign, 80 to 90 percent of the support should be expected from 10 to 20 percent of the contributors (1993, 11). Any university development officer would corroborate these expectations. Why expect that interest groups would rely on a flat dues structure when fund-raising experience makes it clear that a wide range of levels of participation would be expected? Slowly, better understandings of the complexities of membership are coming into the literature. Walker noted the prevalence of split dues structures and the existence of "member patrons"; Bosso noted the limited reliance even of environmental groups on dues; Edles reported the accepted lore of the fund-raising industry.

Membership is a deceptively complicated concept. A focus on the dilemmas of membership recruitment has led interest-group scholars to study certain types of organizations more than their numbers warrant and to adopt a view of the typical group that relies more heavily on individual membership than is often the case. Depending on the theoretical issue being addressed and the type of organization being studied, different definitions of membership are appropriate. As with other areas of the literature on interest groups, these definitional ambiguities make it surprisingly hard to read a series of studies and answer some simple questions, such as the extent of public involvement in the group system or the number of members in various social movements. *Membership, interests,* and *interest groups* are complicated terms to define. So too is *lobbying.*

## WHAT IS LOBBYING?

The word *lobbying* has seldom been used the same way twice by those studying the topic. Lester Milbrath introduced his discussion of the topic by noting that "the words 'lobbyist' and 'lobbying' have meanings so varied that use of them almost inevitably leads to misunderstanding" (1963, 7). Robert Salisbury has written that we should avoid calling interest-group activities "lobbying" at all: "That much-abused word is so fraught with ordinary language meaning, most of it unsavory, as to defy rehabilitation anyway, but it is also true that none of its historic uses comfortably fits what many Washington representatives do" (1983, 71). If one were to compare the daily schedule of a lobbyist with the definitions of lobbying often used in the literature, one would find that much of what lobbyists do is not really at "lobbying" at all. Here we get to the problem of how to deal with indirect lobbying, research and data-gathering, and efforts to monitor what the government is doing. Lobbyists spend much of their time doing such things, but should we call those lobbying? The key point is that, whatever we call these activities, or however we decide to limit our definition of lobbying, we should be clear about what we mean, and we should compare findings in the literature based on similar usages of the term. The careless comparison of unlike definitions of the term generates considerable confusion. Unfortunately, the literature is home to a great variety of definitions of lobbying, and scholars are often tempted to compare the incomparable.

The word *lobby* originally referred to the entry hall in the British House of Commons, where those who were not members of government could meet those who were and plead their case. Thus "lobbying" has been used most often to refer to face-to-face individual meetings between legislators and representatives of an interest. In its most literal form, the word would not even include testimony before Congress. Most interest-group scholars have used a broader definition. "Lobbying" has been used to refer to interest-group contacts in the bureaucracy, the office of the president, and the courts, as well as within the legislature. It has been used to describe grassroots campaigns, use of the mass media, and the creation of research reports, as well as face-to-face contacts. The common thread is that all of these activities must be used in an effort to influence the policy process for them to be called "lobbying."

Milbrath (1963, 7–8) was quite explicit in his explanation of how he reached a definition of lobbying. First, he wrote, lobbying must involve governmental decisions not private ones. Pressuring General Motors to increase minority hiring is not lobbying. Asking the government to pressure General Motors to increase minority hiring is lobbying. Second, lobbying must involve the intent to affect government decisions. Activities that have an impact, but are not necessarily intended to have an impact, are not lobbying. A scientist who discovers a clear link between smoking and cancer would undoubtedly have an effect on government decisions; however, her actions would not necessarily be lobbying. Third, lobbying goes through an intermediary, according to Milbrath. For this author, a citizen directly expressing his own opinion is not lobbying; lobbying occurs only when a group argues on behalf of someone else. (Milbrath sees the potential difficulty with this argument, since voting is the expression of a message often intended to affect government decisions, but we would gain little from a definition that expanded lobbying to include even the act of voting.) Finally, there must be an act of communication. Based on this explanation, Milbrath then arrives at his definition of lobbying: "Lobbying is the stimulation and transmission of a communication, by someone other than a citizen acting on his own behalf, directed to a governmental decision-maker with the hope of influencing his decision" (1963, 8).

The federal Lobbying Disclosure Act of 1995 defines lobbying activities as "lobbying contacts and efforts in support of such contacts, including preparation and planning activities, research and other background work that is intended, at the time it is performed, for use in contacts, and coordination with the lobbying activities of others." It defines lobbying contacts as "any oral or written communication . . . to a covered executive branch official or a covered legislative branch official that is made on behalf of a client with regard to (I) the formulation, modification, or adoption of Federal legislation . . . [or] of a Federal rule, regulation, Executive order, or any other program, policy, or position of the United States Government . . . [or] the administration or execution of a Federal program or policy (including . . . a Federal contract, grant, loan, permit, or license); or the nomination or confirmation of a person for a position subject to confirmation by the Senate." "Covered officials," in the terms of the legislation, are those in a policymaking or policy-advocating position, including congressional and presidential staff. This definition specifically excludes official testimony before Congress, indirect lobbying through the media, filings before the court (like amicus briefs), provision of information requested by the official, and responses to requests for comments published in the Federal Register.

While all would agree that contacting members of Congress and asking them to vote in a particular way is an act of lobbying, many other activities are subject to differing interpretations. Maintaining regular contact, good relations, and easy access to decision makers may involve only occasional efforts to sway votes, for example. Similarly, working to enhance the public image of an industry or a profession is generally not included in definitions of lobbying, but it can be an important source of power. Among the many ambiguities in defining lobbying, the following set of questions offers a sample: Does providing information for legislative allies to use in debate qualify? Working with allies outside of government? Recruiting a particularly influential ally within government to do most of one's lobbying? Keeping one's ties to that person a secret? Conducting membership or public education campaigns without directly asking those contacted to engage in specific lobbying activities? Providing information to a prominent member, who may be a university president, for example, and who in turn may contact a decision maker? Leaking information to journalists? Engaging in legal research for later use in law suits or amicus briefs? Monitoring the activities of government agencies in order to know what decisions may be under discussion? Contributing money to reelection campaigns or to political parties?

Studies of lobbying differ in the degree to which they adopt general or precise definitions. In the literature on policymaking in general, the more informal approach is more common; in the quantitative literature, of course, more precise operationalizations are necessary. The broad surveys of interest-group activities conducted by Schlozman and Tierney (1986), Knoke (1990a), Walker (1991), and Heinz and colleagues (1993) have consistently shown that groups use a tremendous range of tactics in various situations, and this finding is generally corroborated in the informal and case-study literature as well. We will review these findings in some detail in chapters 7 and 8. The range of tactics that groups use in their lobbying efforts is quite broad and has consistently been documented by every major survey of groups in recent decades. Whereas those conducting the broad surveys of groups typically find a great variety of lobbying activities being used, those conducting different types of studies often focus only on one or a few of these lobbying tactics.

Scholars show no consensus on what they mean by lobbying. For some, it represents the range of activities groups engage in as they attempt to maintain links with government officials. For others, it can be so narrowly defined that even many direct contacts with members of Congress would not be included. As scholars have attempted to design more systematic and quantitative research projects, they have shown an increasing tendency to use very precise and often incomplete definitions of lobbying.

As in the other areas discussed so far in this chapter, there is no particular problem with a focus on the use of particular tactic of lobbying. Difficulties ensue when scholars using distinct and sometimes conflicting definitions attempt to compare findings that may not be comparable. In the literature on lobbying, this has often occurred. Economists sometimes discuss lobbying in terms that equate efforts to influence legislators with giving PAC contributions, on the assumption that those who contribute to particular legislators probably also lobby them. Within political science, the emphasis has been on measuring the impact of PACs as distinct from explicit lobbying contacts. Such conflicting definitions and research approaches guarantee that the substantive conclusions about determinants and consequences of lobbying will be difficult to compare.

## WHAT IS INFLUENCE?

Scholars have long attempted to observe and document the exercise of influence in politics. They have yet to succeed. Anecdotes abound in the academic and popular literatures about how a particular vote or decision was manufactured by the skillful exertion of pressure. Never have scholars been able to organize a systematic study that would demonstrate the influence of any particular lobbyist when controlling for all rival factors that might have also affected the decision, however. Scholars continue to design their research projects around a premise that they will be able to "explain" votes or decisions by isolating all the forces acting on the decision makers, even though the process has not worked in the past.

In the last section, we reviewed some of the problems with overly precise and incomplete definitions of lobbying that are common in much of the literature. The appeal of these definitions has to do with a desire to isolate the particular forms of lobbying behavior that most closely resemble "pressure" in the hopes of linking these to subsequent decisions. As Robert Salisbury (1994) has pointed out, the hope to isolate and measure influence is the common thread that links together much of the work on interest groups in recent decades. Almost every study of PACs and lobbying eventually gets around to the linkage between the efforts or contributions of the lobbyists and the votes taken by the targets, Salisbury notes.

The general approach in much of the lobbying and PAC contribution literature is to estimate a baseline of expected behavior using a set of measured variables such as ideological predisposition, district interest, committee assignments, and party, then to ascribe any deviation in voting patterns to whatever lobbying activities might have been measured. Of course the approach requires that all relevant factors be included in the model. This is particularly difficult when dealing with such concepts of what a vote of a member of Congress might have been in the absence of any lobbying or when attempting to insure that all relevant facts that might have influenced the member's decision have been identified and measured. In the absence of a fully specified model, the scholar may hope that the effects of any unmeasured variables will be small and unbiased on average. When taken as a whole, however, the literature attempting to demonstrate these linkages between lobbying and subsequent decisions is characterized by a tremendous lack of consensus given the amount of work that has been done, as we noted in chapter 1 and as we will review in more detail in chapter 7. More important than any individual problems of model specification or measurement, the literature is organized around a chimera. Scholars have long attempted to isolate and measure the exertion of power and influence. In chapter 3 we will review their efforts in the 1950s and 1960s and note how they eventually gave up in the wake of vituperative and inconclusive debates. Rather than learn from this experience, after a brief lull when fewer lobbying studies were done, scholars have returned to the same doomed research idea. Many recent studies have been designed around the false premise that we can observe the actions of influence and power. There is little reason to organize a project on the chimerical promise of measuring the unmeasurable.

One recent approach to the concept of influence is to specify the conditions under which lobbyists would be influential under a set of assumptions concerning the information they control, the information government decision makers would like to have, and the behaviors of rival interests. These "signaling models" of group influence have been much more successful in devising interesting theoretical findings than in demonstrating the empirical usefulness of the approach, however (see, e.g., Ainsworth 1993; Ainsworth and Sened 1993; Austen-Smith 1993). To ascertain the validity of these models, one day scholars will have to solve the problem of how to measure whether these behaviors had the impact that the models predict. More important than only the problem of measuring lobbying is simultaneously measuring a variety of other variables that would allow one to consider a range of rival explanations for the same outcomes.

We can say a lot about the tactics and strategies of lobbyists without discussing influence in particular cases. Spectacular cases of pressure may make for interesting reading, but much of the important work in lobbying is in setting the agenda, in defining the alternatives for decision makers, in gathering evidence, and in convincing others that certain types of evidence are germane to the decision at hand. To the extent that we attempt to define influence narrowly and in the context of a single decision, we inevitably fail in two ways. First, the models are rarely specified fully and are therefore doomed to fail. (This is especially true of the empirical models as opposed to the formal specifications, which are sometimes more complete.) Second, we are led to the adoption of overly narrow definitions of what lobbying is and how influence is wielded in politics. Most importantly, it leads us to study lobbying only at the very last stage of the decision-making process. Ironically, many scholars agree that this is where the possible exertion of influence is at its lowest point. Why search for influence where it is least likely to be found?

## WHAT IS AN ISSUE?

To the extent that interest-group studies are linked with the policy process, they share a problem common to all policy studies (see Greenberg et al. 1977). That is, there is no clear way to determine when an issue or a policy conflict has begun or ended. Three fundamental research problems flow from this simple fact. First, there can be no universe of issues from which to sample. Second, there is no single definition of an issue when issues are easily aggregated into large and interrelated groups or broken down into minute clauses, as constantly occurs in the policy process. Third, issues rise and fall on the political agenda over time, being transformed and redefined in the process. There are no apparent solutions to the difficulties created by the fluid nature of issues in the political process. Scholars must be sensitive to the ambiguities of the concept of an issue if they hope to avoid the confusion that inevitably stems from using similar terms to mean different things.

Issues never begin and they never end. Particular controversies may dominate discussion during certain periods, but policymakers know that issues never disappear forever. Most scholars react to the fluid nature of the issues with which they deal by limiting their consideration of an issue to how it is defined at a particular point in time, often in relation to a particular vote or decision by a certain government agency. This approach allows the identification of a list of participants, the observation of efforts to affect the outcome of the debate, and sometimes the identification of winners and losers. Issues are constantly being redefined in government, however, and when one debate is lost it is often not long before the same issue rises again in another forum. This may be one reason why studies of particular controversies often seem to reach conclusions at odds with those where the author investigates an issue-area over long periods of time. The second approach allows the identification of long-lasting patterns of activity, whereas the first attempts to present a snapshot of an evolving process.

The second ambiguity associated with the definition of an issue is that issues may be aggregated in many different ways, none of which guarantees that the results of a given study will be representative of all issues facing the political system at any particular time. Any given issue is typically part of a broader set of related issues: For example, a decision about whether to modify a fire-safety regulation in poultry plants is likely to be considered in connection with other workplace safety issues. Is the issue the modification of standards as it relates to one industry or across many industries? For a congressman from a particular district, the issue may simply be how the standard would affect one factory. For another policymaker, the issue may be worker-safety standards in general. For others, it may be government regulation of the economy. Since different policymakers may be making their decisions based on different understandings of what the issue is, there is no clear answer to such questions.

The literature on interest-group lobbying and participation in the policy process combines studies at all levels of aggregation. Some studies focus on a single roll-call vote in a single committee whereas others focus on a series of decisions in a broad area such as health-care policy. Some focus on a single issue niche (e.g., how the crop subsidy program works for cotton farmers); others choose huge and heterogeneous issue domains (e.g., telecommunications, health, or defense policy). Some ask group leaders or lobbyists to generalize about their behaviors across a range of issues, or across the previous twelve months (see Schlozman and Tierney 1986 or Walker 1991); other studies are designed around activities in a single case of policymaking. Each approach is valuable but each would be most valuable if it were designed in a way that encouraged the comparison of its findings with those using contrasting definitions.

Andrew McFarland (1991) notes that interest-group scholars are fond of conceiving of the political system as an aggregation of hundreds of smaller issue-areas, typically defined by economic production: Cotton farming, pesticides, higher education, nuclear power generation, and the like. Since interest groups are known to be important in each of these issue-areas, then they must be fundamental in the political system more broadly. He notes, however, that large-scale, macropolitical events can affect hundreds of these issue-areas simultaneously, thereby making it important to understand these macrolevel events as well. Much of the accepted literature concerning the power of various types of groups (for example, Schlesinger's "reform cycles") can be restated in terms of the prominence of certain issues on the national political agenda, according to McFarland (1991, 276–77). In any case it is clear that we reach different conclusions about the nature of the policy process depending on the level of aggregation we choose. The more narrowly we define issues, the more likely we are to find the operation of policy subsystems operating with little public knowledge, partisan bickering, or political oversight. The more broadly we define issues, the more likely we are to note the importance of elections, political parties, and the national political institutions.

McFarland points to an important issue for the study of groups in politics: can the political system be reduced to the aggregation of hundreds of issue-areas, each dominated by a set of groups? The answer is clearly no, for if it were yes, there would be no important role for the president, the political parties, or the institutions of national government. Certainly, "high politics" often matters. The linkage between the politics of issue-areas, where interest groups are commonly studied, and "high politics," where other actors are seen as more important, is the agenda-setting process. Interest-group scholars have provided many important analyses of the roles and importance of groups within their issue networks, but have not done as well in explaining the roles of interest groups in those cases where "high politics" is at work. Issues sometimes rise high into the public consciousness; all political issues are not decided within subgovernments. Giving explicit consideration to the agenda-status of the issues being discussed would resolve many of the difficulties in comparing the results of diverse studies and help reconcile the study of groups with the study of political parties, elections, and national political institutions. Often, these other institutions are seen to be less important in group studies, but this can be only because so many group studies are designed to focus on issues that are off the political agenda.

Baumgartner and Jones (1993) show that the roles of groups may be dramatically different depending on their goals of either destabilizing or reinforcing existing policy communities and depending on whether the issue is on or off the political agenda. Focusing only on those cases with little or no public controversy is incomplete and can be misleading, just as would be a focus only on highly salient issues. Comparison of lobbying strategies of interest groups in cases with little or no public awareness with those in such cases as the Clinton health-care plan, with its massive domination of the entire political agenda, leads to confusion rather than to analytic clarity. The integration of an agenda-setting approach with sensitivity to the roles of interest groups in the policy process promises to resolve many of the apparent contradictions in this literature (see also Heinz et al. 1993, 16–17, 302). In any case, scholars must be sensitive to the fluid nature of policy issues and to their movements up and down the political agenda.

We have reviewed three problems related to the definition of an issue: issues are difficult to identify; issues may be aggregated in different ways; and issues rise and fall on the political agenda, often being redefined as this occurs. These difficulties are not of the type where a single "solution" is apparent. Rather, there are good reasons why scholars find different definitions of an issue best to suit their purposes. Just as with the ambiguities discussed earlier in this chapter, these differences in research approach will always be with us; they simply must be handled carefully and explicitly by scholars so as not to hinder the development of a cumulative and comparable set of findings. Careless comparisons of research findings based on diverse definitions of the same terms renders virtually impossible the synthesis of a variety of findings into a single coherent description of how groups operate in the American political system. If tightly knit issue subsystems are in control in some narrow areas while the issues are off the agenda, but broad and conflictual issue networks obtain in others, especially when the issues are high on the political agenda, what do we conclude about the roles of groups in the system as a whole? Without a clear way to compare studies based on common definitions of key terms, we can have no answer.

## WHAT IS THE NORMATIVE CONCERN?

Interest-group scholars have rarely made explicit the normative bases on which their conclusions might be interpreted. Great ideological and normative debates swept through political science in the 1950s and 1960s, as critics of pluralist thought charged that there were conservative biases in many of the most prominent works. However, as Greenstone (1975) pointed out, the most important debates even in this period combined normative and empirical disagreements. Those with relatively benign interpretations of the system noted certain observations; those who were more critical addressed a different set of empirical facts, never challenging the facts of the others. Rarely have scholars in the area separated the normative and the empirical; rather, both have been linked.

Despite a continued interest in normative issues associated with representation, few scholars have adopted an explicit normative framework. Many works concern the diversity of participation in the group system either through mass participation in groups or through elite participation in the policy process. Rarely does this literature make clear any ideal point toward which a democracy should strive. In the case of mass participation, it seems clear that more participation is normatively preferable to less and that participation should be equitable across social class and other distinctions. In this case, the normative question is relatively straightforward. In policymaking studies where we observe interest groups in their relations with government, however, there is no clear ideal with which to compare observed levels of participation. Scholars are concerned with diversity of participation, how this diversity changes over time, and how it differs from issue to issue. Few have paid attention to such questions as what degree of diversity would be appropriate for which types of issues, how to balance expertise and knowledge against demographic representivity, or how public officials may play a role in guaranteeing public representation, for example.

Studies of policy processes and lobbying often note changes over time in the diversity of lobbying communities. The rise of the consumer, women's rights, civil rights, and environmental movements in the 1960s and 1970s had important implications for the makeup of many policy communities. These were noted in the literature and generally were seen in a positive normative light: Each development seemed to indicate greater equality of participation. Beyond this general observation that greater diversity is to be applauded, scholars have typically not developed very sophisticated models of the normative appropriateness of various types of policymaking communities. If diversity of participation is often the result of a logic of conflict expansion, then do we conclude that only those decisions in government made after the eruption of conflict are made according to a process that is normatively beneficial? Scholars occasionally note the absence of certain interests who perhaps should be involved in important decisions, but without a clear idea of what is appropriate, these efforts are idiosyncratic and incomplete. To interpret the findings of the literature on group participation in government, we need a point of reference: What should be the proper roles of interest groups in policymaking? Does the answer to this question differ dramatically based on the nature of the question at issue? On these questions, the literature has remained resolutely ambivalent.

## CONCLUSION

This chapter has reviewed a series of conceptual problems that has limited the ability of scholars to build a coherent literature on interest groups in American politics. For most of the issues discussed here, no single perspective could be applicable for all potential uses. The conclusion to be reached from this list of ambiguities is not that some single set of definitions should be imposed but rather that scholars should realize how their adoption of any particular usage affects their ability to compare their findings with those of others and to reach broad conclusions. Confusion and contradiction creep into a literature not when people use different definitions as they seek to address different theoretical concerns. Rather, they come when scholars overgeneralize from their studies, reaching conclusions on one set of topics when they have designed their projects in ways that best allow them to address another. Finally, the great range of definitions and legitimate usages of important terms in the literature serves to multiply the difficulties in generating a corpus of comparable findings. For quite some time, interest-group scholars have lived with the hope that the vast investment in empirical studies observed in the past twenty years would inevitably lead to a clear set of collective conclusions about group behavior. With this discussion of the myriad ways in which different theoretical and empirical perspectives produce subtle changes in research designs, measurements, and definitions of key terms, we hope to begin to explain how this accumulation failed to occur.

If we return to our distinction between areas of advance and areas of confusion in the literature, it is clear that if the areas of advance do not benefit from a complete absence of definitional ambiguities, scholars working in those areas have shown a greater ability to share common terms than those working in the areas of confusion. Those working on the collective-action dilemma have focused on a variety of elements of the membership calculus, and they have typically used relatively similar definitions of membership. This literature has grown richer as scholars have noted that not all groups have members, but when solving one particular puzzle most have chosen the appropriate set of definitions and limited their conclusions to those that can be supported by those terms. Looking at the areas where the most important contradictions have taken place, we note that many have to do with efforts to study lobbying in a quantitative manner based on one or a few cases. Notably, these studies have often adopted contrasting definitions of key terms. But the combination of new theoretical insights, new empirical points of reference, and new definitions of important terms can make it difficult indeed to compare findings. We will review these difficulties in detail in chapter 7. The point of this chapter has been simply to note the importance of care in generalization. Many useful definitions of a range of central terms are used simultaneously in the study of interest groups. We propose no imposition of a rigid set of standard definitions; different usages appear useful for different purposes. We do think it prudent, however, for scholars to pay careful attention to the precise terms they are using, especially as they attempt to compare their findings with those of others.

Having reviewed in chapter 1 the uneven patterns of progress in the literature and having noted a range of definitional ambiguities that may help explain these patterns in this chapter, we turn in chapter 3 to a historical overview of the rise and decline of the group approach to politics. To understand the state of the literature in the 1990s, it is important to see from whence it came.

# The Rise and Decline of the Group Approach

THE STUDY OF INTEREST GROUPS was once perhaps the most imperial of literatures, not only in American politics but in political science generally. Scholars of the generation of David Truman thought that a nation's political system could best be understood by looking at how groups formed and interacted with each other and with the government. Studies of interest groups were studies of the entire political system, and students of politics were students of interest groups, virtually by definition. Interest-group research of the postwar years took on the major issues of politics: who wields power and influence and whose views are represented in a democracy. Books focusing on the roles and influence of interest groups such as Truman's *The Governmental Process* (1951) or McConnell's *Private Power and American Democracy* (1966) posed central questions about the nature of representation in a democratic system. Similarly grand questions were the preoccupation in sociology, with books such as Mills' *The Power Elite* (1956), Hunter's *Community Power Structure* (1953), and Domhoff's *Who Rules America?* (1967). Scholars in both fields were concerned with basic questions about power, voice, and representation. The most vibrant research in both areas attempted to answer these questions by looking at groups, corporations, and other institutional linkages between the public and the government. These studies had in common an ambition to use the activities of interest groups as a lens through which to view all of politics. Dahl's *Who Governs* (1961) shared certain elements with this literature, though he disagreed with the view that groups alone could provide the entire picture; his coverage was correspondingly broader, focusing particularly on elected leaders themselves. Still, Dahl reserved an important place for the roles of groups in his study of New Haven, as did most prominent studies of the time.

## THE GROUP APPROACH TO POLITICS

In this chapter, we review the dramatic rise and the precipitous decline of the "group approach to politics." The many difficulties and unfulfilled promises of the group approach affected the discipline for decades. The group approach offered many advantages over what had existed before. It represented one of the first truly behavioral approaches in a discipline that had been dominated by formal and constitutional analyses. On the other hand, the approach foundered on a series of problems including how to measure power, how to devise a series of scientifically testable hypotheses, how to separate the normative from the empirical, and how to analyze a situation where organized interests work in close concert with allies within government, not so much lobbying them as helping them do their work. To understand the nature of the current scholarship on groups, it is important to see how much of it was a reaction against the work of previous generations.

The group approach to politics was important enough that Fred Greenstein and Nelson Polsby included two long chapters on groups in their *Handbook of Political Science*, published in 1975. Greenstone's eighty-page essay focused on group approaches to politics in general, especially the works of Bentley, Truman, Dahl, McConnell, and Lowi. Greenstone notes at the outset that "the group theories tradition has been the most important and sustained attempt to resolve two ancient issues:" the effects of groups on policymaking, institutions, and outcomes, and the effects of these processes and outcomes on the groups themselves (1975, 243). Salisbury's fifty-page essay reviews a broad range of issues dealing with groups, including the definitional ambiguities we discussed in chapter 2, research findings on group origins and growth, the Olsonian dilemma and subsequent research, internal group dynamics, and group relations with government. According to Greenstein and Polsby, then, the state of political science in 1975 required not one but two substantial reviews of research on groups. One focused on the broad theoretical questions of the "group approach to politics" and the other dealt with a range of issues concerning interest-group creation, maintenance, and influence.

Whereas scholars once considered groups to be central to our understanding of politics generally, more recent trends have pushed the topic of interest groups to the very margins of political science. Graduate-level seminars in American politics often overlook current research on interest groups. In stark contrast to the 1975 *Handbook*, a recent compilation of essays published by the American Political Science Association reviewing the state of the discipline includes no general essay on the roles of groups (see Finifter 1993). Clearly, the study of interest groups has receded from its position a generation ago at the core of the discipline (see Garson 1978).

We noted in the introduction that political scientists, philosophers, and commentators of all kinds have long had ambivalent views of the roles of groups in politics. On the one hand, they are seen as a vehicle for popular representation; on the other hand, the biases of group mobilization are acknowledged by continued emphasis on the dangers of granting access to "special interest lobbyists." Groups, at best, are necessary evils that must be controlled before they do too much damage.

Jack Walker noted that political scientists have been much more supportive of the roles of political parties in politics than of interest groups. He noted that more than ten times the number of scholarly articles were published on political parties than on groups in the 1980s but that groups are more commonly active in Washington policymaking than parties are. Why the discrepancies in scholarly attention? "Political scientists devote so much of their resources to the study of political parties mainly because of their historic commitment to the task of convincing anyone who will listen that democracy cannot be successful without the existence of vigorous, competitive political parties" (Walker 1991, 20–21). Whereas parties are seen as encompassing organizations, interest groups are seen as fragmenters of the political process, encouraging the press of particularistic demands rather than helping to develop the conditions necessary for negotiation and compromise. Given these dubious effects, political scientists have abandoned the study of groups while lavishing more attention on parties than they may merit, according to Walker (1991, 20–40).

Kay Schlozman and John Tierney also noted the dearth of attention to the group system in the 1980s. Discussing the rise of the group approach to politics, they wrote: "No sooner had this perspective become dominant than it was questioned seriously" (1986, ix–xii). They foreshadow Walker's arguments that groups were increasingly important in the Washington community but strangely absent from the scholarly agendas of most members of our profession: "In the past two decades we have witnessed what seems to be a virtual explosion in demands by private organizations in Washington. While the media have made much of this development, political scientists have paid it less heed" (ix). In the face of this dearth of attention, they set out in their book "to compensate for the relative neglect by academic analysts of organized interests in contemporary politics by probing what they are up to and what their activity means for public life in America" (ix). For the authors of two of the most important large-scale reviews of the roles of groups in politics in the 1980s, then, part of the motivation was to fill in a perceived gap in the research agenda of the profession. This gap is all the more remarkable, as we will review in this chapter, because it followed a period when the group approach to politics was so dominant.

## GROUPS AT THE CENTER OF POLITICAL SCIENCE

Every literature is in a way a reaction to and often against the work of a previous generation of scholars. Harmon Zeigler and Wayne Peak (1972, 2–6) describe the development of a group approach to politics in the early twentieth century as a reaction to the institutional/legalism of the nineteenth century. The work of the early pluralists clearly indicates that they were dissatisfied with the dominant formal/legal approach of their day. When they looked at the functioning of government, they found that constitutional analysis and description could explain only part of what they observed. Corporations, trade groups, business executives, and others outside of government often played important roles but were absent from the descriptions of the time. Ernest Griffith was most explicit on these points, arguing that a group approach to the processes of government would be more revealing of how the system really works than any analysis of separation of powers or constitutional design:

> One cannot live in Washington for long without being conscious that it has these whirlpools or centers of activity focusing on particular problems. The persons who are thus active—in agriculture, in power, in labor, in foreign trade, and the parts thereof—are variously composed. Some are civil servants, some are active members of the appropriate committees in the House and Senate, some are lobbyists, some are unofficial research authorities, connected perhaps with the Brookings Institution or with one of the universities, or even entirely private individuals. . . .
>
> [H]e who would understand the prevailing pattern of our present governmental behavior, instead of studying the formal institutions or even generalizations in the relationships between these institutions . . . may possibly obtain a better picture of the way things really happen if he would study these "whirlpools" of special social interest and problems. (Griffith 1939, 182–83)

By focusing on the activities of actors inside and outside of government, Griffith and others could be called the first behavioralists in political science. Many of these authors would certainly object to being called behavioralists, since they did not share with the later behavioralists the tendency for systematic quantification or concern for the analysis of individual-level behavior. Still, the early group scholars, like the later behavioralists, studied political dynamics through observation and outside of the formal institutions of government, eschewing the formal/legal approach that was more common before their time. The foundations of behavioralism can be found at least partly in the rise of the group approach to politics, though the two developed differently in later years.

Griffith was not alone in this view of the greater realism of the empirical study of groups as opposed to the formal analysis of structures of government, as David Garson points out:

> In the early years of the twentieth century, the felt need to focus empirically on groups was widely shared among American political scientists. Summarizing popular ideas on government, for example, Albert Hart noted that "more and more people tend to accept the theory that all government in America— national, state, municipal or local—springs from one source, the American people as a whole, who choose to exercise their power through a variety of organizations (Hart 1907, 558)." (Garson 1978, 32)

This "organizational perspective" on political life offered many advantages over strict legalism, in that it allowed many more political variables to come into perspective, but it had the drawback of being all-encompassing as well. Group scholars like Bentley (1908), Odegard (1928), Herring (1929), Schattschneider (1935), Griffith (1939), and Key (1964) made possible some of the most important advances in our understanding of politics by introducing a broader view of the functioning of government institutions, including the informal relations among institutions and outside actors and the dynamics of engaging the public through elections and organized lobbying. Griffith's work is typical of his generation in two ways: Not only did behavioralism supplant formal/legalism as the dominant approach to the study of politics, but many of the first insights about the policy process that this broader view permitted are echoed with almost eerie similarity today. The remaining importance of this early work is of course more due to its broad analytic approach, which allows the simultaneous consideration of the roles of government and nongovernment actors in the policy process, than to any descriptive accuracy that the work might retain decades after it was written. Still, it is surprising to note the degree to which many of the descriptions of the "whirlpools" of policymaking in the works of Griffith and his contemporaries are similar to our more recent discussions of issue networks, policy subsystems, policy domains, and policy communities (see Heclo 1978; Kingdon 1984; Sabatier 1988; Berry 1989a; Browne 1990; Walker 1991; Baumgartner and Jones 1993; Heinz et al. 1993). Policy studies today typically borrow heavily from the work of interest-group scholars in the prewar years.

David Garson (1974; 1978) describes how interest-group theory became the central framework of analysis during the first sixty years of this century. Group theory grew in reaction to the narrow institutionalism of early political science and against assumptions about the absolute sovereignty of the state, he argues. Group theory instead relied on the pluralistic assumption that the best political outcomes would arise as a result of group conflict. Free and active group life was seen as a crucial to the functioning of a democracy. The role of the state was not to dictate outcomes, but rather to arbitrate among various interests. The best functioning democracy would not necessarily be the one with a certain constitutional structure but rather the one with the most balanced, active, and responsive group system. Groups accurately representing the views of their members would be a better guarantor of effective government than any particular institutional design. In the immediate postwar years, one of the explanations of America's success in maintaining democracy while other countries fell to fascism was the vibrant group system based on competition and independence from the state. Pluralism grew partly, then, as an effort to explain the perceived genius of American democracy, and it included both descriptive and normatively charged writings, especially in the postwar period.

The group approach became dominant in these years not only in the study of American politics, but in comparative politics as well. A tremendously influential series of studies was initiated in the 1950s and 1960s, mostly at the urging and with the support of the Social Science Research Council, with the goal of understanding the functioning of democracies around the world through a description of how groups relate to the state. These decades saw an optimism in the possibilities of furthering our understandings of politics by using the broader lens of group politics rather than the narrower and previously dominant perspective of comparative legal institutions and constitutional structures. This approach and this optimism are reflected in such works as Ehrmann's *Organized Business in France* (1957), the essays published in Ehrmann's edited volume *Interest Groups on Four Continents* (1958), Almond's "Comparative Study of Interest Groups" (1958), Eckstein's *Pressure Group Politics* (1960), Brown's "Pressure Politics in the Fifth Republic" (1963), LaPolombara's *Interest Groups in Italian Politics* (1964), Eckstein's *Division and Cohesion in Democracy* (1966), and Lijphart's *The Politics of Accommodation* (1968). These studies shared the perspective that one could understand how a country "really" works not by analyzing its constitutional structures but by observing group-state interactions. In sum, interest groups were the vehicle that political scientists first discovered as they attempted to abandon the constitutional/legal framework that had previously dominated their thinking about politics, and as they attempted to adopt a behavioral framework. (The adoption of the "American" group approach for comparative analysis was not without difficulties, and these were debated at the time; see for example LaPolombara 1960 and Macridis 1961.)

In some ways the group approach became more influential in comparative politics than in American politics. One of the most important components necessary to sustain a vibrant democracy is a healthy network of organizations available to the public, according to Almond and Verba's five-nation study. Their focus on civic culture put organizational affiliations through interest groups at the center of democracy (1965). The importance of local voluntary associations has more recently been picked up by Robert Putnam as he has used organizational affiliations as a centerpiece of his explanation of the basis for a strong and working democracy in Italy and in America (1993; 1995). A research focus on the roles of groups in their relations with state officials is probably more central to much of the comparative study of public policymaking than in American politics today (see for examples Rokkan 1966; Heclo 1974; Suleiman 1974; Dogan 1975; Anton 1980; Aberbach, Putnam, and Rockman 1981; Olsen 1983; Hall 1986; Baumgartner 1989; Wilsford 1991). Major debates concerning the roles of groups and the nature of their relations with government officials dominate the literature on pluralism, corporatism, and related descriptions of the policy process, and these disputes have resonated throughout the field of comparative politics for decades (see Lijphart 1969; Landé 1973; Schmitter 1974; Schmitter and Lehmbruch 1979; Lehmbruch and Schmitter 1982; Richardson 1982; Almond 1983; Keeler 1987; Wilson 1987; Smith 1993). The study of interest groups in comparative politics and in other democratic settings has consistently focused on the lobbying and government relations of those groups, rarely becoming preoccupied with the Olsonian dilemmas of mobilization for collective action. This may explain why group studies are considered more central in comparative politics than in American politics.

Despite its prominence, the group approach was not adopted by unanimous consent in either American or comparative political science. Neither did it ever generate the kind of consensus in its support that is sometimes imagined. Criticisms of the group approach were powerful and continuing. Further, the approach itself was mostly visible only from the outside, and more easily with hindsight. It was never a clear theory of politics with the requisite testable hypotheses, shared definitions, and neat operationalizations; rather it was a set of ideas about what was important to look for in politics, and an idea that representation took place through the group system as much as through the constitutionally mandated institutions of elections and judicial-legislative-executive interactions. Pluralism was so little developed as a theory that proponents of various pluralist arguments objected to being labeled as similar. While they shared certain general orientations, they did not share conclusions or anything as precise as a theory.

The group approach to politics reached its point of greatest acceptance in the 1950s but even then was not the subject of a broad consensus. Problems such as vague definitions, conflicting conclusions, unsystematic research techniques, inability to explain the lack of mobilization by disadvantaged social groups, and other issues had existed for a long time. By the late 1960s, however, the approach was in crisis, criticized on the one hand for failing to recognize the unfair imbalance of power among interests in society, and on the other hand for overstating the influence interest groups wielded over government. By this period, the approach had been largely discredited through a series of internal disputes, external challenges, and by the rise of a new set of research questions that left traditional group studies behind as outdated and irrelevant relics of a prescientific age. By the time of Olson's *Logic of Collective Action*, it was a research agenda on the road to oblivion.

## THE DEMISE OF THE GROUP APPROACH

A great variety of forces combined to cause the demise of the group approach to politics. There were theoretical problems, methodological difficulties, ambiguities of definition, disagreements on how to interpret findings, difficulties of measuring important features such as power and influence, findings of limited group influence in government, and finally the emergence of a new set of research questions based on the question of group mobilization rather than on group influence. We review each of these in turn.

### A Normative Theory or an Empirical Approach?

The most troubling difficulty with the group approach to politics was the lack of clarity about its goals. The most prominent pluralists asserted that their studies were empirical ones, attempting only to explain how democracies operate, but ambiguities remained about whether they were merely explaining and describing, as they asserted, or holding up pluralism as a normative ideal.

In his review of group theories of democracy of the 1950s and 1960s, David Greenstone notes that theorists "disagree with one another over the ethical status of their subject matter. To some, notably Truman and Dahl in his work on New Haven, political interest group activities seem at least comparable with, if not essential to, the health of American politics. To others, such as McConnell and Lowi, interest group behavior often malignly subverts the highest ideals of liberal democracy. This issue, however, has apparently been less empirical than normative; the facts and observations adduced by each side have not ordinarily been challenged" (Greenstone 1975, 244). This confusion of the normative and the empirical rendered each disagreement potentially attributable to the biases or ideology of the author.

Many disputes arose because of ambiguities concerning whether pluralism was a normative or an empirical theory. When Jack Walker raised some of these questions in his 1966 critique of "the elitist theory of democracy," Robert Dahl was particularly forceful:

> One central difficulty with Professor Walker's paradigm is, I think, that he insists upon interpreting as if they were normative or deontological certain writings that were mainly if not wholly intended to set out descriptive, empirical theories. Most (though perhaps not all) of the works cited by Professor Walker are not attempts to prescribe how democracy *ought* to work but to *describe* how some of the political systems widely called by that name do in fact operate and to *explain* why they operate this way. Professor Walker may deplore the neglect of normative questions, as many other political scientists and political philosophers do; but he ought not to confuse attempts at empirical description and explanation with efforts at prescribing how these systems ought to operate in order to attain desirable or ideal ends. I would not argue that every writer cited by Professor Walker has always tried to maintain this distinction, or, if he did, has always succeeded; but I do think that it is a serious misunderstanding to interpret these writers as essentially normative theorists. (Dahl 1966a, 298, emphasis in original)

Whatever the conclusion concerning the original intent of the pluralists, the discipline showed considerable confusion toward these writings. Dahl's response indicates part of the reason: While most of the group studies focused on careful observation, description, and explanation, there was a strong strain of normative content in much of the work as well. To the extent that scholars focused on the diversity of interests active or potentially active in politics rather than on the biases and inequalities present in the pressure system, they seemed to offer an enthusiastic endorsement of the desirability and the justice of the American political system.

The pluralist view rested on an image of the group struggle in which no single group could have significant influence, but where a multitude of competing groups would be the safeguard of democracy through the free competition of ideas. David Garson notes this view by quoting from the presidential address to the American Political Science Association of Quincy Wright in 1950. Wright argued: "'A world with millions of small conflicts in the minds of individuals and in the discussions of small groups is likely to be more peaceful and prosperous than a world divided into two opposing groups each of which commands the exclusive, intense, and blind obedience of the population' (Wright 1950, 11). Thus, Wright's presidential address illustrated the then-common view that the politics of small group conflicts represented both description and prescription of democratic practice. This group politics was cast as the cornerstone of free society" (Garson 1978, 79).

To the extent that this image of competition among the multitude of groups could be challenged, one's conclusions about the nature of American democracy would be altered. In the postwar period, this image came under increasing scrutiny, largely as a result of the growth of large industrial corporations and the development of other large national interest groups. Henry Kariel gives voice to this feeling of unease. If pluralism was built on the notion of perfect competition among groups, as he asserts that it was, then it could no longer function as a justification for, or as a description of, our current form of government, he wrote. Technological innovation and economic change of the postwar years increasingly promoted the growth of organizational behemoths concentrating economic and political power as never before. The growth of such organizations as General Motors, the Teamsters, the Farm Bureau, or the American Medical Association, along with other corporations, unions, and groups boasting millions of members each seemed incongruent with existing notions of democracy. The new postwar economy called into question the competition among a myriad of small groups on which the pluralist perspective relied (Kariel 1961, 1–4).

The nature of pluralist competition among interest groups was the subject of great empirical debates, but these were never too far removed from the normative conclusions to which they led. As we will see in some detail below, the pluralist perspective led to benign normative conclusions regarding the extent to which the pluralist system could be compared to a perfectly competitive economic market. With competition, undue influence would be impossible. To the extent that scholars observed the development of extremely large corporations and other interests, they showed their unease with a theory of political representation that seemed to rely on free competition to ensure normatively defensible outcomes. The obvious links between scholars' justifications of the political system and economists' explanations of the benign genius of the free market only reinforced the suspicion that many pluralists were apologists for the status quo (and that many of those who attacked it were "radicals"). Though nothing about the pluralist approach would imply support for huge special interests able to dominate their parts of the political system, the explanation of the genius of democracy through competition was seen as a broad endorsement of a system that included significant disparities in influence, with some very privileged groups exerting great amounts of political power. The normative and the ideological became confused with the descriptive and the empirical.

Even among those who focused on the diversity of interests present in the pressure system, and who were therefore grouped together as the "pluralists," there was never a strong theoretical structure that joined all the work together. Pluralists lacked a single voice, as Robert Dahl noted (1966a). There was no pluralist "theory" in the sense of the development of testable hypotheses that could orient a school of researchers. Indeed, Mancur Olson used the group approach to illustrate his contention that "science attempts to go beyond descriptions, histories, terminologies, and typologies to genuine hypothetico-deductive theory. Schools of scientific thought that fail to develop deductive theories resting on tested hypotheses never last" (1986, 166). The approach was bedeviled by ambiguities about its goal—empirical description or normative evaluation—but it was further troubled by theoretical incoherence.

### A Theory, an Approach, a School, a Perspective, or What?

Among the most serious intellectual problems for the development of a pluralist view of the roles and activities of interest groups was the fact that pluralism was never a theory at all, but rather a perspective. Those who worked within the approach disagreed with each other on significant points and objected even to being referred to as a school. This can be seen clearly in Robert Dahl's vehement rejoinder to Jack Walker's assertion that there was, indeed, a pluralist school of thought focusing on the competition among elites (see Dahl 1966a and Walker 1966a and 1966b). As Dahl pointed out (1966a, 297–98), those active in the approach espoused a great range of views.

While many of its most influential proponents denied that there was any such thing as a pluralist theory of politics, outside observers continued to note that it constituted at least a school or a perspective (see, e.g., Greenstone 1975). We reviewed in chapter 2 a series of definitional problems that would be unthinkable in a literature that had a clear theoretical structure. Even during the period when the group approach to politics was most widely accepted, it never constituted a clear theory of politics. It held within it the seeds of its demise as scholars proved unable to use the approach for the development of a set of testable hypotheses. We will see in the next chapter that this was one of the greatest attractions of the Olsonian perspective on collective action in the 1970s and 1980s.

Pluralism did not suffer only from a lack of theoretical cohesion. There were also important questions of descriptive accuracy. E. E. Schattschneider's oft-cited remark that "the flaw in the pluralist heaven is that heavenly chorus sings with a strong upper-class accent" (1960, 35) lays at the center of a debate concerning the observable bias in the group system. Was the degree of bias inconsequential, potentially reversible, and benign, or was it an unacceptable demonstration that social class predetermined entry into the group system? In short, how powerful were the barriers to entry into the pressure system?

### Criticisms of the Pluralist Heaven

One of the most appealing elements of the pluralist perspective to many was the concept of the equilibrium of political forces based on the ability of "potential groups" to mobilize when their interests were threatened (Truman 1951). According to Truman's ideas of mobilization in response to threats, in the absence of any overt barriers to mobilization, those groups in society, be they workers, industries, social groups, ethnic groups, or whatever, would form interest groups and mobilize for political action whenever it was in their interest to do so. Of course each mobilization could set off a countermobilization by those with different views, and the end result would be a set of interest groups accurately reflecting the needs and desires of the population. Truman's ideas seemed to explain why many groups formed (and he gave many examples of how groups did indeed organize in response to economic crises, wars, and other threats). Further, they explained the important representational role of groups, casting groups in a more favorable light than was often done by the muckrakers and others who complained of the "undue influence" of the "pressure boys."

While no pluralist writers argued explicitly that the equilibrium that they described was normatively advantageous, many critics charged that these writers exhibited a certain satisfaction with the concept that any threat to important interests would naturally lead those interests to mobilize. If they did not mobilize, the generally unstated but clear implication seemed to be, then it must be because they were relatively satisfied with the status quo. In this "benign view" of the pressure system, barriers to mobilization were treated as inconsequential, or, more often, ignored. V. O. Key describes the pluralist equilibrium in these terms:

> Political systems may exist in a stable, even static, form over long periods. The holders of power are unchallenged; the allocation of rights, privileges, and benefits remains acceptable to all sides; every man knows his place and keeps it. In modern states so serene a political condition does not prevail for long. The equilibrium—the balance, the ordered course of affairs, the established pattern—is disturbed from time to time by some change that generates discontent. Such dislocations tend to set off movements in demand of a correction of the balance or for the creation of a new order. Discontent may find expression through a political movement, a more or less spontaneous rising of the people concerned, or it may be manifested in the intensified activities of existing organized groups. (Key 1964, 40)

Disturbance theories or other equilibrium analyses of the interest-group system or of American politics in general tended to leave the reader with an impression that things are "fair" or "natural" if they are in their state of equilibrium. This is, of course, a misunderstanding of what an equilibrium implies, but it was a common one nonetheless. In a way, the fairness of the pluralist equilibrium was the point of normative disagreement between defenders of the pluralist approach and others. As Dahl argued in his response to Walker, nothing about the fact that an equilibrium may exist suggests the slightest conclusion about the desirability or fairness of that equilibrium: it could easily describe the overrepresentation of privileged groups and the under- or nonrepresentation of the disadvantaged. Still, many pluralist writings were taken to suggest that nothing would stop the disadvantaged groups in society from mobilizing to correct whatever difficulties they might suffer.

Disagreements about the nature of the pluralist equilibrium, centering on the question of barriers to entry to the pressure system, were the base of the combined normative and empirical debates among pluralists and their critics. This is what distinguished Truman from Schattschneider, Dahl from Hunter. Where some saw the mobilization of interests in American society as a guarantor of pluralism, they tended to overlook what Schattschneider called the upper-class accent of the heavenly chorus. One of the most important problems that the literature developed was an ideological one: the pluralists were accused of developing a theory that supported the status quo, which in the 1950s included segregation in the South, obvious advantages in mobilization for those of higher social status, huge organizational advantages for business versus consumer interests, and a variety of other elements that no pluralist felt comfortable defending.

Group scholars since the turn of the century had written dozens of books complaining about biases in what they derisively termed the "pressure system." The "undue influence" of wealthy individuals, large corporations (especially the oil and steel companies in the prewar period), and of business interests in general had been a staple of journalistic and scholarly discussion for decades. Such studies remained common even in the hey-day of the pluralist approach. At the same time as authors such as Truman were describing the great diversity of interests present in the group system and focusing on the possibilities of countervailing power, more narrowly focused studies often found only one side to be active. Garson describes the situation in these terms:

> At the same time [as the pluralists were writing], empirical studies of specific interest groups continued to come to conclusions disconcertingly in tension with the felicitous view of American democracy implicit in the group approach. Charles Hardin's study of *The Politics of Agriculture* (1952) was one example. In this study of the Farm Bureau, Hardin found not countervailing power, but corporatist collusion. Hardin found that the U.S. Department of Agriculture was working hand-in-glove with established farm interests through an extensive system of support (extension services, government advisory committees, appointments, local boards) to perpetuate a particular structure of power. (Garson 1978, 85–86)

The 1950s saw not only the publication of Truman's book describing the great diversity of interests present in America, but also a series of studies focusing on the ills of lobbying: Mason (1950) on the National Association of Manufacturers and the Liberty League; Bailey (1950) on the National Farmers' Union and the Chamber of Commerce; Schriftgiesser (1951) on *The Lobbyists*; Knappen (1950) on shipping; Shott (1950) on railroads. Early findings from mass surveys called the pluralist assumptions into question as well: "The very possibility of representativeness of interests in the group process was called into question by early opinion data showing that less than a third of Americans said they belonged to *any* organization taking stands on national issues" (Garson 1978, 82, emphasis in original).

Just as in liberal economics the best outcomes can only be achieved through active competition and the avoidance of monopoly power, so too did pluralism rely on competition among groups to provide the best political outcomes. The descriptive question of whether there were important barriers to entry in the political marketplace was therefore heavy with normative implications. V. O. Key notes how competition among groups can lead to better government decision making, as those in positions of authority are given freedom by the very conflicts they see about them. However, he notes the corresponding difficulty if the government decision maker is faced only with a single side of a potential dispute:

> To some extent, the outrageous demands of pressure groups are checked by the demands of other groups that may be equally outrageous. In situation after situation legislators and administrators are confronted by groups pushing in opposite directions, a state of affairs that permits government to balance one off against the other and to arrive more easily at a solution thought to represent the general interest.
>
> Though the restraint of mutual antagonism is built into the group system, that check does not operate in many situations. Groups well disciplined and amply supplied with the matériel of political warfare often are countered by no organization of equal strength. The opposing interest may, in fact, be completely unorganized. The lobbyists for electrical utilities, for example, are eternally on the job; the lobbyists for the consumers of this monopolistic service are ordinarily conspicuous by their absence. The representation of these unorganized sectors of society becomes the task of politicians who, bedeviled by the group spokesmen on the ground, may succumb to the immediate and tangible pressures. In short, while group pressures often cancel each other out, this process restrains particularlism erratically and uncertainly. (Key 1964, 150)

The erratic and uncertain functioning of the pluralist equilibrium was emphasized in study after study focusing on particular issues. Not only was this the focus of periodic journalistic exposé, but an entire school of scholarship focused on what Griffith had called policy "whirlpools" in the early part of the century. These authors saw closed systems dominated by special interests with little competition, little room for public involvement or concern, and little in the way of pluralist competition. For Maass (1951), Cater (1964), Freeman (1965), McConnell (1966), Lowi (1969), Fritschler (1975), and other subsystem scholars, pluralism was not erratic and uncertain; it was inaccurate for the cases they studied, and seemed unlikely ever to be a good description of how most issues were decided in government. Lowi's work was especially influential on this score. Lowi's *End of Liberalism* made the case that the congressional practice of delegating authority to agencies inevitably benefits organized interests. These interest groups were seen as seeking narrow and particularized ends. Thus, even a fair and pluralistic fight among those interests would not lead to desirable governmental outcomes, since each group would seek its own selfish goals rather than what was best for the country at large. Lowi's argument convinced many people that the close involvement of interest groups in government would not be advisable even if the system were free of bias. This critical view of groups contrasted sharply with the more favorable pluralist view, and it helped turn many scholars away from the study of groups altogether. Rather than promoting democracy through conflict and competition, groups came to be seen as a drag on the democratic process. From being part of the genius of democracy, potentially explaining the most basic elements of the representational process, groups became part of the problem. Scholars reacted in part by looking elsewhere for explanations of how representation occurred; clearly, they would not find it in a flawed group system.

Schattschneider (1960) was of course the most visible with his simple statement that the membership in the group system was so biased by social class that probably 90 percent of the public could not participate. A developing consensus that the pluralists had overlooked significant and systematic barriers to entry into the group system was one of the most serious difficulties for those who would support the group perspective. Since this debate, of course, the social-class bias of the group system has been studied repeatedly and has been consistently confirmed (for examples, see Verba and Nie 1972; Schlozman and Tierney 1986; Schlozman, Verba, and Brady 1995). In sum, a keystone of the pluralist perspective, that all groups would mobilize if threatened, was never well received and came under increasing attack. This attack was mostly on empirical grounds in the 1950s and early 1960s, but with Mancur Olson it would suffer a fatal blow. Before turning to Olson's criticism, however, it is worth noting that the group approach suffered from a variety of other difficulties. These included a failure to measure the central variables of power and influence and a series of studies that suggested that groups were not as important in politics as had been assumed. By the time of Olson's *Logic of Collective Action* (1965), a great variety of difficulties had disenchanted many with the group approach.

### Problems of Measuring Power and Influence

One of the most troubling difficulties within interest-group research stemmed from the vituperative ideological and methodological debates about where power was located in the political system and how to recognize when, by whom, and how influence was wielded. As Robert Dahl wrote, power can be direct or indirect, reciprocal or unilateral. "One who sets out to observe, analyze, and describe the distribution of influence in a pluralistic democracy will therefore encounter formidable problems" (1961, 90). Dahl was particularly careful in his attempts to measure influence, and devotes an appendix to the discussion of how one can adequately gather indicators for the exertion of political influence. (See Dahl 1961, 330–40. See also his article on the topic, 1957.) Indeed, the 1960s saw vicious debates in political science and sociology based largely on the difficulties of measuring power and on the divergent conclusions that various scholars reached when they used different methods to address the topic.

The debates that separated Dahl (1961) from Mills (1956), Hunter (1953) from Truman (1951), and Domhoff (1967) from Polsby (1963) had in large part to do with their differing conclusions on how wide a stratum exerted significant political power and how permeable this group was to outside influences. The community power studies of the period often reached contradictory conclusions because some used observational techniques, some used reputational methods, and each was based on the intensive study of a single city yet attempted to reach general conclusions. Most importantly, the group of scholars involved in these efforts never was able to reach a consensus on how to measure power, the question at the center of all of their work.

Andrew McFarland (1966, 1969) reviews the literature on the concept of power. He notes the importance in pluralist thought of the dispersion of power across a great many actors, and of the importance of complexity in insuring such a dispersion. For each powerful actor, there should be a countervailing power, allowing no monopolistic situations to develop (see also Key 1964, 150, quoted above, and McFarland 1987). If power is the same as causation, as he argues it is, then "complex causation" is similar to pluralism. (That is, if there are many complex causes of a decision, then power must be relatively diffuse; if there is only one cause, then power is concentrated.) McFarland quickly notes, however, that one can almost always find a complex series of causes if one looks hard enough. He demonstrates the problem of "spurious pluralism," in which decisions appear to be affected by a broad range of actors but are really tightly controlled, with case studies of a Soviet firm and the U.S. Forest Service. Both organizations exhibit a great deal of decentralization on paper. On the other hand, powerful norms limit the nature of the bargaining that actually takes place within each institution. Some issues are just not put on the agenda.

McFarland points to an important and ultimately fatal problem for the pluralists. In the face of any findings of diffused power (or complex causality, as he puts it), critics may argue that the plural elites work within culturally defined parameters limiting the scope of the debate only to the relatively inconsequential. McFarland concludes that this problem is in the end impossible to solve. With no way to guarantee that the bargaining one observes concerns the full range of potential points of disagreement, one cannot be sure that power seemingly broadly shared extends across all the important elements of potential debate.

With the publication of an influential essay in 1962, Peter Bachrach and Morton Baratz showed how ticklish this measurement problem was always going to be. They pointed out that the most important exercise of political power might well be the power to exert agenda-control. The second face of power, as they termed the ability to limit certain items from ever entering the political debate, showed a great gap in most studies of power. However, with a few exceptions (Crenson 1971 and Gaventa 1980), scholars have avoided the difficult question of how one could devise techniques of measuring this second and potentially more important face of power.

After the vituperative debates that characterized these disagreements in the 1960s, the demonstration by Bachrach and Baratz that tremendously important elements of power were potentially unobservable, many in the discipline seemed to agree with William Riker's assessment. In a 1964 article, he reviewed the difficulties and inconsistencies in five major conceptions of power. "The final question, once the full complication of the ambiguities is revealed, concerns the appropriate scientific attitude toward the conception of power itself. Ought we redefine it in a clear way or ought we banish it altogether? My initial emotion, I confess, is that we ought to banish it" (1964, 348). The concept of power was not banished from political science, but scholars for the most part reacted by abandoning their interest in these questions. Community power studies, once a common and prominent research approach in political science and sociology, were largely abandoned or ignored by the broader discipline. Urban politics, once the home of many influential studies, receded as a field within political science. Scholars moved on to other fields that did not have at their core such a difficult concept.

In important ways, one of the most significant failures of the group approach was self-inflicted. Many of its most prominent studies were designed in a way that required the author to devise a mechanism to measure the unmeasurable. Robert Salisbury points out some of the problems with this approach:

> For decades the most common question guiding interest group research has been the question of influence. What group or groups have how much influence over policy-making is the common thread that connects Dahl to Schattschneider, Bauer, Pool and Dexter to Lowi, McConnell to Browne, and Chubb to Stigler. Push it back a step to ask what factors affect group influence, and Truman is brought into the stream. Virtually every discussion of PACs sooner or later comes around to the question of how much influence PAC contributors have on electoral outcomes and/or policy choices.
>
> At first glance, this may seem to be an altogether appropriate focus of inquiry. After all, in many areas of political science, from voting to President-Congress relations to Supreme Court decisions to international relations, a good deal of attention is devoted to who wins, who loses, and why. The trouble is that the game metaphor is profoundly misleading regarding the underlying character of much of the political process. Very often there is no clear resolution, no definitive conclusion to the process by which interests are articulated and pursued. "Play" continues, moving from one venue to another perhaps, the tides of success for particular participants ebbing and flowing, while the structure of the

"game" slowly evolves. As the saga unfolds, individual episodes may be singled out for separate treatment, but unless they are seen in their larger historical/ developmental context, any particular story, however, melodramatic it seems to be, is likely to generate more misunderstanding than insight.

Think of it this way. Does it make much sense to ask who is the most influential member of the U.S. Senate? Or, insofar as we would grasp the essential meaning and impact of their decisions, is it a high priority to determine the influence rank among the Supreme Court Justices? It is not that influence is irrelevant; it is simply not the best way to frame the central questions. (Salisbury 1994, 17–18)

Salisbury points out that one need not organize research projects that require the measurement of the unmeasurable, yet this was precisely what many of the most prominent group and community-power scholars did in the 1950s and 1960s (see also Heinz et al. 1993, 7–8). The failure to devise methods of answering a question that had been set up as the central topic in all these studies led to an abandonment of the community-power approach after it became clear that it would never succeed. It was one more in a series of difficulties for an approach that had been at the center of the discipline.

### Findings of Limited Impact

If the group approach became for a time the dominant approach to politics, it was because of a general feeling that associations, businesses, and other lobbies were powerful. Study after study seemed to indicate that groups were more powerful than government decision makers themselves. The businesses and trade groups in Schattschneider's 1935 study dictated the wording of bills to a compliant Congress. Likewise, the Army Corps of Engineers and local government groups had easily obtained almost unlimited funding from Congress in Maass's 1951 study. Group propaganda could manipulate the public into acting against their best interests, putting pressure on legislators to do whatever the groups desired, according to Crawford's 1939 account. Government officials seemed merely to reflect in their actions those forces that the various lobbies were able to exert upon them. The assumption that groups were all powerful came under attack in the 1960s, however. An influential set of studies gave reason to think that we had overestimated the importance of groups in politics.

Several important studies published in the 1960s took issue with the view of interest-group dominance. Milbrath's (1963) survey of lobbyists, Bauer, Pool, and Dexter's (1963) study of tariff legislation, and Scott and Hunt's (1965) survey of members of Congress all concluded that interest groups wielded much less influence than was generally attributed to them. The findings of these studies were not entirely novel. Even Schattschneider (1935) had showed evidence of interest-group apathy before most legislative issues. Although this book is best known for its description of strong interest-group influence, Schattschneider also noted that most manufacturers affected by the tariff legislation in question did not even take the time to express their support or opposition before Congress. Scholars had long found groups sometimes to be apathetic and ineffectual in some cases, but in the 1960s several studies were taken to indicate that groups were perhaps not the most important place to look for an understanding of the legislative process

Rather than using strong-arm tactics to get what they wanted, the primary role of interest groups was providing information to allies within government, according to this new body of research. Interest-group influence was thus essentially benign, since groups essentially served as adjunct congressional staff. Bauer, Pool, and Dexter's study (1963) is a complex work showing areas of strength and weakness, but it has come to be cited especially for its "service bureau" finding. The authors described the interests they surveyed as surprisingly poorly informed, badly funded, and ill-prepared to do battle in Washington, at least compared to the popular conception that somehow groups were "pulling the strings" in government. The popular scholarly conclusion drawn from these studies was that interest groups did not exert pressure, indeed were not influential. The informational role they played in Washington could easily be supplanted by information from congressional staff. Although these findings of limited impact were at odds with the arguments being put forth by the critics of pluralism, the implications of these contradictory findings were surprisingly similar. Both seemed to justify an abandonment of the previous focus on groups in the policy process.

### CONCLUSION

This chapter has reviewed the rise and decline of the group approach to politics. As the first set of authors to move beyond formal legalism, group scholars offered tremendous advances to the discipline over the institutionalism of their predecessors. Descriptions of the policy process today focusing on such concepts as policy subsystems and issue networks owe a heavy debt to scholars of the generation of Griffith, who first wrote of policy whirlpools in 1939. Even as it developed a great number of important insights that remain central to our views of the policy process today, the group approach also suffered from a series of difficulties, as this chapter has reviewed. Only a fuzzy line separated the normative and the ideological from the descriptive and the empirical (and even this line was not always respected). No clear theoretical structure was ever developed, leading to a wide range of contradictions in the literature. Huge barriers to entry were found to restrict participation in the pluralist competition among groups, challenging the view that politics could be understood through the observation of groups active in the pressure system. Fundamental issues remained unresolved about how to observe or measure the central concept of pluralism, influence. And findings accumulated with the suggestion that groups were not all that important to the governmental process in the first place.

Into this declining literature Mancur Olson added a crushing blow. *The Logic of Collective Action*, published in 1965, demonstrated convincingly that the group system could never be counted on for providing a fair system of interest representation, taking away any normative appeal that the group approach might once have had. Olson's elegant demonstration of the differential barriers to organization effectively put an end to the group approach to political science. Not only did Olson provide a devastating critique of the previous literature, which was suffering from the many problems we have reviewed in this chapter, but more importantly, he provided a new set of research questions for subsequent scholars to investigate. Olson's ideas paved the way for the creation of a new literature on interest groups. This new literature was quite different from the old, addressing a much narrower set of questions, but doing so with much greater analytic care and sophistication.

# CHAPTER 4.

# Collective Action and the New Literature
# on Interest Groups

THE GROUP THEORY of politics became increasingly discredited as a result of the trends described in chapter 3. Political scientists had two reactions to these developments. First, many turned away from the study of interest groups altogether, focusing instead on the workings of governmental institutions, voting and elections, and other topics not so liable to the problems that had plagued the group approach. Second, scholars developed new approaches to studying interest groups. The new literature that developed in the 1970s and 1980s was less grand than the older literature in that it aspired to answer much narrower questions, but to answer them with greater certainty. It was more scientific than the previous literature in that it aspired not merely to discuss important topics of group influence, but to test real theories of how groups mobilize for political action. Group scholars focused on internal dynamics rather than on the group system as a whole or on the external activities of groups.

One way to note the shift in research emphases is to compare the approaches used and the topics covered in articles published in the profession's top journal. We have reviewed every article on interest groups published in the *American Political Science Review* (*APSR*) since 1950 (our appendix provides a chronological list of citations). We note a sharp decline then a resurgence of attention to interest groups. During the hey-day of the group approach to politics, the *APSR* devoted considerable space to the study of groups: There were twenty articles on interest groups in the 1950s and twenty-eight such articles in the 1960s. (Our list of articles does not include those focusing on groups outside the United States.) A dramatic decline in attention to groups is visible immediately after the group approach was discredited in the mid to late 1960s: There were just twelve articles on groups in the *APSR* during the 1970s. After this period of decline, studies of interest groups became substantially more common: The *APSR* featured forty-one interest-group articles in the 1980s and published twenty-two from 1990 to 1995. The percentages tell the same story. Articles addressing interest group topics made up 5 percent *APSR* articles in the 1950s and 7 percent in the 1960s. The proportion of articles dropped to 2 percent in the 1970s before rising to 8 percent in the 1980s and 7 percent in the first half of the 1990s. Groups are back in political science: after a decline in interest in the 1970s, while a previous research paradigm was severely attacked, a new literature on groups has emerged. The discipline's top journal publishes studies on groups at a rate higher than in any decade in the postwar period.

Most of the articles in the new literature are far more systematic and quantitative than the studies that preceded them. Learning from the debates that proved insoluble in the past, scholars focus on topics that can be addressed more systematically. Accordingly, we have seen tremendous advances in understanding certain elements of group behavior, notably how groups mobilize for political action and how they overcome the collective-action dilemma. A resurgence of interest in groups has made it easier to fill graduate syllabi with high-quality studies using the best research approaches, the latest theoretical modeling strategies, and the most appropriate statistical techniques. The new literature, being more systematic, features fewer disagreements on the fundamental questions of group power and bias in the group system. This consensus is more apparent than real, however, because scholars have not solved these points of disagreement; they have avoided them.

In the new literature questions of collective action and mobilization have replaced group power and influence as the primary foci of interest. In our review of articles in the *APSR*, we compared studies that focused on questions of internal versus external activities of groups. Internal questions include how groups recruit members, how they govern themselves, and how they raise money; external activities include lobbying the government, filing suits, and the like. In the 1950s and 1960s, few studies on groups dealt with internal questions. For the pluralists, the mobilization of groups was simply not a problem. Mancur Olson (1965) showed how wrong the pluralists were to ignore questions of mobilization and internal maintenance. One of the most important consequences of Olson's work was to create a whole set of research questions that the pluralists had wrongly taken for granted: how groups mobilize and maintain themselves.

Comparing articles published before and after 1965 shows some important differences in emphasis. Before 1965 the predominant topics of studies of interest groups were studies of lobbying in the legislature or the bureaucracy (fifteen articles published) and normative essays on pluralism and groups (twelve articles). There were only two articles published during this time on internal operations of groups. Beginning in 1966, an important shift in focus is apparent, as the topic of internal operations became the single most common topic of articles on groups in the *APSR*: twenty-seven articles appeared on this topic, as compared with only twenty-six studies of lobbying and eight normative reviews. (Other topics of coverage also grew since 1965, including the study of campaign contributions, lawsuits, protest, social movements, and the nature of the overall group system.) All in all, it is clear that the new literature on groups reflected the impact of Mancur Olson in a reduced interest on external activities and a tremendous curiosity about the internal dynamics of group membership and maintenance. Olson created a new research agenda, pulling scholarly energies away from the study of lobbying.

The new literature on interest groups has not eschewed the study of lobbying completely. Articles still appear regularly in the *APSR* with a focus on external activities. Every major book on groups published in recent years, including all those based on large-scale surveys of groups, has focused extensively on lobbying. Important studies have appeared focusing on policy processes within a single policy domain or in a series of issues. Book-length reviews of the activities of single groups give great attention to lobbying activities. Edited volumes on groups consistently include several chapters on their lobbying activities. Conceptual essays continue to deal with questions of influence and power. (See, for examples of the large surveys, Schlozman and Tierney 1986, Knoke 1990a, Walker 1991, and Heinz et al. 1993; for examples of the single-domain studies, Vogel 1989, Hansen 1991, McFarland 1993, and Browne 1995; for prominent single-group studies, McFarland 1984 and Rothenberg 1992; for collections of essays, see Petracca 1992a and Cigler and Loomis 1995; for important conceptual works, see McFarland 1987 and 1991.) When we compare the literature of the 1980s and 1990s with that of the 1950s and 1960s, however, and in spite of these and other exceptions, the new literature is notable for the decline of interest in external activities, for the rise of interest in collective action and mobilization, and for the increasing prevalence of a research strategy that puts its emphasis on analytic tractability rather than on empirical generalizability. As we will review in chapter 7, many of the new studies of lobbying are surprisingly narrow in their empirical scope. Many new studies of lobbying adopt a research strategy that focuses on a single decision at a single point in time, even if authors include measures of the activities of dozens of groups and apply sophisticated statistical and modeling tools to the evidence. It is interesting to note that the one branch of scholars who did not abandon the study of group external activities in the 1970s were economists with elegant deductive theories. Interest groups remained primary actors in formal models created within the Virginia and Chicago schools of economists. These scholars tended to model the policy process as deal-making between legislators and groups, with votes and campaign contributions as the currency and the courts as contract enforcers. (See, e.g., Tullock 1967; Stigler 1971; Posner 1974; Peltzman 1976; Becker 1983. For a review, see Mitchell and Munger 1991. On the role of the courts in an interest-group system, see Landes and Posner 1975.)

Chapter 1 reviewed areas of advance, avoidance, and confusion in the current literature on interest groups. According to most reviewers, the areas of greatest advance are in those domains most centrally affected by Mancur

Olson's insights in his 1965 *Logic of Collective Action*. The arguments presented in that book not only put an end to the pluralist perspective on group mobilization, but they also provided the framework for a great range of new research. The wealth of new hypotheses generated by Olson provided the grist for many scholarly projects. These new projects tended to focus on more specific questions than had been posed before and often made use of experimental, modeling, and statistical techniques that had been all too rare in the literature. The same research philosophy that allowed for many advances in our understandings of collective action had some costs as well. With a focus on the dilemmas of mobilization, scholars ignored those lobbying organizations that did not have members; with attention riveted to the internal dynamics of groups, scholars neglected to relate those dynamics to the groups' external lobbying activities; with a desire to emphasize the internal validity of their research projects, scholars paid less attention to questions of external validity. Each of these impacts was in stark contrast to the practices and traditions of scholars of a previous generation. Just as the pluralists had reacted to the legalism that had been dominant when they began to write, developing behavioralism as a dominant paradigm, those coming after the pluralists reacted to the broad generalizations of the pluralists, adopting a distinctively narrow approach to the study of groups. Olson's book ushered in a new literature on interest groups.

## OLSON'S DEVASTATING *LOGIC*

With the publication of his book in 1965, Mancur Olson delivered the fatal blow to an approach that was already wounded. His simple and elegant demonstration of the dilemmas of organizing for collective action showed the critical flaw in the pluralist assumption that all potential groups would have an equal chance of participating in the pressure system. Some groups, notably small, business-oriented ones, had great advantages in organization and were likely to mobilize as Truman described. Other groups, notably those with many potential members and seeking only collective benefits, were at a considerable disadvantage and were unlikely ever to mobilize even to a fraction of their potential. Consumers would never rival producers as interest groups. The economically disadvantaged, the jobless, the poor would never overcome the obstacles to mobilization with the ease of other groups. The group struggle would never be fair. Differential intensities of preference would be reinforced, not lessened, through the group system.

With the publication of this book, the pluralist perspective was essentially dead, since there was no way for most scholars after that date to accept the idea that the natural working of the group system could be expected to generate a set of active interest groups that would be representative of interests in society. Some interests would always be more equal than others. Olson's influence went beyond this fundamental insight, however. By providing a deductive framework on which scholars could focus, he helped address the scientific failings of the pluralist approach. While the group approach never generated a set of testable hypotheses amenable to scientific testing, the Olsonian approach allowed scholars to focus on a narrower set of propositions that could be disproved or confirmed with greater precision.

The benefits of the new approach have been significant, as scholars have searched for greater scientific precision by isolating small parts of a complex system of interactions for detailed observation and analysis. We have a much better idea now than we did in the 1950s of the costs of collective action, of the nature of bias in the mobilization of groups, of the effects of group campaign contributions on incumbency reelection rates, and on a myriad of other particular topics. The costs of this approach have also been high: the marginalization of interest group studies as they lost their relation with the core issues of democratic governance. The unintended consequence of Olson's work has been to encourage the development of theories and research projects on relatively narrow topics related to the internal functioning of groups, incurring tremendous opportunity costs as an entire generation of scholars focused on the collective-action dilemma rather than on other topics related to groups.

## THE NEW LITERATURE ON COLLECTIVE ACTION

A wide range of theoretical extensions, tests, confirmations, and challenges to Olson's theory took place in the decades following his book. Some of the most significant theoretical extensions concerned Clark and Wilson's (1961) discussion of solidary and purposive incentives that groups might use to attract members in addition to the material incentives that Olson had discussed; Salisbury's (1969) introduction of the role of an entrepreneur, who would invest in the creation of a group hoping for future gains from being its leader; Moe's (1980a, 1980b, 1981) demonstration that individuals might systematically overestimate their own importance in the achievement of a group's collective goals; reviews by Hardin (1982), Ostrom (1990), and Lichbach (1996) of the range of ways in which institutions in many areas of society have been organized to overcome collective-action dilemmas; experimental work by many authors discussing the degree to which individuals can be expected to follow their individual self-interest in the context of joining a collective effort; discussions in American and comparative politics about how large social movements have been organized through the efforts of leaders and with the knowledge that social pressure and expectations of future benefits may play a great role in inducing contributions to seemingly hopeless collective causes; and other findings and theoretical extensions. In this section, we review a number of these.

## Solidary, Expressive, and Material Benefits

Extensions to the Olsonian perspective on membership recruitment have focused on the different types of incentives that groups may offer. Olson focused on selective material incentives that groups might use to attract members and he noted that noneconomic collective action groups face a serious disadvantage because their most important benefits are neither selective nor material. Extensions to his theory have focused on the abilities of groups of all types to offer more than only this type of membership inducements. This area of the literature is rooted in an article by Peter Clark and James Q. Wilson (1961; also see Wilson 1973 and 1995). The typology set forth by Clark and Wilson distinguishes three types of membership incentives: *material*, *solidary*, and *purposive*. Material incentives are the same types of tangible selective benefits described by Olson. Solidary incentives arise from the act of associating, and "depend for their value on how the recipient appears in the eyes of others" (Wilson 1973, 40). They include such intangibles as social relationships with other group members and increased status in the eyes of nonmembers. Friendship, enjoyment, status, and other intangibles can be important inducements for many potential group members. Further, these can often be provided by groups at little or no cost. Purposive incentives are even less tangible than solidary benefits, involving the good feelings people get from contributing to a cause in which they believe.

Robert Salisbury (1969) first adapted this typology to an Olsonian framework, and illustrated how such incentives could help explain group origins as well as group maintenance. Salisbury refined the typology slightly to note that a purposive benefit is, strictly speaking, a public good, since one might enjoy seeing that a group is advocating a certain cause even if one is not a member of that group. He introduced the term "expressive benefit" to focus on its selective nature: One can feel good about one's contribution to a group because the group expresses values that one holds dear. This is similar to a purposive benefit, but is selective rather than collective in nature, providing value only to those who contribute to it. In any case, scholars since Clark and Wilson have steadily built on the notion that groups may have many types of benefits to provide for their members, and that many of these benefits may be available only or mainly to groups suffering from the dilemmas of collective action that Olson noted.

Olson discussed the use of selective incentives to overcome the collective-action dilemma but never suggested who or what would provide those incentives in the first place. Robert Salisbury's classic article "An Exchange Theory of Interest Groups" (1969) proposed that individual entrepreneurs create groups, offering potential members selective incentives to join. In exchange, entrepreneurs whose groups succeed benefit by having a job, by controlling potentially substantial resources, and by having an opportunity to further their own political agendas as the leader of an organization rather than as a private citizen. The role of entrepreneurs has been recognized by virtually every researcher of group origins and maintenance since Salisbury introduced the concept.

Terry Moe (1980a, 1980b, 1981) and Lawrence Rothenberg (1988, 1992) showed the importance of Olson's assumption that individuals have perfect information about membership decisions. Moe argues that people join groups in part because they overestimate the importance of their contribution to the provision of the collective benefit. Moe's survey of Minnesota group members found that people who reported strong feelings of efficacy also were more likely to cite political reasons (a collective good) rather than material or solidary reasons for joining a group. In effect, these people joined groups because they made a mistake: Had they more accurate information about the importance of their own contribution, they would not join. Since people commonly overestimate the importance of their own contribution toward achieving a collective outcome, this tendency could serve to mitigate some of Olson's most pessimistic conclusions concerning the ability of collective-action groups to mobilize. They can mobilize, Moe argues, because people systematically overestimate their own importance.

Rothenberg (1988, 1992) studied membership decisions within Common Cause and concluded that people may join a group they know little about, since the investment in time and money is usually nominal. Once members, they decide through a process of "experiential search" whether to retain their memberships. Although Rothenberg's data stem from a cross-sectional survey of members, he showed that long-standing members knew more about the group and were more committed to remaining with the group than neophyte members. Membership recruitment and retention are often discussed interchangeably, but Rothenberg's work suggests that the processes affecting them may be different. The important differences in knowledge of group activities that distinguish longstanding members from recent joiners indicate that members learn considerably about the efforts of their group to further collective goals not merely about the material benefits they may enjoy through membership. This knowledge of collective action seems related to a stronger commitment to the group.

The development of the Olsonian perspective on membership decisions had led to many efforts to test these ideas. Virtually every survey of groups in the 1970s and 1980s included extensive questioning about the types of services groups provide their members and how they raise their annual budgets. (See, for examples, Berry 1977; Schlozman and Tierney 1986; Knoke 1990a; Rothenberg 1992; Walker 1983, 1991. For a review from sociology see Knoke 1988.) Solidary and purposive incentives often are cited as important by group members and leaders. Walker's surveys of fifteen hun-

dred interest groups showed that solidary and purposive benefits were offered by most of the groups and that personal material benefits like insurance and merchandise discounts were less common.

Scholars have noted a variety of ways in which nonmaterial benefits can
be important in overcoming the collective action dilemma. Groups with few
material incentives to provide can nonetheless create an atmosphere of social inclusion and emphasize to their members the degree to which they are
"making a difference" in achieving some cherished goal. Nothing is to stop
groups from leading their members to overestimate the importance of their
contributions; indeed incentives to do so are clear from this literature. Explaining decisions to join groups in terms of solidary and purposive incentives is problematic, however, because such benefits are difficult to measure
and because the concept of a purposive incentive can be expanded to "explain" virtually every possible case. In the case where two individuals of
similar characteristics contribute widely differing amounts of time or money
to a certain organization, one is tempted to conclude that they enjoy different levels of solidary or expressive benefits from doing so. Since these benefits are almost impossible to measure with great accuracy, it is hard to dis-
confirm a theory that states that individuals contribute to groups because
they get a variety of benefits, some of them purely psychological, in return.

Mancur Olson recognized that selective incentives need not be limited to
material benefits, but he thought his theory was best applied to economic
interest groups where the dominant forms of selective benefits were material. He wrote that stretching his argument to nonmaterial benefits would
not be useful since the resulting theory would not be subject to any possible
empirical refutation (1971, 160n). This admonition has generally not
stopped authors from applying Olson's perspective in areas where the predominant inducements to participation are clearly altruistic or expressive.
Jack Walker (1991, 47) suggests that instead of trying to include purposive
incentives within an Olsonian framework, researchers should focus on determining the conditions under which individuals will join groups to advance purposive or collective goals. In any case, much of the literature on
the collective action dilemma now focuses on the provision of psychological
rather than material benefits, pushing research into an area fraught with
great difficulties of measurement and testing.

### Experimental Tests

Considerable effort has been made in devising experimental studies to test
theories of contribution to collective causes. These studies have a number of
advantages over surveys of members. First, both contributors and noncon-
tributors are included. Second, greater control over the range of incentives

is possible. In these experimental studies, subjects are typically given tokens representing a small amount of money and offered the opportunity to "invest" it in a public good that will only be provided if enough others agree to invest in it. If the collective action "succeeds" and the public good is provided, all subjects receive a benefit. If the collective action fails, those who contributed to the collective good lose their original "investment," while free riders keep theirs. Taken as a group, results from a variety of experimental studies are mixed but tend to show that many people will indeed join groups to further collective goods. The level of contribution is often seen as "suboptimal," however. That is, not everyone who would benefit from a public good agrees to contribute to creating that good.

A series of experiments by Marwell and Ames (1979, 1980, 1981) on high-school subjects indicated that most would not choose to free-ride, while Dawes, Orbell, Simmons, and van de Kragt (1986) found that free ridership decreased when researchers promised that free riders would be forced to pay their share should the collective action succeed. Isaac, Walker, and Thomas (1984) found widely varying degrees of free ridership within their set of eight experiments and suggested that group size and marginal per capita returns may explain at least part of the variation. Although the results of these studies are provocative, the question is often raised whether results from a laboratory setting involving a few dollars would be replicated in the real world. A wide range of experimental studies within psychology and economics have also been devoted to exploring various elements of the collective-action dilemma.

### Nonexperimental Tests

Researchers have rarely sampled both activists and free riders in a nonlaboratory setting. Two exceptions involve studies that analyzed community mobilization stemming from the Three Mile Island accident of 1979 (Walsh and Warland 1983) and from environmental threats to Lake Tahoe (Sabatier 1992; also see Sabatier and McLaughlin 1990). Free riding was found to be more widespread than indicated by the experimental studies: Only 12 percent of residents who described themselves as discontented contributed even a token amount of time or money to the antinuclear efforts, and only 6 percent of people who owned second homes in the Tahoe Basin area joined the environmental efforts. Contrary to what Olson's theory would predict, however, lack of information about the mobilization effort was seen as the primary reason for free riding in the TMI case, although calculations of self-interest were also important. The Lake Tahoe study found that joiners believed more strongly in group goals than nonjoiners, suggesting that collective benefits rather than selective benefits may explain member-ship decisions.

In general, research testing Olsonian hypotheses has provided support for his prediction that large groups pursuing collective goals will not organize to their full potential. This research has also shown, however, that Olson's pre-ferred explanation for why some individuals do join a collective action, se-lective material benefits, fails to explain the motivations of all individuals. Olson's focus on suboptimality also brushes aside the question of whether the group, no matter how small in proportion to the number of people who agree with their goals, might still be large enough to achieve significant results. Both the environmental movement and the civil rights movement, for example, attracted few active members compared with the number of people who stood to benefit from their collective goals, and yet both move-ments were successful on a number of fronts.

### *Theoretical Extensions: Social Norms and Structures*

Scholars have attacked the set of problems Olson laid out from a variety of theoretical perspectives. Knoke (1986) reviews a number of these, as do Salisbury (1975), Garson (1978), Walker (1991), and Cigler (1991). In gen-eral, all have noted the importance of Olson's insight, but none has pinned down the degree to which this suffices to explain which groups do and do not mobilize. Hardin (1982) and Axelrod (1981, 1984, 1986) point out, for example, that collective-action situations are often continuing relationships and that in such a case one may observe the development of norms of reci-procity and cooperation. Such a range of potential solutions to the dilemma has been noted in the literature that we are left with the knowledge that a dilemma exists, but with little guidance about exactly how common it is for groups to overcome it.

In the introduction to his book published in 1994, Sidney Tarrow writes:

> In the past twenty years, heavily influenced by economic thought, political scientists and sociologists have focused their analyses of social movements on what seems like a puzzle: that collective action occurs even though it is so difficult to bring about. Yet that puzzle is a puzzle—and not a sociological law—because, in many situations and against many odds, collective action *does* occur; often on the part of people with few resources and little permanent power. (6, emphasis in original)

Dozens of scholars have developed ideas about the circumstances that make it possible for many groups around the world to solve the puzzle of collective action. Recent and prominent examples include Chamberlin

(1974), Taylor (1987), Ostrom (1990), Sandler (1992), and Lichbach (1995 and 1996). These and other scholars focus on the roles of social institutions, the importance of continuing social relationships, the development of norms, the ability of social pressure to work in large groups as well as in small groups, the roles of leadership and related organizations, and on other factors that have been observed to help disadvantaged groups mobilize in the face of the obstacles of collective action.

### Patrons, Philanthropies, Occupational Interests, and Institutional Sponsors

Perhaps the best-known finding from the surveys of membership interest groups conducted by Jack Walker in 1980 and 1985 concerns the importance of patrons (Walker 1983, 1991). While most of the previous empirical work applying Olson's theory had focused on the problem of convincing individual members to contribute their fair share, Walker's surveys demonstrated the importance of large contributions from foundations, government grants, corporations, and wealthy individuals. Thirty-four percent of profit-sector groups and 89 percent of citizen groups surveyed said they received start-up money from some type of patron (1991, 78). Citizen groups reported that about 35 percent of their annual budgets were funded by such patrons (1991, 82). Walker argued that an increase in patronage was the primary reason for the rapid increase in the number of interest groups during the 1960s and 1970s.

Walker emphasized that group formation could not be understood by looking solely at individual-level variables. Of crucial importance were "the incentives, constraints, and opportunities" created by governmental, economic, and social institutions (Walker 1991, 49). For instance, major social legislation often includes provisions to create citizen advisory groups and creates a material benefit that potential group members now join to protect. Important Great Society programs of the 1960s included the requirement of "maximum feasible participation" by the public, thus creating important incentives for government agencies to encourage, and sometimes to subsidize, groups representing diffuse interests such as those benefiting from new social programs. (On the Community Action Programs of the Johnson Administration's War on Poverty, see J. Wilson 1995, chap. 5, and Peterson 1970.) Clearly, the group system is not a result of individual-level incentives acting alone. Large institutional patrons of political action, including the government itself, affect the abilities of groups to mobilize. (Such behaviors are not peculiar to the American government, either: Baumgartner and Walker [1989] discussed similarities in the willingness of French and American governments to subsidize educational interest groups.)

By far the most common type of interest group is associations representing various professions and trades. As Olson's by-product theory would predict, these associations originate for nonpolitical reasons, then use some of their excess organizational capital to lobby. Walker's study of membership associations found that more than 75 percent were in some way associated with occupations. About half of these occupationally based groups were nonprofit groups like the Association of American Medical Colleges and the National Association of State Alcohol and Drug Abuse Directors (Walker 1991, 59–60). Many interests that would not be expected to mobilize on their own—such as children, retarded people, and poor people—nonetheless have organizations that lobby on their behalf. Social-service professionals and other entrepreneurs sometimes form these clientele organizations to serve groups of people to which the entrepreneur does not belong. Walker (1983, 1991) argued that broad-based organizations of this type tend to arise after a major piece of social legislation has been passed, creating bureaucratic patronage for the service-providers in question.

Many of the entities often referred to as "interest groups" are not really groups at all, as Salisbury (1984) points out. In addition to the clientele groups serving various social groups, a large percentage of the organized interests represented before government are entities like think tanks, local governments, universities, hospitals, and corporations, for which collective-action problems are minor or nonexistent. This points to the question of whether the problems discussed by Olson may have been given more prominence in the interest-group literature than they deserve.

While researchers studying group members have focused on assessing the extent of free riding and describing the type of person who contributes to a collective good, other scholars have suggested ways in which groups might overcome or at least minimize the collective-action dilemma. By turning the focus away from the rank-and-file member, they note the importance of patrons and entrepreneurs, and find many interest groups are not really groups at all. Institutions, professions, and social movements provide additional ways for organized interests to manifest themselves.

### Social Movements

The process through which social movements arise is essentially a membership process, and thus scholars of social movements often invoke Olson's theoretical framework. Gamson (1990) presents data on 53 protest groups supporting Olson's by-product theory: Groups that offered selective incentives in addition to solidary benefits were more than twice as likely to succeed as those who offered only solidary benefits. Walker (1991, 52) and Oliver, Marwell, and Teixeira (1985) suggest, however, that Olson's work is an incomplete description of the creation of social movements. While Walker stresses the importance of patrons and the political environment, Oliver, Marwell, and Teixeira take issue with Olson's assumption that individuals make decisions about a collective action independently of other individuals. The authors argue that while this assumption may hold true in economic markets, it seldom is true in social group formation. Individuals make their decisions based in part on the actions of others and on their expectations of others' future actions. Oliver, Marwell, and Teixeira mathematically outline a theory that predicts the conditions under which an unorganized interest will succeed in compiling the "critical mass" of members needed to begin a collective action (see also Marwell, Oliver, and Prahl 1988; Marwell and Oliver 1993). Chong (1991) builds on this theory, using the case of the civil rights movement. His explanation stresses the importance of individuals' monitoring the decisions of others and using social pressure to encourage cooperation. A number of scholars have noted the importance of social pressure on collective action. Olson also recognized this to be important, but he considered it more likely to work effectively in small groups rather than in large ones. He is certainly right about that, but evidence from a range of studies indicates that social pressure can nonetheless be important in many large-group situations as well (see, e.g., Granovetter 1978; Crenson 1987; Bikhchandani, Hirshleifer, and Welch 1992). (A voluminous literature on important social movements of the United States continues to thrive. Studies of the civil rights movement and the women's movement have been particularly influential, noting a wide variety of ways in which groups have successfully overcome the problems that Olson described. For further examples, see Lipsky 1968; Jenkins and Perrow 1977; McCarthy and Zald 1978; Mitchell 1979, 1981; Zald and McCarthy 1979, 1980, 1986; McAdam 1982, 1983, 1986, 1988; Morris 1984; Jenkins 1985; Jenkins and Eckert 1986; Morris and Mueller 1992.)

A wide range of studies in comparative politics has focused on the growth of revolutionary movements and rebellions. An obvious question is how broad social movements can develop in the face of active opposition, and in many cases, violent confrontation, from the forces of the state. More than most collective-action groups, revolutionary movements face the dilemma of public goods in the starkest terms. Since their goal is the replacement of one governmental regime with another, by definition it will be experienced by those who did not work for its cause as well as by those who were fervent supporters. Of course, there may be expectations that supporters will be treated with preference by the new regime if it is established. One of the most difficult challenges in the Olsonian perspective is to explain social movements, rebellions, and revolutions. Considering the range of countries that have experienced important social change in recent decades, it is clear that many groups around the world have found ways of overcoming the problems Olson described. (On social movements in comparative politics, see, among others, Gurr 1970; Paige 1975; Tilly 1978 and 1986; DeNardo 1985; Kitschelt 1986; Muller and Opp 1986, 1987; Klandermans and Oegama 1987; Taylor 1988; Finkel, Muller, and Opp 1989; Tarrow 1994.)

Comparative studies of social movements remain a vibrant and active area in political science and sociology. A recent volume (McAdam, McCarthy, and Zald 1996) presents a variety of studies focusing on three elements of sociological explanations: the political opportunity structure afforded by the actions and institutions of the state, the mobilizing structures or the organizations that attempt to channel the efforts of the social movement, and the concept of cultural framings, or the ways in which ideas are presented to support the social movement and/or to discredit the regime against which the movement is struggling. Social movements face serious problems of mobilization but also a wide variety of solutions to their dilemmas.

Since the publication of Olson's book in 1965, scholars have focused on a variety of questions related to the severity, the impact, and the solutions to the dilemmas of collective action. A range of important studies have appeared focusing on different types of individual benefits, on experimental and nonexperimental tests of the accuracy of the predictions that Olson made, on social institutions that help mitigate the problem of collective action, and on the paradox of broad social movements has shown that Olson identified a serious problem with important consequences for politics. However, it has also shown that individual-level motivations explain only part of the puzzle of group mobilization.

## INTEGRATING MODELS OF INDIVIDUAL BEHAVIOR WITH THEIR SOCIAL CONTEXT

One of the most compelling elements of the new set of questions posed in the Olsonian paradigm of collective action was the shift of attention away from the group and toward the individual. Olson asked under what conditions a rational individual would choose to contribute to a group, and he noted that many of the implicit assumptions of those who had come before had no basis in individual rationality. Previous scholars erred in positing models of group mobilization with no basis in models of individual behavior. In Truman's view, people were assumed to react naturally to social forces or economic threats that affected them. Olson's emphasis on individual motivations for action corresponded with broader disciplinary trends in favor of methodological individualism. The individual approach was attractive in part because it allowed a range of new research approaches to be applied to the new questions he posed.

The group approach to politics placed its emphasis on contextual factors, generally to the exclusion of the internal factors that Olson demonstrated to be so important. Disturbance theory, in which groups formed simply because their interests had been jostled by societal changes or governmental actions, ignored important internal factors limiting organization. But to say that Truman's ideas were incomplete does not mean that they were wrong. Just as Truman was incomplete by ignoring important internal dynamics in the mobilization of potential groups, so was Olson's view incomplete because of its focus only on internal factors. Both internal and contextual factors must be taken into account. Beginning in the 1980s, a group of scholars began to develop more complete views of the problem of group mobilization combining elements of the individual and the contextual. Until then, attention had traditionally focused on either one or the other.

An almost exclusive interest in solving the dilemmas of individual collective action had many impacts on the literature on interest groups in the 1970s. Its most positive impact was of course that scholars elucidated a great number of issues that had previously been taken for granted. In this process, scholars began to equate the study of groups with the study of group's efforts to mobilize their potential memberships. At the very least, scholars expected that any important book on the topic of groups should examine the question of membership recruitment in some detail. Jack Walker's surveys of interest groups were limited to membership organizations largely for this reason. Even though Walker was primarily concerned with the nature of the group system and its effect on government, he limited his study only to membership organizations so that he could discuss in detail these mobilization questions. Such decisions come with a cost, as Walker notes in the beginning pages of his book (1991, 4–5). There are many important interests represented in Washington with no members, which therefore fall outside the scope of his observations. A generation after the Olsonian perspective was first developed, Salisbury (1984) had to remind us that many interest groups have no members at all, so much had our attention shifted, almost unconsciously, to equate interest groups with the dilemma of individual collective action. Just as Olson noted the pluralists were wrong to ignore individual motivations, an increasing number of scholars have come to note that the new literature developed in the wake of Olson was wrong to ignore the roles of government, group leaders, social movements, large institutions, and other contextual factors. Not only did scholars focus only on membership organizations, but their views of membership focused nearly exclusively on individual-level explanations rather than on the social context of membership and collective action.

Jack Walker (1991, 41–48) discussed the irony of scholarly attention being focused on the difficulties of collective action precisely during that time when so many American social movements and groups were demonstrating that its limits could be overcome. The 1960s and 1970s were simultaneously the period of ascendancy of the Olsonian perspective and the setting for massive marches on Washington by exactly those types of groups that Olson argued faced such powerful hurdles to collective mobilization. Walker concluded: "So many powerful forces have been identified that prevail against the mobilization of large social groupings that it is surprising that any such groups exist. Despite the theories, however, many such groups do exist, and, furthermore, their numbers are steadily increasing" (Walker 1991, 48; see also Jordan and Maloney 1996). For a generation before Olson, scholars ignored the problems of individual motivation. For a generation after Olson, scholars ignored questions of social context. Increasingly, in the 1980s and 1990s, scholars have been developing a more complete view that incorporates both perspectives.

John Mark Hansen's (1985) analysis of the membership records of five disparate membership organizations indicated that people are more likely to join groups when their interests are threatened, as Truman had argued. Jack Walker's surveys (1983, 1991) showed that group formation often followed the creation of government programs affecting the potential group in question, as Truman had also argued. Walker noted how governmental agencies occasionally acted as patrons or otherwise encouraged the growth of groups, providing start-up funds and support to potential interest groups. In any case, new government programs created new interests to be defended. Robert Salisbury (1994, 12) has defined *interest* as resulting from the interaction of a private value held by a political actor and some authoritative action or proposed action by the government. It follows from such a definition that the behavior of government officials is an important contextual element in any interest-group action. The existence of competing interests and the activities of government officials are important contextual variables in Virginia Gray and David Lowery's (1996) theory of interest-group populations. Their study of organized interests in six states indicates that system-level influences have a profound effect on individual-level actions and the resulting population of interest groups.

Attention to the context of individual decision making increased not only in studies of group mobilization during the 1980s and 1990s but in studies of political participation in general. Contextual variables are used to explain much of the variation in individual-level mobilization for political activity that demographic and psychological variables alone could not. Schlozman, Verba, and Brady note that a model explaining individual political activities must include efforts at recruitment: "Those who have the motivation and the capacity to become active are more likely to do so if they are asked" (1995, 3). Many contextual factors affect the decision to join, including the simple fact of having been asked (see also Huckfeldt and Sprague 1992, 1995; Rosenstone and Hansen 1993; Leighley 1995). Since many people will respond to a request to participate, or to join in a group, even if they would not do so of their own initiative, a complete model of this behavior must include discussion of recruitment efforts. As Rothenberg (1988) pointed out, many individuals join groups with little knowledge of what the groups do, but in response to some contact. The task for group leaders is to encourage membership retention as much as new member recruitment. As groups are active in such recruitment drives and retention efforts, an explanation of group mobilization should include discussion of their effects. A recent study of effects of direct mail recruitment by Paul Johnson suggests that "collective interests do not explain group membership—recruiting activities do" (1995, 29). This is a far step from where we stood in 1970.

In the generation preceding the publication of Olson's *Logic*, group scholars typically ignored the dilemmas of individual motivation that he showed to be important. In the generation following the publication of his book, most scholars investigating the new questions he posed ignored contextual factors in order to isolate the newly discovered individual-level factors. Today, as scholars develop models of group mobilization that are sensitive both to individual and to contextual variables, we note some important revisions to both the earlier group approach and to the later individual-level approach. Olson demonstrated the flaw in the pluralist assumption that groups would naturally mobilize when threatened. However, the conclusion, reached by extrapolating from the difficulties of collective action, that a nation's group system would inevitably and increasingly become so biased as to clog a nation's political arteries with an evermore voracious set of narrow-minded interest groups (see M. Olson 1982 and Rauch 1994) has also failed the test of time. The group system will never be as perfect as Truman hoped it might be; nor is it likely to be as biased as Olson described either. Individual behavior does not occur in a vacuum, but in the context of large social forces, institutions, governmental policies, existing interests, and other factors that temper the problems of collective action for many groups in society.

## CONCLUSION

When Robert Salisbury introduced a collection of essays on interest groups (1970), he noted that scholars had been so preoccupied with the grand questions of who rules America that they had ignored a range of smaller and more tractable research problems. For interest-group studies to advance, he wrote at that time, a wide range of more narrow issues needed attention: Who joins groups? How do groups overcome the collective action dilemma? What types of inducements work better than others? What are the roles of group leaders in developing their memberships? How have some prominent groups grown? How do groups govern themselves? These were just a few of the multitude of smaller-scale issues that had been neglected as scholars of the previous generation focused on the grand questions of power and influence.

In the generation that has followed the publication of Salisbury's 1970 reader, one might wonder whether his advice was taken too seriously. Looking at the state of the literature today, one can observe that scholars have attacked such a range of disparate and small research problems that interest-group studies collectively suffer from a problem opposite to the one that they faced thirty years ago. Certainly some important research dilemmas have effectively been addressed, notably in the area of collective action. However, such a wide range of issues have been abandoned or studied only in ways that preclude direct comparison of the results that a massive investment in research has not produced an equivalent payoff in the advance of our collective knowledge. If Lawrence Rothenberg can write, with perfect accuracy, a generation after Salisbury's book was published, that "exactly how associations fit into the political world remains somewhat mysterious" (1993, 1167), then we must wonder why such a large investment in so many well-designed studies has not led to a greater accumulation of findings. Groups are all around us, and are often the subject of scholarly and popular inquiry; why should they remain a mystery? In the new literature on interest groups, the big questions remain unresolved.

The group-mobilization literature reviewed in this chapter tells us little about what groups do in Washington. To carry forward an analogy begun by the late Jack Walker, we have spent so much time expounding learnedly about whether the laws of aerodynamics should allow the bumblebee to fly that we have ignored what to do when it is ready to sting. Our intensive research in demand aggregation has focused enormous energies on the topic of how groups overcome or are affected by the collective-action dilemma. All groups are not affected by this difficulty; those that are have proven that there are many ways around the problem; and in any case attention to mobilization questions has diverted attention from important questions of what the tens of thousands of groups controlling billions of dollars are doing in Washington.

The group-mobilization perspective has led to many insights about the biases of mobilization and the resulting biases of the interest-group system. It does not offer the promise of resolving all the difficulties in the literature on groups, however. First, many questions remain unanswered concerning the relative importance of different types of incentives for mobilization. Many groups overcome the difficulties of collective action, even if some do not. Second, the distinction between privileged groups and disadvantaged groups, so central to the collective-action perspective, is irrelevant to many political conflicts. Many, if not most, political disputes involve privileged groups on many sides of the debate. To state that disadvantaged groups are absent from the debate is an important insight, but it does not explain the sum total of what a political scientist observes. The collective-action dilemma, in sum, is central to many debates, but it does not by itself explain all of them.

In our review of the group approach to politics in chapter 3, we noted the problem scholars faced in dealing with evidence. Some noted diversity and concluded that the group system was truly representative of society; others noted barriers to entry and concluded that the system was elitist at its core. In the new literature on interest groups, with its focus on collective action and mobilization, we can see a similar trend. Scholars have spent a generation focusing on a set of narrow questions associated with the various ways in which groups face the problem of mobilizing their potential members. Such a range of problems and solutions have been presented that it is unclear exactly how serious the problem is. Faced with a single piece of evidence, scholars still interpret that finding based on their theoretical starting point rather than on a shared perspective on what the appropriate interpretation might be. The Olsonian perspective on collective action has led to a number of insights but it has also suffered from some of the same problems in interpretation that plagued the group approach that Olson criticized so effectively.

Thirty years have now passed since the publication of Olson's *Logic*; more than forty-five years separate us from Truman's *Governmental Process*. Only recently have scholars begun to develop models that take seriously the insights of both authors. We have oscillated from a position of ignoring the importance of individual decision making, to focusing on individuals to the exclusion of broad social forces that provide the context for their behavior. Finally, many scholars are making serious efforts to include both perspectives into our understandings of how the interest-group system generates support. This more complete approach to the study of individual bases of group mobilization allows some significant progress. In the next two chapters, we review the evidence on the nature and degree of bias in public participation in the group system and in the structure and biases of the Washington interest-group system. In both cases, we note some disturbing tendencies, reminiscent of the debates between the pluralists and the elitists, for different scholars to reach their conclusions on the basis of their theoretical starting point rather than on the basis of the evidence. Similar tendencies are apparent in the works discussed in this chapter. Scholars have succeeded in pointing to the causes of bias in the group system, but not in demonstrating clearly how severe it is, exactly what consequences it has, or whether it is growing worse or less severe. We turn now to consider the evidence on bias and diversity in the interest-group system.

# CHAPTER 5

# Bias and Diversity
# in the Interest-Group System

FOR AS LONG as observers have focused their attention on the mobilization of interest groups, they have noted the vast numbers, the great variety, and the vitality of associations in American life. De Tocqueville, one of the first and most astute observers, saw the development of groups in the young American republic as an inspiration, noting the good works and public-minded orientations of many of the associations. Since his initial observations, popular observers have continued to note the vitality and growth of the group system, but rarely have they shared his enthusiasm. Many have noted the paradox inherent in the group system: the group system is seen simultaneously to be a route for popular representation and a threat to good government because of the biases that it allows. In this chapter, we review the contradictory stances that political scientists and other observers have taken on the value of interest groups as vehicles of popular representation.

In a democracy groups are at once the means by which many disparate voices are heard and the scapegoats for complaints about the powers of great corporations, industrial barons, highly paid influence peddlers, and special interests of all kinds. In this and the following chapter, we review theoretical stances and empirical evidence on the question of interest-group representation. This chapter focuses on the question of bias in both popular involvement in groups and the nature of the Washington lobbying community. The next chapter discusses evidence that this bias differs across time, across issue domains, and among different types of issues. We end chapter 6 with a discussion of the difficulties that scholars have shown in coming to shared interpretations of the findings in this area. In spite of a great range of interesting and provocative research results, few strong conclusions emerge from this literature, partly because scholars cannot agree on a shared point of reference.

## INTEREST GROUPS AND REPRESENTATION

In general, those who have focused on the growth and development of the interest-group system in America have worried about the consequences of this growth for the process of governing. Groups are often seen as inhibitors of democracy, as "special pleaders" using unseemly tactics to wrangle favors from legislators. This is not only a recent phenomenon; the view of the lobbyist as agent of undue influence has a long history. Frederick Cleveland, writing in 1913, describes the plight of the legislator in these terms:

> At the present time two state constitutions and the statutes of seven others make some provision for the protection of members of the state legislature against undue personal influence. This interference . . . usually emanates from the hired agents of great corporations who seek favors through special legislation. . . .
>
> So serious has this interference become that popular resentment has expressed itself in drastic measures. The constitutions of California and Georgia declare lobbying a felony. The former constitution defines lobbying to be the seeking to influence the vote of a member of the legislature by bribery, promise of reward, intimidation, or other dishonest means. (Cleveland 1913, 372)

So strong have been these negative views of lobbying that agent registration laws generally were enacted with the intent to prohibit lobbyists from personally contacting legislators and allowing them to participate only in public hearings. For example, in Wisconsin the law of the time "forbids any legislative agent or counsel to attempt to influence legislation in any other way than by arguing before committees and filing printed briefs with the members of the two houses" (Cleveland 1913, 373). Similar laws were on the books in several other states.

The strength of business opposition to many Rooseveltian innovations was powerful enough in the 1930s to cause many commentators to complain about the influence of their hired lobbies (and for many state legislatures to enact restrictive laws such as those described above; for a further review of these efforts and a discussion of their general failure, see Lane 1964). Senator Hugo Black, before his appointment to the U.S. Supreme Court, considered regulation of lobbyists to be a priority and sponsored legislation in the Senate to this effect. (The legislation died in conference with the House, after passing the Senate.) In a 1935 radio speech, he summed up his conclusions on the matter in a widely quoted summary of the problem: "Contrary to tradition, against the public morals, and hostile to good government, the lobby has reached such a position of power that it threatens government itself" (quoted in Crawford 1939, 4; see also Schriftgiesser 1951, chap. 5).

Members of government have long complained of the powers of the lobbies, and their terms of complaint have changed little over the decades. In an NBC radio broadcast of March 28, 1933, James K. Pollack, a political scientist, discussed "the lobby problem" with U.S. Senator Edward P. Costigan. After discussing the largely ineffectual efforts to regulate lobbyists, Senator Costigan shows his exasperation. Some lobbyists, he notes, are men and women of high purpose, unusual intelligence, and full information. What they have to say is for the most part helpful, important and accurate. Others, and regrettably the larger group, endlessly pursue legislators with the desires and requests of the interests they represent. They add confusion and tumult to the already over-crowded days of those members of Congress who are striving to discharge their official duties faithfully, fairly, and wisely. They prevent necessary conferences and uninterrupted examination of problems by insisting on interviews during limited office hours. They destroy continuous attention to debate and effective participation. They call members of the Senate needlessly from the floor. They interrupt at dawn, midnight, and meal times. They permit neither privacy nor freedom. They stimulate countless other persons to plead, demand, and even threaten by letters and telegrams, sent in such numbers that the mere task of answering must exhaust the energies of the best staff and the strongest individual. Some of them for their own selfish financial gain even try to deceive and spare no expense to influence Congress and public opinion. (Pollack et al. 1933, 5)

In the senatorial view, lobbyists take up so much time that little is left over for careful consideration of weighty policy matters. Sixty years later, as the Senate was considering legislation again to regulate campaign contributions, Robert C. Byrd voiced almost identical views on the demands placed on members of the Senate by the need to raise large amounts of money, generally from lobbyists:

The incessant money chase is an insidious demand that takes away from the time we have to actually do our job here in Washington. It takes away from the time we have to study and understand the issues, to meet with our constituents, to talk with other senators and to work out solutions to the problems that face this nation. (Quoted in Clymer 1996)

Mancur Olson argued that the development of a nation's interest-group system is likely to follow a pattern of increasing bias against the general interest because of the difficulties of overcoming the collective-action dilemma, as discussed in the previous chapter and in his 1965 *Logic of Collective Action*. In his later book, *The Rise and Decline of Nations* (1982), he presents a theory that special interests will mobilize consistently at a higher rate than representatives of collective interests, inevitably leading the country into economic decline as the political system is overwhelmed by an increasingly voracious set of interest groups intent on pleading their special cases.

This argument corresponds closely to a long string of popular and scholarly works published throughout the century. Important books have appeared over the decades with such titles as *The Impasse of Democracy* (Griffith 1939), *Economic Power and Political Pressures* (Blaisdell 1949), *American Democracy under Pressure* (Blaisdell 1957), *The Deadlock of Democracy* (Burns 1963), *The End of Liberalism* (Lowi 1969), *Can the Government Govern?* (Chubb and Peterson 1989), and *Demosclerosis* (Rauch 1994). An important scholarly and popular tradition, traceable across the century, views lobbyists and interest groups as special interests likely only to push government officials away from making decisions in the public interest. The increasing diversity of society and the larger role of government in American life conspire to lead to the creation of more and more groups. In this view, the only hope for continued good government lies in the ability of government officials to resist group pressures. Strong political parties, powerful government agencies, and an authoritative judicial system are seen as the greatest protection against the ever-increasing powers of the special interests.

There is another view of the interest-group system, one that focuses on the range of interests active in political life and speculates that this remarkable diversity must be broadly representative of the interests in society. This view was perhaps at its strongest during the 1950s and 1960s, the heydays of pluralist thought. It has much deeper roots than this, however. Like its rival train of thought, this tradition spans at least the present century. In his study of group activities in the U.S. Congress during the mid-1920s, Pendleton Herring wrote that when individuals face a political problem, they naturally look to see what organized interest group might be able to support their view before the government. Further, he argued that "it is a rare point of view, indeed, that does not find . . . some society or national association that is not already sponsoring whatever the most fertile mind of man can conceive" (Herring 1929, 2). To Herring, and to other pluralists following in his footsteps, this diversity was so great that it seemed to ensure that every interest imaginable was indeed present in Washington. He writes:

> Not only are almost all sorts of interests and classes represented but also all sides of most questions as well. For example, the motorists have the American Automobile Association; the manufacturers are represented by the National Automobile Chamber of Commerce, while the distributors speak through the National Automobile Dealers Association. Makers and sellers of accessories, tires, batteries, and parts have their national associations. What of the poor pedestrian? There is the American Pedestrian Protective Association, organized in 1926, with national headquarters in Washington. There is the Lord's Day Alliance on the one hand and the Association Opposed to Blue Laws on the other. . . . Instances could be multiplied indefinitely. (Herring 1929, 22)

The optimistic view of representation through the group system finds perhaps its greatest expression in Truman's *The Governmental Process* (1951).

For Truman, those faced with a problem are likely to form groups; therefore, any potential group in society would be organized to ask for redress if its problems were really serious. A focus on the diversity of organized interests active in America can be seen in the works of de Tocqueville, Herring (1929), Truman (1951), Milbrath (1963), and Key (1964). While these writers do not assert that the representation of interests through the group system is perfect or without bias, they emphasize the diversity of interests present not the barriers to participation through groups or the bias of this form of interest representation.

In the years following Olson's 1965 *Logic*, the assumption of unfettered organization of all potential interests has not been taken seriously. Important barriers are known to prevent many potential groups from organizing, so few scholars take the existing group universe to be representative of those interests that might need to be represented. The most reassuring version of pluralism—focusing on the value of a diverse set of groups actively representing virtually every imaginable point of view, and assuring good government through negotiation and persistence—has been discredited. Still, a great variety of interests are represented, and important social movements have indeed left strong organizational legacies. Groups representing women, minorities, environmentalists, antinuclear power activists, and many other diffuse goals do indeed exist, and they sometimes prevail.

Many scholars throughout the decades have argued with de Tocqueville that interest groups not only provide representation for a broad range of views, but also that they perform important educational roles: Participation in interest groups makes people better citizens. In this view, the growth of more groups can be seen as a good thing because Americans learn important skills of communication, collaboration, and political efficacy through their contacts with local and national associations. Robert Putnam (1994, 1995) discusses the "social fabric" of society in his look at of how groups give citizens useful experiences of working together. His view is that there are too few, not too many, associations in American life (especially those groups that promote discussion and common action, as opposed to mere "checkbook" membership). Sidney Verba and colleagues (1995) also discuss the important socializing role of groups. Robert Wuthnow remarks that "Tocqueville recognized that voluntary associations make an important contribution to the *cultural health* of a nation" (Wuthnow 1991, 4, emphasis in original). This view of the positive role of groups in fostering greater social cohesion also has a long history, even if it is not shared by all.

Jane Mansbridge (1992) provides one of the few efforts to deal explicitly with the normative questions of the role of groups in a democracy. She focuses on the role that groups play in encouraging deliberation among their members and on the positive informational role that groups play in their relations with government. Groups can be a positive force for democratic development if they play an important role in explaining, airing, and discussing the issues of the day. Members learn of public policies that affect them through their group affiliations; she notes the importance that Schlozman and Tierney (1986) ascribed to communicating with their own members in their study of group leaders.

Two long-standing traditions persist to this day in our understanding of interest groups in American politics. Each view has been modified by decades of research and new findings, but the central theme of each remains. One sees the interest-group system as hopelessly biased in favor of powerful economic interests and narrow special pleaders; another sees a greater diversity of interests in the Washington policy community and a positive role for groups in the creation of better citizens. The relative emphasis that scholars have placed on each of these points of view has changed from decade to decade, but neither has been shown to be completely accurate; a complete view must recognize elements of both views. Just as the framers of the Constitution fretted about the "mischiefs of faction" but at the same time included the petition of government as a constitutional right for all, scholars and activists in each generation since then have debated the dual roles of interest groups in government.

Intellectual trends giving greater attention to the positive or the negative aspects of representation through interest groups have followed important social trends. During the more socially quiescent 1940s and 1950s, scholars were more likely to focus on the value of groups in representing all those who seemed to be attempting to speak. The massive riots and social movements of the 1960s and 1970s discredited this view substantially. But the social movements and protests of this period led to two reactions; one immediate, the other delayed. First, scholars leveled a much more critical assessment of the existing set of interest groups, in a series of important criticisms of the "pluralist heaven" (see Schattschneider 1960). So many important social groups were manifestly left outside of the mainstream system of representation that it became difficult to support the view that such a system was neutral or unbiased (see Walker 1966a and 1991). Second, however, came a delayed reaction. The new social movements often were successful in spawning new interest organizations in the areas of civil rights, women's rights, and the environment, and scholars became more likely to accept a view that the interest-group system really was, or at least could be, diverse. Even if the system was not without bias, neither was it completely frozen or incapable of adjusting to new social realities. In the literature on policy making, such concepts as iron triangles and policy subsystems, focusing on shared interests, bias, and consensus among the self-interested, gave way to such metaphors as issue-networks and advocacy coalitions, both emphasizing relative openness and conflict. One constant throughout this progression of views has been the centrality of interest groups to our views of the representative process and to our evaluations of the quality of representation in American government. Unfortunately, another constant has been the lack of consensus on how to interpret evidence. Just as the pluralists and elitists differed by citing different pieces of evidence to prove their points, scholars attempting to discuss the diversity and bias in the American group system share no common point of reference that would allow them to interpret a given piece of evidence about the degree of bias that all observe. We will return to this point towards the end of chapter 6.

## MASS PARTICIPATION IN INTEREST GROUPS

An important element in determining the value of the group system as a vehicle for representative government is to ascertain the degree and type of popular participation in voluntary associations. Research on this topic has been plagued by many methodological difficulties, but it nonetheless can help us understand both the remarkable degree of participation in the interest-group system, and its strong biases in terms of social class, education, income, and occupation. Most Americans are members of interest groups and many more have their interests represented by groups of which they are not formal members, but overall there remains a strong overinvolvement in the group system by those with greater social and economic resources. The occupational basis of most interest groups ensures that business owners and members of certain professions are dramatically overrepresented in Washington.

Many of the definitional problems discussed in chapter 2 are illustrated by the literature on mass involvement in groups. Depending on the definitions used, researchers show tremendously broad activity by virtually all Americans in the group system or activity only by the narrowest stratum of wealthy elites. Membership in overtly political organizations, for example, has been typically found to be on the order of only about 8 percent (Verba and Nie 1972, 31, 42). Some studies report even lower levels. The General Social Survey consistently reports levels of membership in "political clubs" of only 3 to 5 percent from the 1970s onward (see Davis and Smith 1994, 300). Including religious organizations, charities, professional associations, labor unions, veterans' groups, ethnic or nationality organizations, parent-teacher associations, neighborhood groups, sports and hobby organizations, and other types of groups inflates the numbers considerably.

Despite this and other methodological problems associated with determining exactly how many Americans are members or supporters of interest groups, we can note certain core figures. First, almost every national study finds that a majority of adult Americans are members of at least one group of some kind. In the General Social Survey, the most prominent national survey systematically to include questions about group membership, approximately 70 percent of Americans have been found to have at least one membership, a percentage that has held steady since the early 1970s (Davis and Smith 1994; Baumgartner and Walker 1988, 910). This number is subject to some dispute. Using a more generous set of questions, Baumgartner and Walker (1988, 1990) found higher levels of involvement. Using a more restricted set of questions, Hyman and Wright (1971) found less involvement. In spite of these problems of precision, it remains clear that the American public is largely involved in the interest-group system.

On the basis of their monumental two-stage survey of Americans focusing on their participation in various forms of community activities, both political and nonpolitical, Sidney Verba and colleagues (1995) report much higher figures of affiliation with groups than other studies have found. Like Baumgartner and Walker, Verba and colleagues use an extensive list of questions about organizational affiliations. They report that 79 percent of Americans are members of groups; 61 percent of these report that the organizations take stands on political issues at the national or local level (Verba et al. 1995, 63). "Almost half of the respondents (48 percent) reported being affiliated with—that is, being a member or making a contribution to—an organization that takes stands in politics. These data testify to the important role of voluntary associations as a channel for citizen activity" (50). They report further that affiliation with nonpolitical organizations, even church involvement, has implications for subsequent political engagement: Citizens learn important skills that later give them greater ease of participation in political issues.

On the basis of their large study of political participation in America, Verba and colleagues conclude that overall levels of activity are extremely high when compared with previous studies. Partly, this is due to a more generous set of definitions. Still, as they measure involvement, overall levels of activity in either politics or nonpolitical community activities are remarkable, covering the vast majority of American citizens in one way or another. "In spite of the contemporary image of Americans as a nation of passive spectators mesmerized before their television screens, these comparative metrics suggest that there is a great deal of voluntary activity in the United States, both within and, especially, outside politics. The activities may be intermittent and peripheral to Americans' basic concerns, but they are there" (Verba et al. 1995, 81–82). Their data show some 95 percent of Americans with some activities; 65 percent with activities in political organizations, and 29 percent with activities only in non-political organizations (83). Clearly, Americans complain about the roles of interest groups in politics, but they participate massively in national and local associations involved with many elements of public life.

A second core finding is that popular participation in the group system includes both a great majority of people who are only loosely attached to the group system and a thin stratum of extremely active individuals. Many Americans have just one or two affiliations with local or national groups, but some are involved with many organizations. These differences in levels of activity make representation through the interest-group system dramatically different from such activities as voting: The same individual may be active simultaneously in a great number of interest groups, whereas each person can vote only once. Our understanding of the role of the group system in the representative process must therefore be tempered by this overrepresentation of a thin stratum of extremely active individuals. For example, in a series of questions added to the 1985 Pilot Study for the National Election Study, approximately 90 percent of the respondents had at least one group affiliation (including financial contributions) and 78 percent had at least one group membership. So there is evidence of broad involvement in the system, as Verba and others have also noted. On the other hand, about 5 percent of the 1985 sample were members of six or more organizations, giving these people much more involvement in the group system than others (Baumgartner and Walker 1988, 919). These extremely active individuals are distinctive by their education, their social class, their occupations, and their income. Any assessment of overall levels of involvement by Americans in the group system should also consider that a large percentage of the total membership activity may be generated by a surprisingly low percentage of the public.

A third core finding is that Americans join interest groups and contribute to charities at greater rates than citizens of other democracies. One may argue whether the overall levels of participation shown by Americans are high or low on an absolute scale, and one may question whether the group system may simply allow a small segment of extremely active individuals to multiply their own voices, but when one compares survey data collected in this country with those from other similar nations, one finds that Americans join at higher rates. The most recent and complete study on this topic, that done by James E. Curtis and colleagues, showed Americans to have the highest rate of joining in fifteen countries studied (Curtis, Grabb, and Baer 1992; see also Almond and Verba 1965, chap. 10; Curtis 1971; Verba et al. 1995, 71, 80). A recent study of volunteerism reached similar conclusions: Whereas 48 percent of Americans report that they volunteer, the highest figures in Europe were considerably lower: 38 percent in the Netherlands, 36 percent in Sweden, and 34 percent in Great Britain, and 18 percent in Germany (Stehle 1995, 15).

Contributions to charities in the United States sustain a large and influential set of institutions such as the American Red Cross, the American Lung Association, and other major organizations in health care, culture, education, social services, and other areas of public life. Total giving increased from $92 billion in 1975 to $144 billion in 1995, measured in constant 1995 dollars. Contributions from foundations doubled in this period, from $5.32 to $10.44 billion; gifts from corporations grew similarly from $3.72 billion to $7.40 billion, again in constant 1995 dollars (Murawski 1996). More than one-quarter of all American taxpayers declare a deduction for charitable giving, with the mean amount declared being approximately $2,300. IRS figures drawn from tax returns in 1993 and 1994 thus show a total of approximately $70 billion per year in donations from individuals (Blum 1996). Whether one considers these figures to be high or low depends, of course, on one's point of comparison. We can conclude two things, however. First, the aggregate amounts of charitable giving in the United States, measured as they are in the hundreds of billions of dollars, are enough to sustain some important and influential organizations that are active in Washington. Second, charity and philanthropy have steadily been growing over the past generation. Even measured in constant dollars, overall contributions grew by nearly 60 percent from 1975 to 1995.

In sum, one can point to a number of studies that lead to a conclusion that mass involvement by Americans in the voluntary sector is considerable. Most Americans participate in groups through membership, and many make additional contributions to the causes of their choice through financial contributions or by volunteering. Membership, contributions, and volunteerism are higher in the United States than in any other democracy. Do these facts guarantee that representation through the group system is equitable? Not by any means.

A fourth core finding of research on mass involvement in the interest-group system is that strong social class and occupational biases affect mass participation in groups. Since Schattschneider's charge that the "flaw in the pluralist heaven is that the heavenly chorus sings with an upper-class accent" (1960, 35), scholars have repeatedly found evidence for the social class bias in participation in interest groups. Although Schattschneider was referring mostly to the contours of the Washington lobbying community, public opinion surveys have consistently shown his observation to hold at the level of the mass public. A majority of Americans are involved in the group system in one way or another, but those with higher social status are much more involved than others (see Verba and Nie 1972; Rosenstone and Hansen 1993; Verba et al. 1995). Many Americans become active in interest groups through their professions; the unemployed and those with low-skilled jobs have fewer such opportunities. In the case of voluntary associations, we can see a clear link between these individual-level explanations and others based on analyses of the group system at the national level. Walker (1991, 59) found, after all, that three-quarters of all Washington-based membership groups had their origins in the occupational structure of the American economy. This systemic factor helps to explain why the individual-level bias can be so high. Professions, businesses, industries, and career-oriented occupations pull members into the interest-group system almost automatically, whereas those outside of the labor force or in low status jobs are much less likely to be afforded this sort of representation.

One way to look at the roles of interest groups in American democracy is to question who joins groups. In this quick review of some of the major findings in this area, we have seen that most Americans are represented and that Americans are more likely to join groups than those in other countries, but serious problems of bias remain. Certain types of interests are much more likely than others to be represented forcefully and with greater resources. Likewise, when we turn our attention to the universe of groups active in Washington, rather than to the mass basis of support for interest groups in the public, we find a much more concentrated set of groups than we might be led to expect.

## THE WASHINGTON INTEREST-GROUP COMMUNITY

Just as scholars have long noted that many Americans are linked in one way or another to the interest-group system and yet important biases remain apparent in this form of representation, so too have scholars simultaneously marveled at the diversity of interests present in the Washington interest-group system and complained of the biases inherent in this system. There is no question that the organized group system accentuates many differences in political advantage. Jeffrey Berry (1994a) notes, for example, two types of bias. At the individual level, clear tendencies exist for those of higher social, educational, income, and professional status to participate more in groups than those of lower status. Perhaps even more important than this individual-level bias, however, is the organizational bias that causes groups to form surrounding professions and industries at much greater rates than around other potential causes, such as shared beliefs, ethnic background, or habits. Combined, these tendencies make clear that the constellation of interest groups active in the nation's capital should never be assumed to mirror the set of interests in society.

As easy as it is for scholars and observers to agree that there are important elements of bias in the representation of organized interests in America, it has proven extremely difficult to pin this down empirically. The absence of a clear point of reference makes it difficult for scholars to agree on the degree to which the Washington interest-group system is biased. There is no question that the greatest degree of overrepresentation through interest groups is within the business community. Businesses and industries are extremely active in the Washington pressure community, and they have been for decades. Economic interest groups enjoy several advantages for mobilization when compared with noneconomic groups, as Olson (1965) described. This advantage in mobilization is even greater when we note that corporations are active in Washington not only through their trade and professional associations; they often have direct representation through their own offices of government affairs as well. As we discussed in chapter 2, research findings on the degree of business advantage in representation are often affected by the method of selecting the elements for inclusion in a study. A consensus about the important advantages enjoyed by business interests in the group system is apparent, however, across a number of studies in the area despite differences in research approach and design. Schlozman and Tierney (1986) noted the distribution of interests, including private businesses, active in the Washington community; Heinz et al. (1993) traced who was influential or active in four policy areas; Danielian and Page (1994) noted which organizations appeared in the news, also including private corporations; Golden (1995) traced participation in bureaucratic rule-making procedures; Caldeira and Wright (1990) tracked Supreme Court amicus briefs. Each drew different conclusions about the degree of business dominance, but each noted the importance of private interests in the Washington lobbying community.

A long line of observers has documented the advantages that accrue to business interests in mobilizing for Washington lobbying activity. Herring (1929, 276–83) listed hundreds of organizations active in Washington at the time of his research in 1927; this list included a great diversity of interests but was dominated by economic interests. When Blaisdell updated this list, he showed more than three hundred organizations active, with a similar predominance of manufacturing and business interests (1941, 197–201). To be sure, these lists include a great range of organizations, including such ones as the Association of American Producers of Domestic Inedible Fats, the Committee for Repeal of the National Labor Relations Act, the Make Europe Pay War Debts Committee, and the Association of Quality Ice Cream Manufacturers. Still, the list is heavy with trade associations, unions, and others with their base in the business community. So prevalent have these economic interests been that scholars such as Blaisdell fretted openly about the excesses of business lobbying and the unforeseen consequences of the increased concentration of economic power into fewer large hands. In a theme that Kariel would pick up twenty years later, Blaisdell worried about the ability of the nation's eighteenth-century institutions to deal with the powers generated by the economy of the twentieth century (see Blaisdell 1941; Kariel 1961).

Writing a decade after Blaisdell, and directly following the Second World War, David Truman noted that the predominance of economic groups was so great "that many writers have fallen into the error of treating economic groups as the only important interest groups" (1951, 61). One of the reasons for the prevalence of occupationally based groups, according to Truman, was the disturbances that often affect modern industry. New technologies, changes in tax laws, or the simple functioning of the business cycle regularly produce turmoil within the economy, and each wave of disturbances may generate new economic interest groups. Truman's disturbance theory, in which each large disruption leads to the creation of new interest groups to defend a group facing a threat, may have been relatively accurate where it concerned businesses, and it helps explain the rapid mobilization of economic interests in the first half of the century. Truman's explanation makes business-sector advantage in interest-group mobilization seem to be an inevitable consequence of the business cycle and of technological advance.

Data cited by Truman from a 1949 study by the Department of Commerce show that business interests were vastly overrepresented when compared with other types of organizations. Each of the largest sets of organizations was affiliated with business affairs. Of a total of four thousand organizations active in national affairs in that year, the largest categories of groups were as follows: eight hundred organizations of manufacturers; five hundred organizations of professional and semiprofessional persons; four hundred organizations of transportation, finance, insurance, and other industries; three hundred organizations of distributors; and three hundred organizations of other businesses.

In contrast to these organizations from the business world, Truman lists two hundred labor unions and a variety of other categories of groups (including women, veterans and military, farmers, Negroes, commodity exchanges, public officials, fraternal, sports and recreation groups), none of which included more than one hundred groups. Not counting one thousand organizations listed from "all other fields," then, more than three-quarters of all the organizations listed in this 1949 census of national associations, and all of the largest categories, were business-related organizations (1951, 58).

Just as Truman noted, Schattschneider also documented (and lamented) the huge bias in group organization in favor of the business community. Among other figures similar to those just mentioned, Schattschneider cites the "*Lobby Index, 1946–1949* (an index of organizations and individuals registering or filing quarterly reports under the Federal Lobbying Act) published as a report of the House Select Committee on Lobbying Activities. In this compilation, 825 out of a total of 1,247 entries (exclusive of individuals and Indian tribes) represented business" (1960, 31). His summary of the situation is well known: "The business or upper-class bias of the pressure system shows up everywhere" (Schattschneider 1960, 31).

Given these facts, there is no wonder that Truman and Schattschnieder noted that many scholars equate the interest-group system with business interests. Studies from the 1920s, the 1930s, the 1940s, and the 1950s all documented the predominance of business in the lobbying community. More recent studies of the Washington interest-group landscape confirm the continued importance of business interests in politics. The large empirical studies conducted by Jack Walker (1983, 1991) and by Kay Lehman Schlozman and John Tierney (1983, 1986) provide the broadest recent empirical descriptions of the Washington interest-group population. They are therefore a good place to start in any assessment of the current state of bias in that community. Walker surveyed more than one thousand groups in his two surveys, although he limited his investigation to membership groups. Schlozman and Tierney surveyed fewer than two hundred groups but included corporations and some other organizations without members, and they supplemented their survey with an analysis of a list of more than five thousand groups and firms active in Washington from *Washington Representatives*. Laumann and Knoke (1987) included all people or organizations cited by informants as influential, including professional lobbying firms, while Heinz et al. (1993) combined published sources and informants' reports to compile their sampling frame. These last two studies are limited to specific policy domains: Laumann and Knoke consider energy and health policy; Heinz et al. studied agriculture, health, energy, and labor.

These national studies provide a clear set of findings on certain aspects of the question of bias (though our next chapter will review some points of dispute concerning whether these biases are growing worse or are being attenuated). Clearly the finding that business interests predominate—at least in terms of numbers of organizations represented in Washington—is quite robust. Walker and Schlozman and Tierney found that about three-fourths of their groups were associated in some way with occupations. Walker's finding was especially striking because he did not include businesses themselves in his sampling frame. His survey of membership organizations active in Washington lobbying showed that 76 percent of all groups were associated with the professional backgrounds of their members (1991, 59). Scholzman and Tierney reported that 72 percent of those organizations having Washington representation in 1980 were either corporations or trade and business associations. An additional 8 percent were professional associations, for a combined total of 80 percent of all groups with Washington representation. This number compares with those for citizens' groups (5 percent); civil rights, social welfare, and those representing the poor (2 percent); and those representing women, the elderly, and the handicapped (1 percent) (1986, 77).

Not only are occupations and businesses vastly overrepresented in the Washington lobbying process, but there are further biases inherent in the group system. When threatened some groups can mobilize more easily than others. Unfortunately for those who would hope to see the group system as an accurate reflection of society, businesses have further advantages here. Greenstone (1975) notes Dahl's example of how interests can be mobilized out of their normal position of relative political apathy. This question of the ease of political mobilization is central to our understandings of the fairness of the group system. Truman's evaluations were relatively positive because he focused on the abilities of any "latent group" to mobilize to protect its interests if threatened. Two important empirical refinements have come since Truman's writings. First, the mobilization of the apathetic is indeed central to the outcomes of political battles (see Schattschneider 1960; Dahl 1961; Greenstone 1975; Baumgartner and Jones 1993; Gray and Lowery 1996). Second, the ability of different types of groups to mobilize for political action differs greatly, and these differences generally reinforce rather than dilute the social class and business-oriented biases of the existing group system. Certainly it is true that citizens' and other "outsider" groups often have advantages in terms of the numbers of potential members, and such groups are at an advantage when an issue becomes broadly politicized. On the other hand, professional and business organizations often have an existing set of communication ties allowing them to mobilize quickly and relatively efficiently when a new threat or opportunity is observed. Gray and Lowery (1996) note, for example, that the business associations in their sample often seemed to go into "hibernation" during periods when there was little legislative activity of concern to them. They did not disappear completely, however, and were capable of reappearing on short notice when they recognized the renewed need for political action. Membership in a variety of trade associations is a low-cost way for many corporations to be alerted when their interests are at stake. The importance of this is reflected in the frequency with which interest-group representatives in Washington report that one of their most important functions is "monitoring." These organizations spend a great deal of time observing activities in a wide range of governmental departments and committees in Congress, making sure to notify members when anything ominous appears. Clearly, the ability to monitor government activity and to mobilize quickly once a threat is observed is an advantage not shared equally by all potential groups.

What can we conclude about business advantage in the group system? It seems clear that many of the largest interest groups are those representing business interests, that these groups are among the best endowed, the most professional, and the best able to achieve access in their areas. However, there are other elements that lead us away from a conclusion that would equate the interest-group system with unfettered and unrestricted business advantage.

First, we have seen the rise of citizens' groups and the mobilization of new types of interests in the decades since 1960. A much greater range of interests are present in Washington than was once the case. Second, increased economic diversity has created more conflicts within existing policy communities, creating the opportunity for those not so well endowed with organizational resources to forge coalitions based on shared interests. This surrogate form of "vicarious representation" is an important element of the interest representation process in the 1990s. Mancur Olson was right: Small groups with intense preferences have an organizational advantage over large groups with diffuse interests. The interest-group system is lopsided because of the vast overrepresentation of certain types of groups. However, this picture is increasingly incomplete as some groups overcome the problems of collective action and as these groups find that political cleavages over particular issues frequently cause fissures within the business community itself. These create strategic opportunities, which are rapidly exploited where possible, making representation through interest groups much more complete than it might otherwise be.

One of the most powerful examples of the influence of special interests, and one of the favorites of interest-group scholars, has been the huge tariffs that support American sugar producers (see Cater 1964). During the 1995 budget debates, as agricultural subsidies in general were under consideration for cuts, important battles raged over the continuation of a system that allows Americans to support a sugar price roughly double the world market price, through a combination of import controls and price supports. As is often the case where the great diversity of business interests in Washington clash, this debate did not pit producers against the national federations of consumers but rather producers against large industrial manufacturers of sugar-laden products: the Coca-Cola corporation, Hershey's, and breakfast cereal manufacturers were the natural allies of the consumers in this case (see Bradsher 1995). Political conflicts on specific issues do not tend to break so neatly along a line that would pit "consumers" against "businesses." Often, divisions among well-endowed commercial interests put one side of the debate in at least a temporary alliance with a broader interest. Businesses are consumers as well. All in all, we can conclude that clear evidence points to far greater resources for businesses in American politics than for any other type of group. The degree to which this simple fact suffices to summarize all political conflict is another matter, however.

## CONCLUSION

The consistent efforts of scores of scholars working in this area for the entire postwar period have led to no consensus on the degree of bias in the system nor even to an understanding of how one would reach such a conclusion. It is clear to all that important tendencies point to the overinvolvement of individuals of higher social and educational background in the group system. Further, the occupational basis of most interest groups is well documented and adds to the tendency for the well-off and professionally secure to be more adequately represented than the poor or those with low-status jobs or no professions at all. Finally, there is no doubt that businesses are greatly advantaged in the fight for mobilization and for representation in Washington.

If it is clear that important elements of bias characterize participation in the American interest-group system, there are also important elements of diversity. The relative degrees of bias and of diversity in the group system have been seen to change over time, from area to area, and from issue to issue. Some political outcomes are clearly the result of a one-sided mobilization of political interests that represent only one side of a potential conflict. Others are home to well-publicized disputes among hundreds of organized interests, each with a different understanding of the issue and with its own information and resources to bring to the policy debate. The group system at once provides a biased representation of views, and an ever-changing set of interests active before government. In chapter 6, we review findings considering the dynamics of bias.

# The Dynamics of Bias

WHATEVER may be the biases stemming from differences in public involvement and the occupational bases of many interest groups in America, these biases are not the same at all times, for all issues, or in all areas of political life. The set of interest groups active in Washington is anything but stable: it has undergone dramatic transformations over time; it differs from area to area; and it varies from issue to issue.

## THE RECURRING DISCOVERY OF AN "INTEREST-GROUP EXPLOSION"

In a field where constants are few, it is reassuring to read the descriptions of the "explosion" of interest-group activity in Washington in almost every book on the subject. In virtually every decade of the century, observers have noted the increasing numbers of lobbyists in the nation's capital. Mark Petracca gives a review of many of the studies noting increased numbers of groups active in Washington, and he remarks with irony that one can scarcely distinguish those descriptions published in the 1920s from those published in the 1940s, the 1960s, or the 1980s. Scholars of all generations have described the "explosion" of interest groups in similar ways. Among those cited by Petracca (1992b, 11–13) are the following:

1. "A large number of voluntary associations have sprung up during the past twenty years, devoted to the propagation of special economic interests or special political and social ideas." (Croly 1915)

2. "In the last decade, there has been an amazing development of the practice of employing legislative agents to represent special interests during the sessions of legislative bodies. . . . [N]ever before have legislative bodies been subjected to such a continuous and powerful bombardment from private interests as at present." (Pollock 1927)

3. "The lobby army—small enough to be overlooked in normal times, but big enough to fight a Central American boundary war—still is busy in Washington burning the bridges between the voter and what he voted for." (Crawford 1939)

4. "During the past few decades the number of pressure groups has rapidly multiplied, the scope of their activities has vastly expanded, and their methods and tactics have become more professionalized and subtle. Today, the more

highly organized groups have lobbyists in Washington and in many state capitals, well-staffed bureaus of press agents and research personnel, and active membership groups across the nation." (H. Turner 1958)

**5.** "There has been an increase in the amount, tempo, and intensity of pressure group activity in recent decades." (Mahood 1967)

Rare is the text on interest groups in American politics today that does not contain a discussion of the "interest-group explosion" (see Berry 1997). Difficulties of agreeing on exactly what should be counted make it impossible to compare the findings of one study precisely with those of another, so it is hard to document or to follow this explosion carefully. As Salisbury notes, "estimates of raw numbers [of interest groups] for earlier years are neither plentiful nor, probably, very reliable" (1984, 72). Still, one can construct a rough continuity from the estimates of growth reported by Petracca (1992b, 14–15), Walker (1991), Schlozman and Tierney (1986), Salisbury (1984), Berry (1984a, 18–26), Truman (1951), Crawford (1939), and Herring (1929). Each notes a dramatic increase in the numbers of interest groups, lobbying organizations, trade associations, law firms, or public relations companies active in the nation's capital. Further, each concludes that the decline of the political parties is one of the major elements of this interest-group explosion (including, interestingly enough, Herring, who wrote in the 1920s).

In a typical discussion (and one of the earliest), Herring describes the situation in 1927:

> An observer on the scene for many years states that there are certainly more than a thousand representatives of organized groups in Washington and probably nearly five thousand, if their clerks, aides, statisticians, publicity helpers, and others be included. This takes no account of the volunteer spokesmen that come to Washington from time to time to impress their views upon officials of the government. . . .
>
> Observers state, moreover, that the number of representatives or organized groups established in the capital to watch legislation and speak for their membership is on the increase. Between ten and fifteen years ago the situation was entirely different. In little more than a decade this descent of Washington representatives of national associations has been witnessed. (Herring 1967 [1929], 19–21)

Since Herring's findings, observers have only multiplied the excited conclusions that vast numbers of interest groups are descending upon the lawmakers in Washington. Furthermore, with the notable exception of any claims that these changes are unprecedented, they have been correct in their assertions. The interest-group system has grown dramatically throughout the century. Even though these studies have not used precisely the same definitions and even if not all of them have been as systematic as the others, they have collectively painted a picture of increased growth over the years. In this chapter, we attempt to add some more systematic evidence to this literature and to point to some important changes both in the size and composition of the Washington lobbying community. Not only has the group system become larger over the years, as many writers have noted, but it has also changed internally. As the overall number of groups has expanded, each sector of the interest-group system has not grown at the same rate. This leads us to a further discussion of whether the American interest-group system is characterized by increasing bias in favor of business and upper-class interests, as some have asserted (see Schlozman 1984 and Schlozman and Tierney 1986), or whether it varies in the degree of such advantage at different periods or across different issue areas. Finally, we note the difficulty that scholars have shown in interpreting evidence in this area. A lack of a shared point of reference makes it unclear how one should interpret a demonstration that bias is growing less severe or differs by issue-area or by case. This concluding section refers to the works discussed in chapters 4 and 5 as well as in this one.

## GROWTH AND CHANGE IN THE WASHINGTON LOBBYING COMMUNITY

There can be no doubt that the American interest-group system has grown dramatically over the decades, but some types of interest groups have grown at much greater rates than others. Table 6.1 shows the results of a review of groups listed in the annual *Encyclopedia of Associations*. The compilers of the *Encyclopedia* update their list each year, and they list the organizations by type. Therefore it is possible to trace the growth in numbers of each type of organization since the first edition in 1959. These data are presented in table 6.1. It lists the different categories of groups in order by growth rates, and shows that the past 35 years have seen remarkable changes in the nature of the American interest-group system.

Note the increase in the total number of groups listed from fewer than 6,000 in 1959 to more than 23,000 in 1995. Mark Petracca reports an increase in the number of interest representatives listed in *Washington Representatives* from 4,000 in 1977 to 14,500 in 1991, an increase similar in scope to that reported here (1992b, 14–15). The ability to break down the *Encyclopedia of Associations* data by category allows us to show clearly that different parts of the interest-group system have grown at different rates. To take a simple but important example, the category of trade associations shows an impressive increase from 2,309 associations in 1959 to 3,973 in 1995. Some version of this figure is often used as a rough indicator of the interest-group explosion (probably because this figure is published in the

**TABLE 6.1**
Uneven Patterns of Growth among Associations of Various Types

| Type of Association | Number of Associations Listed in | | | | | Ratio of Growth |
|---|---|---|---|---|---|---|
| | 1959 | 1970 | 1980 | 1990 | 1995 | |
| Public affairs | 117 | 477 | 1,068 | 2,249 | 2,178 | 18.62 |
| Hobby and avocational | 98 | 449 | 910 | 1,475 | 1,579 | 16.11 |
| Social welfare | 241 | 458 | 994 | 1,705 | 1,938 | 8.04 |
| Athletic and sports | 123 | 334 | 504 | 840 | 850 | 6.91 |
| Veterans, hereditary, and patriotic | 109 | 197 | 208 | 462 | 740 | 6.78 |
| Educational | 563[a] | 1,357[a] | 976 | 1,292 | 1,312 | 5.77[a] |
| Cultural | | | 1,400 | 1,886 | 1,938 | |
| Health and medical | 433 | 834 | 1,413 | 2,227 | 2,426 | 5.60 |
| Legal, governmental, public administration, and military | 164 | 355 | 529 | 792 | 781 | 4.76 |
| Engineering, technological, and natural and social science | 294 | 544 | 1,039 | 1,417 | 1,383 | 4.70 |
| Fraternal, foreign interest, nationality, and ethnic | 122 | 591 | 435 | 572 | 555 | 4.59 |
| Religious | 295 | 782 | 797 | 1,172 | 1,243 | 4.21 |
| Environmental and agricultural | 331 | 504 | 677 | 940 | 1,136 | 3.43 |
| Trade, business, and commercial | 2,309 | 2,753 | 3,118 | 3,918 | 3,973 | 1.72 |
| Chambers of commerce, trade, and tourism | 100[b] | 112 | 105 | 168 | 168 | 1.68 |
| Labor unions, associations, and federations | 226 | 225 | 235 | 253 | 246 | 1.09 |
| Greek and non-Greek letter societies | 318 | 336 | 318 | 340 | 338 | 1.06 |
| Fan clubs[c] | — | — | — | 551 | 514 | — |
| Total | 5,843 | 10,308 | 14,726 | 22,259 | 23,298 | 3.99 |

*Source: Encyclopedia of Associations,* years indicated. For 1995, the CD-ROM version; for earlier years, printed volumes.

[a] The educational and cultural categories were combined before 1972. Their combined growth rate is presented in the last column.

[b] Before 1970, thousands of local chambers of commerce were also listed in the national *Encyclopedia.* Since 1970, they have been listed separately. The 1959 figure is an estimate for the number of national groups in that year.

[c] Fan Clubs was not a category before 1987. No growth rate is calculated.

*Statistical Abstract of the United States* and is widely available). Table 6.1 makes clear that trade associations are a declining force, however, when considered as a proportion of all groups. Other types of groups have vastly outstripped the growth among trade associations. Trade associations represented fully 40 percent of all associations listed in 1959, but had declined to only 22 percent of those listed in 1975. By 1995 they represented only 17 percent of the total. Public affairs, social welfare, health, educational and cultural, and many kinds of professional associations saw growth rates considerably above average.

Clearly, the interest-group explosion that many have noted has had great consequences not only for the absolute size of the American group system but also for the relative strengths of various parts of that system as well. As Jack Walker (1983, 1991) has pointed out, different periods of history have been particularly prone to the development of different types of groups. We can see from table 6.1 that different types of groups have indeed grown at dramatically different rates.

How can we explain these differential rates of growth? Virginia Gray and David Lowery (1993a, 1996; see also 1993b, 1994, 1995) note that one would not develop an explanation of the overall population of any animal species without taking into consideration such environmental factors as the amount of food available, the climate, or the presence of competitors. They further note that political scientists following in the Olsonian tradition have often developed explanations for group growth that ignore equivalent questions of the social, economic, and political environment. At most, scholars have assumed that interest-group diversity would increase with increasing wealth or the passage of time (see Olson 1982). Using data collected on state interest groups, Gray and Lowery (1993a) present evidence showing the effects of economic diversity, wealth, and the scope of the economic system on the size and diversity of the interest-group population. The states provide an excellent laboratory for testing their theory, because they provide cross-sectional variance on these variables; something researchers who study only Washington interest groups lack. They found that economic size and diversity were related to the diversity of the interest group systems, while wealth was not. They also found that larger interest group populations were not necessarily more diverse. They note that their model left much of the variance unexplained, and suggest that political factors most likely need to be added to the economic factors they listed in order satisfactorily to explain interest-group diversity.

Gray and Lowery (1996) also have paid substantial attention to the role that interest group mortality plays in the distribution of groups within a population. For Gray and Lowery, *mortality* refers not necessarily to the death of an organization but rather to its withdrawal from lobbying. Their focus is lobbying populations and the forces that lead groups to enter or exit these populations. Using data from lobbying registrations in six states from

1980 and 1990, Gray and Lowery found that interest group populations tend to be fluid, marked by groups dropping in and out of the influence game. While they found that the creation of new groups (or the decision of existing groups to begin lobbying) had a greater impact on the growth of lobbying populations, mortality did greatly influence the diversity and density of the interest group system. This was especially the case in more crowded populations; greater group density was associated with higher mortality rates. Mortality affected some categories of groups more strongly than others. Institutions (a term that encompasses such organizations as businesses, universities, and hospitals) were more likely to quit lobbying for a while without the organization itself disappearing. As a result, institutions have the ability to drop quickly in and out of the lobbying arena, depending on the circumstances. For membership groups and associations, however, withdrawal from lobbying usually was equated with the death of the organization.

Such events as the new government programs of the New Deal, the need to coordinate industrial output during times of war, or the social transformation associated with such movements as those in favor of civil rights, women's rights, or environmental concern, clearly have a great impact on the likelihood that different types of organizations will emerge. Writing in the late 1920s, Pendleton Herring noted the tremendous impact of the First World War on the organization of interests:

> The government at Washington, in recruiting the national resources in that time of emergency, found it difficult to deal with separate industries and individual business concerns scattered all over the country. . . . The war witnessed a great increase in the number of these group associations; but in many cases the end of the war did not witness their dissolution. Even those organized originally for war purposes discovered increasing fields of usefulness in times of peace. This trend toward organization along lines of common interest, whether vocational, industrial, moral, or social, was too fundamental to be affected by the end of the war. (1967 [1929], 51)

Writing a generation after Herring, David Truman made some similar points. Pointing to the impact of the First World War, he mentions that "an estimate by the Department of Commerce and Labor in 1913 indicated that there were about 240 regional, national, and international trade associations; this number grew to approximately 2000 in 1919" (1951, 76). Truman reports that within six years there was an increase of more than 800 percent in the number of such groups. Truman believed that not only could government encouragement during times of war cause a great number of groups to form, but so could economic dislocations. Accordingly, he looked at the numbers of groups before and after the Depression and in the years surrounding the Second World War. He found that each of these major events corresponded with the creation of many new interest organizations. "A careful study in 1938 indicated that nearly 23 per cent of the associations then extant had been formed in the years 1933–5. . . . That a somewhat similar development occurred during World War II is suggested by a 1949 estimate from the Department of Commerce that there were in that year 2,000 national and regional trade associations. This figure indicates an increase of 500 over the number estimated to be in operation in 1938." He sums up a discussion of the role of government by noting that "various cases illustrate the role of government encouragement in the establishment of trade associations" (Truman 1951, 76), and he gives a number of precise examples.

Writing forty years after Truman, Jack Walker (1991) also noted the importance of broad societal trends in affecting the growth rates of interest groups. For Walker, the most important recent examples focused on the social movements and increased wealth of the 1960s and 1970s. He discussed the importance of government grants, the activities of patrons, and the role of social movements in encouraging the growth of certain kinds of groups at certain times, and he noted the great impact of these trends in making the group system less biased than it once had been. We can see from this quick review of three generations of interest-group studies that broad social factors affecting the entire economy bear heavily in any explanation of growth in the interest-group system. Further, different types of events are especially helpful to different types of organizations. Clearly, new groups are created not only as a result of the internal dynamics of their potential memberships, but also in part because of encouragement by outside forces.

### The Dynamics of Business Advantage

Virtually all studies of changes in the interest-group system over time have come to the conclusion that different types of groups have grown at different rates, but they have not all agreed on the significance of these differential growth rates. Kay Lehman Schlozman and John Tierney argue, for example, that in spite of the growth in many new types of organizations since 1960, these groups "do not form a more significant component in the pressure community. Many new citizens' groups have also been born over this period. As in the case of the [civil rights, social welfare, women's, elderly, and handicapped groups] just mentioned, there are still too few of them to figure significantly in the pressure community" (1986, 81; see also 387–88). What is the evidence for the persistence of business dominance?

Schlozman and Tierney reach the strongest conclusion about continued business advantage in the interest-group system. Indeed, they argue that this bias is growing worse, whereas other authors consistently point to the growth of new types of interest groups based on social movements that have made important inroads into the traditional dominance of business in Washington. Based on a review of information taken from *Washington Representatives—1981* and *The Encyclopedia of Associations* (also 1981), they argue that corporations make up more than 45 percent of the organizations represented in Washington. More than three-quarters of the organizations represent business or professional interests of some type, with citizen groups, civil rights, social welfare, and ideological organizations vying for about 20 percent of the total (Schlozman and Tierney 1986, 67). Further, they argue that the degree of advantage for business interests through the interest-group system is growing more severe:

> If anything, the distribution of organizations within the Washington pressure community is even more heavily weighted in favor of business organizations than it used to be. If all organizations having representation in Washington are considered, the proportion representing the interests of business has risen from 57 percent to 72 percent since 1960. The proportion of citizens' groups decreased from 9 percent to 5 percent of all organizations, and the proportion representing labor fell from 11 percent to 2 percent. Thus, while the single most appropriate word to describe the changing number of organizations involved in Washington is "more," in an important sense what we have found is "more of the same." (Schlozman and Tierney 1986, 388)

Many scholars agree with Schlozman and Tierney that business is an important player in the interest-group system, but fewer agree with them that the degree of business advantage is growing over time. There are several reasons for this. One has to do with the evidence presented by Schlozman and Tierney themselves. For example, at one point they report that 56 percent of the civil rights groups and 79 percent of the social welfare groups listed in a 1981 directory of lobbyists were founded after 1960, while only 38 percent of the trade associations and 14 percent of the corporations were that young. This finding fits in with several others indicating a more recent growth for nonbusiness interests in Washington. Still, they conclude that even this influx of citizen- and public-interest groups has not stopped business dominance from growing even greater than before (87). More importantly, Schlozman and Tierney do not present a complete set of comparable data on which to base their conclusion. Their over-time comparison is based on two distinct sources: their 1960 data come from a Congressional Quarterly *Almanac* listing 523 organizations; their 1981 data come from a much more comprehensive and not necessarily comparable listing of more than five thousand organizations taken from the *Encyclopedia of Associations* and the 1981 edition of *Washington Representatives* (see Schlozman and Tierney 1986, 75–82, esp. fn 30, p. 78; see also Gray and Lowery 1996, 6.) In sum, the evidence that business dominance has increased since the 1960s is limited at best.

Walker makes the strongest case for change in the nature of the American group system. His data show the rapid increase in mobilization in the non-profit and the citizens sectors of the group system. Since the 1960s, he demonstrates, the proportion of interest groups in Washington from the profit sector has declined even if the absolute numbers of such groups have grown. Similar conclusions can be drawn from table 6.1, presented earlier. While business is clearly an important actor, if not the most important actor, few studies have corroborated the findings reported by Schlozman and Tierney concerning the direction of change.

Baumgartner and Jones (1993, chap. 9) reviewed important changes in the environmental interest-group landscape, and documented tremendous growth in the numbers of groups and in the resources available to the environmental advocacy groups. The number of groups almost tripled in the three decades from 1960 to 1990, and the combined staff reported by those groups grew by almost a factor of ten. Whereas the beginning of the 1960s saw 119 environmental groups with a combined staff of only 316 active at the national level, the beginning of the 1990s saw almost 3,000 staffers working for more than 300 groups (see Baumgartner and Jones 1993, 187). These changes in the interest-group landscape of course were reflected in many policy changes as issues that were once handled within consensual policy communities dominated by business and producer interests were torn apart by the intrusion of these newly organized groups (see Baumgartner and Jones 1993; Bosso 1987). Baumgartner and Talbert (1995) have documented dramatic changes in the nature of the groups active in the area of health care; from relative dominance of a small number of powerful professional associations, the health-care field has now developed into a complicated network of vociferous and powerful groups with a great range of conflicting interests. Similar changes occurred in civil rights, women's rights, and other areas.

Andrew McFarland gives an extended discussion of cycles of reform in American politics, which he equates with the impermanence of business dominance. Cycles of reform come through the American political system, he writes, as issues of business dominance rise on the national political agenda every so often. As increased business access leads to certain "excesses," the political system reacts for a time, increasing its attention to more reform-minded proposals. American politics, he writes, can be summarized as a series of alternations between business dominance and reform (see McFarland 1991). In his aptly titled book, *Fluctuating Fortunes*, David Vogel (1989) also discusses surges and declines in business influence. In sum, scholars have noted not only that the numbers of business organizations varies over time but also that their political influence seems to vary as well.

## Documenting Change in the Group System

One way to consider the overall levels of bias in the group system is to compare those groups in existence at various points in time using a comparable data source. Figure 6.1 shows one such comparison. It shows the propor-

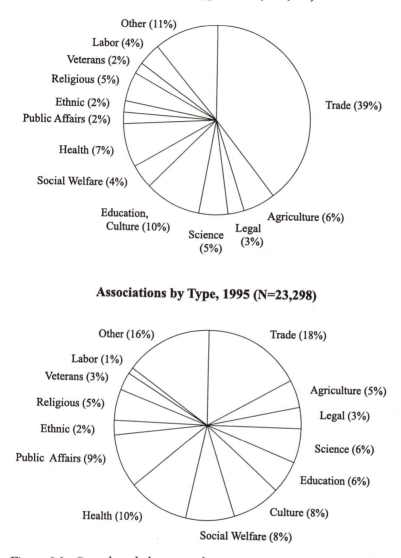

## Associations by Type, 1959 (N=5,843)

Other (11%)
Labor (4%)
Veterans (2%)
Religious (5%)
Ethnic (2%)
Public Affairs (2%)
Health (7%)
Social Welfare (4%)
Education, Culture (10%)
Science (5%)
Legal (3%)
Agriculture (6%)
Trade (39%)

## Associations by Type, 1995 (N=23,298)

Other (16%)
Labor (1%)
Veterans (3%)
Religious (5%)
Ethnic (2%)
Public Affairs (9%)
Health (10%)
Social Welfare (8%)
Culture (8%)
Education (6%)
Science (6%)
Legal (3%)
Agriculture (5%)
Trade (18%)

Figure 6.1. Growth and change in the American interest-group system.
*Source: Encyclopedia of Associations*, years indicated.

tion of groups of various types listed in the *Encyclopedia of Associations* in 1959 and in 1995 (the absolute numbers are listed in table 6.1, above).

Figure 6.1 makes clear that important changes have indeed taken place in the Washington lobbying community over the past forty years. Rather than being dominated by any single type of organization, as was the case in 1959, the groups active in 1995 are much more widely dispersed by type. Whereas the 1959 data show a clear predominance of trade associations in Washington, justifying Truman's complaint that many observers seem to equate such groups with interest groups in general, the situation was much more complex by 1995. Trade associations remain an important part of the interest-group landscape, of course, but other types of groups are increasingly important. Particularly impressive is the growth of various types of organizations from the nonprofit sector: health, social welfare, cultural, educational, public affairs, governmental, and religious groups together represent 59 percent of the groups present in 1995, whereas they accounted for only 31 percent of the group universe in 1959. From 1,813 groups in the first year of the period, there were 13,754 such organizations by the last.

Baumgartner and Talbert (1995, 105) showed the extent of change in the resources controlled by health-care interest groups. Whereas there were just under three thousand staff members working for the largest health-care organizations in 1961, there were more than eleven thousand staff members employed by the largest such groups in 1990. Jack Walker made similar points concerning changes in the bias of the Washington group system, based on questions about the founding dates of groups included in his 1980 and 1985 surveys (1983; 1991, chap. 4). He showed how citizens groups in particular grew dramatically during the 1960s, whereas other types of organizations had their periods of mobilization earlier. His data stem from a single 1985 survey (rather than a series of annual observations), unlike the *Encyclopedia* figures just reported. Because of this unavoidable limitation to his single cross-sectional data set, there is the possibility that differential mortality rates could have led him to spurious conclusions. Table 6.2 shows how closely the results from the Walker survey parallel those of the *Encyclopedia*, however.

It shows the different rates of growth of the four types of groups Walker distinguishes in his typology. Using this simple typology, based on his 1985 survey of membership organizations, Walker concluded that about three-fourths of all groups in Washington were occupationally based. He also showed, in an often-reproduced figure, how each group sector had differential growth rates at different periods in history (Walker 1983 and 1991). This is clearly evident when we compare the numbers of groups of each type in 1985 with the numbers of these groups that had been created before 1960. The occupational bias that Walker pointed to in 1985 was much stronger in the earlier period. Citizens groups, representing 24 percent of the groups in 1985, represented only 15 percent of those groups in existence in 1960. The occupational basis of the group system, so remarkable in the 1985 survey, was even stronger in 1960. The citizens sector almost tripled its size in twenty-five years, whereas the group system as a whole grew by only about

**TABLE 6.2**
Groups by Type, 1960 and 1985

|  | 1960 | | 1995 | | Percent Change in the Number of Groups |
|---|---|---|---|---|---|
|  | N | % | N | % |  |
| Profit sector | 217 | 44 | 326 | 38 | 47 |
| Nonprofit | 174 | 35 | 281 | 33 | 65 |
| Citizens | 72 | 15 | 206 | 24 | 180 |
| Mixed | 31 | 6 | 50 | 6 | 73 |
| Total | 494 | 100 | 863 | 100 | 75 |

Source: Calculated from Walker 1985 dataset.

75 percent during this period. Taken together, the data presented here make it clear that different parts of the interest-group system have mobilized at different rates over the past generation.

Clearly, a consistent finding that business and profit-sector organizations have an advantage in the process of mobilization is one of the most important elements of the nature of bias in the Washington interest-group community. Nonetheless, we should not assume that this bias, because it is great, is necessarily growing. Walker's data, those from the *Encyclopedia*, and others indicate that diversity, not business dominance, has increased since 1960. Schlozman and Tierney seem to come to a contrasting conclusion in part because of their comparison of two different data sources.

It is interesting to compare the set of interests active in Washington at the time when Olson wrote his *Logic of Collective Action* with that which has developed since that period. When Olson wrote, trade associations and other professional groups clearly dominated the interest-group landscape. Since that time, these organizations have continued to maintain a powerful presence in Washington. However, other types of organizations, including many of those whose difficulties in mobilization Olson explained so clearly, have multiplied at unprecedented rates. The changes in the numbers of different types of interest groups active in Washington makes clear that there is an important dynamic element to bias in the American interest-group system. Groups of different types seem to prosper during different periods.

## FROM SUBSYSTEM TO ISSUE NETWORK

In recent years many scholars have noted that particular issue-domains have been transformed by the rapid growth of an ever-more complex set of interest groups, even within the same issue-area. These studies point to the conclusion that important changes in the nature of policymaking have taken place: issue-areas where one could previously conceive of business dominance based on a one-sided mobilization of groups are now prone to important internal divisions. Partly, these divisions are a result of the increased mobilization of groups from the nonprofit or citizens sectors. However, much of the increased conflict within Washington policy networks results from divisions within the business community itself, stemming inevitably from the growing complexities of the marketplace, technological change, and the changing nature of competition.

Heinz et al. (1993, 63) show in their study of national policymaking that business interests are the predominant type of organization overall, but they also document considerable variation across the four policy domains included in their study. For instance, trade associations represent 51 percent of the organizations active in agriculture policy but only 16 percent of those active in health-care issues. Similarly, citizens groups are more common in the agriculture and energy domains (where they constitute 14 and 11 percent of the groups, respectively), than in health and labor (where they represent only 7 and 4 percent of those involved). Across the entire political system, then, we can note increased diversity since the 1960s and considerable diversity from domain to domain. We can also observe change within particular issue domains.

Dramatic examples of the increasingly complex and conflictual nature of many policy networks are easy to find. Health care—once the domain of a relatively small number of powerful actors centered in the medical community, hospital administrators, and the largest insurance providers—has been transformed into a tremendously conflictual interest-group battlefield (see Baumgartner and Talbert 1995). Health-care policy cannot be made without the involvement of a great range of powerful interests representing a great diversity of views. Providers, insurers, researchers, those who pay premiums (usually businesses), the elderly, and many of those suffering with particular diseases are all represented (even if some are represented more adequately than others). It is not clear that problems in health care stem from the bias of the set of groups active in Washington: so many diverse interests are active that one cannot reasonably blame oligopolistic control of the policy process by a narrow set of providers' groups for the policy solutions being debated. Indeed, in searching for an explanation for difficulties in reaching policy consensus, one would point to the difficulty in reaching agreement in such a diverse and conflictual interest-group environment rather than to the bias or restrictive nature of representation through groups. Health care may be an extreme example, but it is not an unusual one.

Telecommunications policy is another area where technological change has led to a complete transformation of the industry and to the dramatic reversal of a pattern that once saw a small number of major corporate actors dominate the area. Jeffrey Berry has documented these changes in some detail. He compares a schematic mapping of interests and actors in telecommunications policy active in 1988 with one for 1994. In that short period, he shows a change from a relatively comprehensible "industry niche model" of representation and influence to a bewildering assortment of actors only six years later (see Berry 1994b, 1997).

Of course consumer interests are not well represented in some important debates, and this bias remains an important element even of these transformed issue-areas. For example in recent telecommunications debates relating to cable television provision, consumers were at a fundamental disadvantage, especially in those cases where a great majority of businesses have shared interests against them or in those cases where their rights are best guaranteed by the existence of large and competitive markets, leaving great gaps in competition in rural areas, for example. Without arguing that such cases are rare, there appears nonetheless to be an increasing tendency for broad interests to find shared cause with private interests. In other words, it seems increasingly common for a form of surrogate representation to occur: Consumers and other broad causes increasingly find that conflicts within complex issue-networks afford them the opportunity to find a natural, if temporary, ally. Groups are often represented by those businesses or trade associations that seek advantage over other businesses. This is of course a hollow form of political representation, but it can be an important one in those areas where the diversity of the established interest-group system is sufficiently great.

Vicarious representation is unlikely to serve as a sufficient substitute for direct representation, even if on particular issues it can sometimes be an important means by which the unmobilized have their views presented in government. In their study of issues related to workers compensation, Kay Lehman Schlozman and Sidney Verba note, for example, that labor unions sometimes do argue in favor of the unemployed. But, since this is not their sole concern, unions cannot be expected to argue as consistently or as vociferously in their favor as would a group directly representing the unemployed (see Schlozman and Verba 1979, 338–44). Verba, Schlozman, and Brady (1995, 177) make a similar case. In spite of occasional efforts by labor unions or churches to represent the poor, the poor would be better represented if they had their own associations. In their conclusion, they note, for example: "It has long been part of the union mission to represent the less advantaged in the halls of government. Although religious institutions sometimes take on this function—the Catholic Church, for example, often acts as an advocate for the poor—the economic needs of the less well-off rarely top their lists of political priorities" (1995, 521). (On the relative effectiveness of vicarious representation, also see Schlozman and Tierney 1986, 401–5; Walker 1991; Verba, Schlozman, and Brady 1995, 176–77). Vicarious representation is not a long-term solution to the needs of the unmobilized, but the old adage that "politics makes strange bedfellows" sometimes remains true. On a given political issue, the interests of the unmobilized often happen to coincide with one or another set of established interests.

We noted in the previous chapter the example of the relative merging of interests in discussions of sugar price supports between the relatively unmobilized consumer interests and the relatively powerful lobbies for those businesses that use large amounts of sugar. Where there is conflict within the business community, as there often is, there is the possibility for vicarious representation. A recent example of diversity and conflict within a single domain, created by a combination of outside interests and internal divisions within the business community, has to do with an apparently unintended clause in the General Agreement on Tariffs and Trade (GATT). As a result of an oversight, the patent protection for certain U.S. drugs was extended from the seventeen years of normal protection under U.S. patent law to twenty years under GATT. With three years of additional protection against competition from producers of generic drugs, pharmaceutical companies stood to gain billions of dollars on certain lucrative products. Consumer groups, of course, were opposed to this extension. Consumer interests were not alone in a David and Goliath battle against the giants of the pharmaceutical industry in this case, however. Their allies were other pharmaceutical companies who wanted access to the market and who were anxious to produce those generic drugs. The result was a constellation of interests with powerful players on each side, not a one-sided mobilization as one might imagine (see Lewis 1995). As policy networks and as economic markets have grown more complex over past decades, Washington observers have noted a qualitative change, not only a quantitative one. Conflict among well-funded advocates for a variety of interests within a single policy domain is increasingly the rule rather than the exception.

Increased economic diversity and the conflicts that inevitably stem from this diversity have led to the break-up of previously powerful policy subsystems in a great number of issue-areas. Conflict among interests is more common than it once was. These conflicts create opportunities for consumers and other interests to find allies with greater resources, creating the possibility of increased representation through alliances and coalitions. In any case, increased competition among powerful interests is more often the case in the 1990s than it was in the 1950s, with important implications for representation through the interest-group system, according to a range of studies in many issue-areas (see Heclo 1978; Bosso 1987; Jenkins-Smith et al. 1991; Baumgartner and Jones 1993; Heinz et al. 1993; Sabatier and Jenkins-Smith 1993; Berry 1994b, 1997).

## THE AMBIGUOUS POINT OF REFERENCE

One of the greatest ironies of the new literature on group mobilization, given its efforts at scientific precision (chapter 4) and the massive and continual efforts throughout the century to document the extent of bias in the system (chapters 5 and 6), has been the difficulty that scholars have shown in dealing with the evidence. Just as Greenstein noted that many of the arguments between pluralists and elitists in a previous generation went on largely without reference to disputes about evidence (see chapter 3), so too do arguments about the impact of the collective-action dilemma, bias, and the nature of the Washington interest-group system often occur in the absence of standards of falsification. For a given observation, some argue that it proves the point that the group system will never be representative and others argue that it shows the abilities of groups to overcome the dilemmas of collective action. The Olsonian perspective on collective action was built up as a method of understanding the nature and the biases of the national interest-group system. Olson pointed out that previous scholars had overlooked the dilemmas of mobilization that made some organizations less likely to form than others. We discussed the growth of the theoretical literature in chapter 4 and a variety of empirical studies on the scope and bias of popular participation and of the Washington lobbying community in chapters 5 and 6. Here, we point to a problem in all these discussions: the degree to which scholars can agree that a given observation constitutes support or a challenge to the Olsonian perspective.

Olson's insights are noteworthy because of their implications for the nature of the interest-group system. They are significantly more pessimistic than Truman's, and more accurate in many ways. Most research following up on Olson, however, has focused on better modeling of the individual-level questions rather than on estimating the severity of the system-level problems of the scope and bias of the system, as we noted in chapter 4. The few studies that have attempted to address these system-level questions (e.g., Schlozman 1984; Schlozman and Tierney 1986; Walker 1983, 1991; Gray and Lowery 1996) show a system that cannot be explained entirely either by Olson's or by Truman's logics. Groups with a concentrated economic interest are certainly overrepresented, as Olson predicted, but there are also many "aberrant" groups that have somehow overcome the problems of collective action. Case studies of individual groups and social movements illustrate a similar point: some groups manage to solve the collective-action dilemma and to be effective.

Empirical work on the implications of the collective-action dilemma has been faced with an evaluative quandary: Does a given result show that the collective-action glass is half empty or half full? In a revealing exchange of views, Harriet Tillock and Denton Morrison (1979) noted the success of Zero Population Growth in overcoming the collective-action dilemma. Clearly this group, which offered few material benefits and sought a collective good that could be obtained only if people all over the world participated in its achievement, demonstrated that material incentives were not necessary for groups to form. True to his logic, Olson (1979) argued in response that the case proved his point: if billions of humans are to benefit from the goals the organization seeks but only a few thousand bother to become members, then it is hard to say that the group has "overcome" the dilemmas of mobilization. Olson's logic would continue to hold even if the group had grown to have hundreds of millions of members or had been successful in lobbying for important changes in government policies. In the case of growth, it would still be only a fraction of its potential; in the case of lobbying success, that would be irrelevant to its mobilizational efficiency.

Examples of interpretive disputes abound in the literature on collective action. Is a certain amount of mobilization a sign that the dilemma has been overcome, or is there always a higher, theoretically possible, point by comparison with which any observed level of mobilization seems paltry? For example, comparative studies consistently indicate that Americans overcome the collective-action dilemma in greater numbers than do citizens of other countries: Our nonprofit sector is greater, our tradition of charitable giving is stronger, and our public-interest groups are better endowed than those in most other countries of similar standard of living. To some, this might be taken as evidence that we have "overcome" the collective-action dilemma, but others could argue simply that no matter how much higher the level may be here than elsewhere, or in the 1990s as compared with the 1940s, it remains "suboptimal" when compared with the number of affected interests and free riders.

In a study conducted in the wake of the nuclear incident at Three Mile Island in 1979, Edward Walsh and Rex Warland found that only 12 percent of those living in the area who opposed nuclear power had actually participated in any collective action (1983, 778). On the other hand, even fewer of those who supported nuclear power joined any organizations sharing their views. It is also worth noting that organized opposition to nuclear power grew sufficiently after 1979 to put an end to the growth of the domestic nuclear power industry (see Baumgartner and Jones 1991 and 1993). There is no doubt that Olson pointed out an absolutely fundamental conundrum that must be addressed, but few have evidence to show how serious it is, whether it is getting worse, which groups can or cannot overcome it and how, or even how to evaluate the findings of those studies presenting information on these topics.

The literature on collective action raises the question of what degree of mobilization is sufficient to matter in politics. From the point of view of the prospective entrepreneur who may seek to mobilize a latent constituency (Salisbury 1969), there are certain benefits in appealing to an extremely large and diverse population: Even a low response rate can translate into millions of dollars of support. Billions of dollars are donated to charities annually in the United States; millions of Americans have joined groups and contributed money for causes that they know to be collective. From the perspective of a student of collective action, the implicit point of reference seems to be the mobilization of all who share a goal; many large organizations appear to be hopelessly inefficient by this standard. From the perspective of a Washington policymaker, on the other hand, these same groups may appear to be formidable. In any case, this debate has no clear winner, since each side begins with its own point of reference. One side observes what appears to be a great deal of diversity in the existing set of interest groups, marvels at it, and then attempts to explain how such a great amount of diversity could have arisen. The other side takes an individual-level puzzle and uses it to demonstrate that a hypothetically perfect reflection of society is not likely to be seen in the group system. These different starting points are enough to allow debate to continue indefinitely without any resolution. Conclusions depend more on theoretical starting points than on evidence (for other examples on a similar point, see Green and Shapiro 1994, 41; Lowenstein 1982).

Even if scholars agreed that the point of reference for any evaluation of the diversity of the interest-group system were the degree to which the observed mobilization of interests corresponds to its theoretical potential, they would not resolve these disputes. There is little chance of defining the potential mobilizational capabilities of most groups. If all the members of a given ethnic group were members of a formal organization, one could still debate about whether their contributions were as high as they "might be." In the end, scholars have most often ignored this problem of the arbitrary or nonexistent point of reference by assuming the theoretical potential level of mobilization for most groups to be extremely high and by then concluding that the observed level of mobilization falls far short. There may be some merits to this approach, but scientific rigor is not among them.

Kay Lehman Schlozman and John Tierney (1986, 87) make the case quite clearly in their discussion of the nature of the Washington pressure community. They note that it may be impossible to state exactly what the perfect interest-group system would look like, but, "whatever the contours of that utopia," it would not look like what they observe. Schlozman and Tierney are of course correct in noting that the group system does not correspond perfectly to what an unbiased one would resemble, but they also point to a serious problem in the literature. Whether one is discussing popular participation in the group system or the set of groups organized and active in Washington, the lack of a shared point of reference prevents the debate from being focused on the evidence. Rather, scholars reach disparate conclusions based in large part on their individual points of view.

There is no question that we have a better view now than in 1960 about the barriers to collective action and the ways around these barriers. But, as Jack Walker noted (1991, chap. 3), perhaps instead of dissertating so eloquently about the difficulties of collective action even while groups by the thousands are demonstrating their abilities to overcome these obstacles, scholars would be better off shifting their attention to the workings of the Washington lobbying community. Maybe rather than asking if a given level of mobilization corresponds to some hypothetical level of perfect efficiency, we should ask whether observed levels of mobilization are sufficient to affect the distribution of political resources, or whether important groups are left out of the pressure system. Instead of arguing about whether and how groups overcome the collective-action dilemma, we might admit that many do and go on and study the degree to which the observable bias in the system varies over time, from area to area, or from issue to issue.

## CONCLUSION

This chapter has described some of the enormous changes in the size and diversity of the American interest-group system over the past decades. Many complications attend the discussion of the severity of the bias in favor of business in the interest-group system, whether these tendencies are growing worse over time, and whether they are more severe in some areas of the economy or surrounding some political issues than others. Further, there is no guarantee that the gross typologies into which scholars typically classify interest groups represent important analytical categories or real political cleavages. Many political disputes are likely to pit certain business interests against others, for example, but few interest-group scholars have designed their studies to be sensitive to the constellation of interests that may mobilize in different disputes in order to determine whether groups of similar type are often on the same or on opposing sides of different issues. Analyses that lump "business interests" into a single category are only slightly less helpful than those that implicitly treat all groups in the area of "health and medicine" as if they were uniform in their political stance. Certainly we can trace important elements of bias in the interest-group system to the sources and professional backgrounds of the constituent groups, but this analysis will not explain the details of political conflict nor will it give a complete picture of whose interests are being represented, since interests of various groups often coincide or diverge unexpectedly. In sum, bias is there and everyone knows it. But we know little about the forms, extent, and consequences of this bias as it affects public policy.

The inability to pin down the question of bias results largely from a research strategy that has not yet allowed the merger of studies based on particular issues with those studies attempting a more generalizable range of coverage. Heinz and colleagues (1993) focused on a great number of particular policy issues in their study of policy influence and relations in four national policy domains. However, the research approach that combines both a large number of policy decisions with the systematic treatment of interest-group strategies and activities in these different cases remains all too rare. In our next chapters, we focus on how political scientists have addressed lobbying strategies; we will see that their approaches have not typically allowed them to answer the question of bias because of the wall that has separated the broad studies of tactics on the one side from the study of lobbying behavior in particular cases on the other. In the end, we will argue for a merger of these approaches and show how it might be accomplished.

While there are many disputes about the degree and nature of the bias of the group system, there is no ambiguity concerning the growth of the group system overall. This transformation, which has been documented in a variety of ways by virtually every student of the topic, has tremendous implications for the process of lobbying.

# CHAPTER 7

# Building a Literature on Lobbying,
# One Case Study at a Time

SCHOLARS, journalists, and policymakers often conclude that interest groups are among the most important forces in American politics. Studies of policy subsystems have often depicted the cozy relationships between "captured" agencies and allied congressional committees. More polemical work has decried the negative effects of interest-group "pressure" on legislators. Quantitative analyses of the effects of political action committees have shown that campaign contributions are often related to the outcomes of congressional roll-call votes. Journalists often report on the activities and effectiveness of powerful lobbyists getting their way. Reformers often complain about the abuses of power by well-heeled lobbying organizations. Groups are powerful, as observers of all types have often noted.

At the same time, others conclude that interest-group influence is trivial or vastly overstated. Beginning in the 1970s, studies began emphasizing how expanded issue networks have diluted interest-group control of subsystems. Since the 1960s scholars have noted that group leaders spend more time providing information and rendering services to lawmakers who already agree with them than twisting the arms of those who might vote the wrong way. Quantitative analyses of political action committees have often shown that campaign contributions have no effect on roll call votes. Working from a great range of scholarly and applied perspectives, observers have sometimes concluded that groups dominate the political process, and they have sometimes concluded that groups have little effect. Lobbying and related activities have been studied by dozens of scholars during the past thirty years, and yet we can draw few firm conclusions about interest-group behavior. How is it that with so much research we still know so little about interest-group influence and the strategies they use to affect public policy? Why are these studies so contradictory?

In this and the following chapter, we review what political scientists know about the lobbying behavior and political influence of interest groups in the United States. Hundreds of case studies of how groups have sought to influence the outcome of particular political issues have been conducted over the years, from Peter Odegard's descriptive study of the temperance movement, published in 1928, to the highly quantitative studies of PAC contributions more than half a century later. In addition to the case studies, we will also review a number of larger-scale surveys of interest groups and their lobbyists. Each of these approaches has complementary strengths and weaknesses. Together, the reliance on these two approaches helps explain the contradictory nature of the state of the literature on lobbying. The idiosyncratic nature of the case studies makes it impossible for these to serve as the basis for effective generalizations; the general nature of the surveys causes them to ignore important variation in what groups do, and to what effect, in different circumstances. We can conclude that groups are often influential and that they are often not influential, but the combined case-study and survey-based literatures tell us little about the conditions of influence.

In this chapter we begin by reviewing studies of interest-group lobbying on particular policy issues, saving our discussion of the surveys of interest groups for chapter 8. We first discuss older policy studies, which did not focus exclusively on interest groups but which nonetheless paid close attention to their roles. We discuss some of the reasons for contradictions and disagreement within this literature before turning to studies of interest groups per se, a literature that has been divided among those who see interest groups and lobbyists as "pressuring" legislators and distorting democracy and those who see lobbyists playing a more passive role. Finally, we discuss a more recent body of research about interest groups, far more systematic and quantitative than the classic studies, which attempts to assess the type and degree of interest-group influence. Despite its mathematical approach, this more recent literature is also fraught with contradictions and faces many of the same problems that plagued the more descriptive case studies in the past.

## THE POLICY APPROACH

A vast and venerable literature surrounds the concept of the policy subsystem (a few of the best known studies in this tradition are Griffith 1939; Maass 1951; Bernstein 1955; Cater 1964; Freeman 1965; Redford 1969; Fritschler 1975; Heclo 1978; and Berry 1989b). Although these works all discuss direct contacts between interest groups and members of Congress or the bureaucracy, these studies are not cited in recent interest-group research as often as one would expect. An invisible line seems to be drawn between these "policy studies" and "interest-group studies," and there is little cross-reference between the two bodies of research. This is a serious flaw in the more recent literature, because policy studies have much to say about the ways in which interest groups are involved in the policy process.

### The Power of Subsystems

Research in the tradition of the policy subsystem routinely portrays interest groups as quite influential because of their position in a symbiotic relationship; groups at times are able to dictate policy because what is good for them is also in the best interests of the agencies and committees in the system. The relationships between legislators, bureaucrats, and interest-group representatives are portrayed as generally friendly and involving frequent contact among a relatively small group of players. These studies have clear implications for studies of groups, even though their focus is typically broader than only the groups themselves. They make clear that groups are often influential by working closely with their allies. Influence is achieved not by lobbying enemies, but by insulating the policy subsystem as a whole. Autonomy from "political interference" is the sign of a powerful subsystem, and of powerful interest groups.

Arthur Maass (1951) described such a self-protecting system operating within national water policy. The only interest groups presenting their case to the Corps of Engineers and congressional committees were groups that wanted large-scale water projects built. Taxpayers as a whole were too diffuse to be represented; likewise environmental interests were not well organized before the 1970s. Cater (1964) described similar systems benefiting the defense industry and sugar producers. The defense industry, members of Congress whose districts benefited from military spending, and the Pentagon all favored more defense spending; opposing voices were virtually nonexistent. Domestic sugar growers also were long successful in maintaining trade legislation that benefited them but cost consumers more: Consumers were not organized, and they were not a part of the subsystem.

While some scholars have portrayed subsystems as rigid, excluding outsiders and dissenting voices, Freeman's study of the Bureau of Indian Affairs (BIA) during the 1930s and 1940s depicts conflict within a subsystem (1955; 1965). Native Americans opposed to federal government involvement in their affairs sided with allies within the Senate subcommittee system, while Native Americans seeking more federal aid sided with the BIA. Disagreements remained mostly contained within this narrow group of players, however, with neither side escalating the controversy through appeals to the general public.

Other studies have depicted subsystems as much less fixed. The sugar subsystem described by Cater (1964) broke up when Cuban sugar interests took their case to the media and changed the definition of the issue from protection of domestic sugar farmers to the need to support (then-democratic) Cuba from economic failure and communism. Likewise, health interests won a battle in their war with the tobacco lobby and its entrenched subsystem after the interest of the general public was aroused (see Fritschler 1975; for a discussion of reasons for subsystem breakup and a series of case studies of such breakups, see Baumgartner and Jones 1993).

The classic policy studies agree that relationships between interest groups and government officials are usually close, but the studies disagree about how open the system is and the degree of conflict involved. These disagreements most likely simply reflect the variance among the different cases each of these scholars chose to study, but for the most part these scholars give scant theoretical attention to the reasons behind the differences they describe. Emmette Redford (1969), however, did provide a framework for thinking about subsystems. A subsystem is not a rigid iron triangle, barring all dissenting voices, but it does provide a stable structure for the existing relations among interests, according to Redford. Subsystems contain conflict, they do not eliminate it. As Redford puts it: "While the systems tend to maintain the interests represented in the existing equilibriums, they still provide some access to other interests. And those which find the door to one forum shut may turn to another door, for the subsystems provide multiple channels of access" (105).

Although subsystems provide some access for outsiders, substantial changes in the balances among interests can occur only through a large-scale political intervention from outside the subsystem, just as we saw in the case studies described by Cater (1964) and Fritschler (1975). Subsystems thrive on the avoidance of conflict, publicity, and "meddling" by those from outside the affected industry or policy area. Most studies of subsystems, it is worth noting, have focused on particular industries: arms manufacturing; sugar production; tobacco production; and the building of harbors, dams, and other water projects. None of these studies could conclude anything about the prevalence of the patterns they described, but they collectively painted a portrait of powerful groups getting their way in government, with the help of sympathetic members of Congress and agency administrators also intent on fostering the growth of the particular policy in question. Further, subsystem studies tended to base their analyses on issues that were not part of the national political agenda. By looking beyond the headlines, the subsystem scholars attempted to show the power of vested interests operating in every nook and cranny of government. Still, their empirical base suffered from a definite selection bias. We will see below that more recent studies of group influence suffer from the opposite selection bias—they include only issues that figure more or less prominently in the headlines.

### A Subsystem by Any Other Name

Hugh Heclo published an influential essay in 1978 in which he argued that the old view of rigid subsystems was outdated because of the growth of the bureaucracy and the interest-group system. He suggested instead that we should think of policymaking taking place within "issue networks":

> The notion of iron triangles and subgovernments presumes small circles of participants who have succeeded in becoming largely autonomous. Issue networks, on the other hand, comprise a large number of participants with quite

variable degrees of mutual commitment or of dependence on others in the environment; in fact it is almost impossible to say where a network leaves off and its environment begins. . . . Rather than groups united in dominance over a program, no one, as far as one can tell, is in control of the policies and issues. (Heclo 1978, 102)

Jeffrey Berry expanded substantially on this point ten years later, noting that the "interest-group explosion" of the 1970s did not simply lead to bigger subgovernments, but to a more complex system in which "the likelihood of conflict between competing coalitions increases" (Berry 1989b, 239). He suggested that issue networks may offer greater chances for participation and more closely fit the pluralist ideal than subgovernments ever did.

While most scholars agree that the interest-group system is more crowded today than in the past, and that this crowdedness must certainly change the dynamics of the system (see Browne 1990, 1995; and Schlozman and Tierney 1983), the evidence that the "old" subsystems were closed is less clear. Riley (1990) reviews classic policy studies of subsystems and points out that they often involved conflict, players other than the triad of powers from the iron triangle (committee, agency, and interest group), and actors with ideological rather than merely narrow economic interests. He points out that "subsystem operations—and, in particular the relationship between system and subsystem—will vary dramatically from one type of issue to another" (Riley 1990, 26). Indeed, this is what we saw above in our brief review of some of the best-known subsystem studies. While some systems are narrow and closed to conflict, such as the water project subsystem described by Maass (1951), others are not. The degree of openness can also vary across time, with a consensual system suddenly facing dissent and controversy.

Considering the theoretical value in explaining variation in subsystem power or autonomy, these questions have received scant empirical attention because few have designed studies to trace such variation across subsystems or within a single subsystem over time (but see Kollman 1997). Policy subsystems (or issue networks, for that matter) have for the most part been studied one at a time, and generally over only a limited period of time. Although anecdotal evidence suggests that some policy domains are more open than others, there is little systematic evidence to indicate the degree of such variation across domains, and little effort to test theories about when and why some domains are more open than others. Substantial exceptions to this general trend include Laumann and Knoke (1987), who consider two large domains in some detail; Heinz et al. (1993), who look at four policy domains; Bosso (1987), who reviewed pesticide issues over a long period; and Hansen (1991), who considers change in the agricultural policy subsystem over time. Each of these authors noted important variability in relations among subsystem actors and between subsystem and system-level players. Domain studies like these differ from previous studies of subsystems in that they tend to be more theoretically oriented: they attempt to systematically answer particular research questions rather than simply describe a policy area. They differ too from the narrower, quantitative case studies that we will discuss later in this chapter because they consider multiple issues within the domains they study, often over time or across multiple domains.

Questions about the relative openness of various policy areas are of critical importance because of their implications for the democratic nature of the political system. The critics of pluralism may have been more on target for some areas of government than others, and scholars should want to know why—what characteristics of a policy arena enhance broad participation and wide-ranging debate? What characteristics of a policy arena enhance the autonomy of those with a vested interest? What encourages interest-group power; what mitigates it? These large questions of group power are at the center of the literature on policy subsystems, but with a few exceptions, the literature offers few clear answers to them because most studies are not designed to allow broad generalizations based on evidence featuring variation on the key elements of theoretical comparison.

## THE GROUP APPROACH

At the same time as a broad literature developed surrounding the policy approach, another important approach developed, focusing much more narrowly on the roles of groups rather than on policy subsystems more generally.

### The Early Studies of Group Power

Early interest-group studies shared the outlook of early subsystem studies. Interest groups were enormously powerful, and insider groups had the advantage. Organized interests were "pressure groups," which achieved their political goals through strong-arm tactics and cronyism. These were networks of insiders whose campaign contributions and friendships with legislators often allowed them to dictate the content of bills (see Odegard 1928; Schattschneider 1935; Zeller 1937; and Crawford 1939). If that strategy was unsuccessful, advertising budgets, friendships with newspaper owners, and devious stunts could be relied upon to produce favorable "propaganda" that would "manipulate" the public to put pressure on legislators (Crawford 1939 and Zeller 1937 provide extensive discussions of this "newer, now more favored technique"). Although there is a tendency to exaggerate the findings of these studies—it is seldom remembered, for example, that Schattschneider's (1935) study of "pressures" found that most manufacturers affected by the tariff legislation in question did not even take the time to express their support or opposition before Congress—nonetheless the emphasis is on strong interest groups "manipulating" public opinion and "persuading" members of Congress.

Several important studies published in the 1960s helped challenge this view. Milbrath's (1963) survey of lobbyists, Bauer, Pool, and Dexter's (1963) study of tariff legislation, and Scott and Hunt's (1965) survey of members of Congress all concluded that the primary role of interest groups was providing information to allies within government. Rather than persuading members of Congress, interest groups simply acted as "service bureaus" supplying information (Bauer, Pool, and Dexter 1963). Interest-group influence was thus benign, since groups essentially served as adjunct congressional staff. While Bauer, Pool, and Dexter's study detailed instances of group members helping draft legislation and in many ways depicted a process not unlike that detailed by Schattschneider's study thirty years before, what was remembered from their work was their service bureau finding. They described the interests they surveyed as surprisingly ill-informed, ill-funded, and ill-prepared to do battle in Washington. The popular conclusion drawn from these studies was that interest groups did not exert pressure, indeed were not influential. The informational role they played in Washington could easily be supplanted by information from congressional staff.

If it were that simple, this chapter could end here. We could simply say that interest groups were once seen as all-powerful, but more recent studies have shown this to be wrong. About this same time, however, policy studies were still being published that portrayed interest groups playing important roles within subsystems, and three important books were published: Bernstein's *Regulating Business by Independent Commission*, published in 1955, McConnell's *Private Power and American Democracy*, published in 1966, and Lowi's *The End of Liberalism*, published in 1969. All three books portrayed a policy process in which interest groups were the dominant players. Regulatory agencies were "captured" and served the needs of the regulated interests, according to Bernstein. McConnell described a political world in which private organizations wielded quasi-governmental authority without democratic control. Lowi decried congressional delegation to agencies controlled by special interests. In these books interest groups were powerful and threatened democracy.

### Making Sense of Contradictions

Descriptive works about interest groups are full of mutually contradictory examples. That is not to say, however, that one set of studies or another is wrong. Interest groups at times probably are weak and ineffectual, and at other times very effective at getting what they want. Interest groups may devote themselves to informing allies at some times, while turning to strong-arm tactics involving constituency pressure and media campaigns at other times. The question becomes not which of two descriptions of interest-group behavior is accurate but rather: Which interest groups behave in which ways and under what circumstances? When do they succeed in influencing policy and when do they fail? What often appear as simple contradictions in the literature are really variations that need to be explained.

Attempts have been made to uncover those variables and make sense of disparate findings. For instance, Hayes (1978) compares the two cases of trade legislation described by Schattschneider (1935) and Bauer, Pool, and Dexter (1963) and suggests that the difference in the findings might be the result of the way costs and benefits were distributed in the two cases. Hansen (1991) compares the same two cases and suggests that the difference may be the result of differential attention: members of Congress are faced with so many demands that the issue becomes which groups they decide to grant access. Baumgartner and Leech (1996a) suggest that variation in how conflictual and salient the issues were might help explain seemingly contradictory findings. In addition, point of view makes a difference. Looking at the legislation from the perspective of groups, as Bauer, Pool, and Dexter did, it appears often that groups were ignored, or granted access only to members of Congress who already agreed with them. Looking at a broad issue from the perspective of Congress, as Schattschneider did, one observes that the members are collectively paying a great deal of attention to outside interests. This question of perspective also helps explain why scholars using the "group approach" could conclude that groups were ineffectual because they "merely" worked closely with their allies, even while other scholars, working from the "policy approach" could describe the enormous implications of these cozy relations.

There are of course many potential explanations for why a group might have been successful in one case and not in another, or for why groups chose conflictual strategies in some cases and cooperative strategies in another. The cases suggest potential hypotheses, but do not provide adequate information across cases to allow us to test those hypotheses. Although each case study suggests reasons behind the choice of strategy adopted by a given interest group, comparisons across cases remain problematic. The cases simply vary on too many points, not only the substance of the particular issue studied but the decision-making venue, whether the issue generated conflict among groups, whether the issue was highly salient, and whether the group in question had effective allies within government for that issue. Does one study come to a different conclusion because one case was highly salient and the other was not, or simply because one occurred decades before the other and interest-group strategies have changed over the years? There is no way to determine, in retrospect, which was the decisive factor.

Another reason for the difficulties in comparing cases in the literature concerns a point we emphasized in chapter 2: each scholar adopts a different approach to what constitutes influence and how it should be measured. While some researchers define influence as effect on votes (e.g., Rothenberg 1992, 203–22; or Fritschler 1975), others define influence as access (Hansen 1991) or impact on policy outcomes (Maass 1951). The conclusion often drawn from Bauer, Pool, and Dexter (1963) is that interest groups are ineffectual, and yet they describe a legislative world in which group members sometimes help legislators draft legislation and decide which aspects of an issue are important. Is the glass of influence half empty or half full? Does influence mean winning a roll call vote or is agenda-setting or mere damage control enough? For the most part these studies do not agree on the dependent variable. Such problems also plague a more recent and prominent style of research, that based on a more quantitative approach.

## QUANTITATIVE STUDIES OF LOBBYING

It is easy to understand how the qualitative literature on interest-group effects failed to develop a common set of definitions or to consider the same set of theoretical variables in a range of studies. In the quantitative literature, on the other hand, one might expect a greater ability to generate comparable findings, since similar indicators could be used across a variety of cases. Part of the attraction in the quantitative approach is the ability to be more systematic. This, in turn, should promote a cumulative science, with each study comparable to those that had come before it. In contrast to the ambiguities that often characterized the qualitative studies, quantitative studies require both the theoretical model and the indicators to be made explicit. While more descriptive studies may be based, at least in part, on anecdotal or impressionistic evidence, the quantitative studies should be replicable and may be less dependent on the personal outlook of the researcher. If we have a series of studies looking at the same research question, we should be able to consider them together and come to broad, generalizable conclusions about that question.

Here we consider the two most common types of quantitative lobbying studies—analyses of direct congressional lobbying and the legislative effects of PAC contributions—in an attempt to support such generalizable conclusions. We focus on fifteen lobbying studies and thirty-three PAC studies, which comprise all such studies that have been printed in major political science and economics journals during the past twenty years, as well as all other PAC and lobbying studies cited in those articles. There is no question that the quantitative approach to lobbying has a great number of merits, especially when compared with an impressionistic and unsystematic case study. However, the promise of replicability has not been met. In both the quantitative studies of lobbying and studies of the impact of PAC contributions, we note a number of problems that preclude the development of a cumulative literature. In particular, the scope of most of the studies is small and scholars tend to approach each case slightly differently, either methodologically or theoretically, making comparisons and generalizations across studies difficult. While each individual study may be designed in such a way as to test a particular set of hypotheses, there is little common perspective. Despite its statistical sophistication, the quantitative literature is no more cumulative, unfortunately and surprisingly, than the qualitative literature that preceded it. We will first sketch out the type of evidence presented in the studies—focusing on the breadth of the data—before discussing the conclusions that can or cannot be drawn from this body of research.

### The Scope of the Evidence

If we consider the fifteen quantitative studies of interest-group lobbying influence that we have collected in table 7.1, we can see why it can be difficult to draw broad conclusions from any single piece of research. The limited scope of the typical study is made clear simply by glancing down the columns that list the number of issues, the number of votes, and the number of groups analyzed in each of the studies. These numbers show that for the most part, the evidence presented in any single study tends to be narrowly focused. The median number of issues studied in these projects is one; the median number of groups studied is two.

More than half of the studies in table 7.1 analyze the impact of lobbying using a single policy issue; only three of the studies (Segal et al. 1992; Smith 1984; Heinz et al. 1993) analyzed more than five issues. Even those numbers are deceptively large. With the exception of Heinz and his colleagues, who analyzed eighty issues, and Wright (1990), who considered two issues, all of the other studies are focused on a single topical area or single policy domain. The number of votes analyzed in this collection of studies is also typically in the single digits.

In addition to the limited number of issues and votes considered, most of these studies consider the activities of very few groups. In nearly a third of the studies, the model includes data about only one interest group (or one coalition of groups assumed to be working toward the same goal on the given issue, for instance "labor groups" or "environmental groups"). This is despite the fact that in the case of issues like the environment, there is almost always an opposing business interest whose activity ought to be measured if the

**TABLE 7.1**
Studies of Lobbying Influence

| | Topics Studied | Number of | | | Measure of Lobbying | Lobby Influence? |
|---|---|---|---|---|---|---|
| | | Issues | Votes | Groups[a] | | |
| Fowler and Shaiko 1987 | Environmental issues | 5 | 5 | 1 | Group activity in each state | Minimal |
| Heinz et al. 1993 | Various | 80 | 80 | 316 | Self-reports of lobbying activity | N/A[b] |
| Kabashima and Sato 1986 | Trade: auto imports | 1 | 1 | 1 | COPE score | Yes |
| Kalt and Zupan 1984 | Coal strip-mining | 1 | 21 | 7 | Group membership, coal consumption | Marginal |
| Kau and Rubin 1982 | Public interest issues | 5 | 5 | 2 | Group membership by district | Yes |
| Langbein 1993 | Gun control | 1 | 6 | 3 | Self-reports of lobbying activity | Yes |
| Langbein and Lotwis 1990 | Gun control | 1 | 6 | 3 | Self-reports of lobbying activity | No |
| Quinn and Shapiro 1991 | Corporate taxation | 1 | N/A | 1 | Number of registered lobbyists | No |
| Rothenberg 1992 | MX missile | 1 | 8 | 2 | Self-reports of lobbying activity | Marginal |
| Salamon and Siegfried 1977 | Corporate taxation | 2 | N/A | 114 | Size of firm or industry | Conditional |
| Segal et al. 1992 | Supreme Court nominations | Many | Many | 2 | Hearing testimony | Yes |
| Skocpol et al. 1993 | Mothers pensions | 1 | N/A | 3 | Group membership by state | Yes |
| Smith 1993 | Create Dept. of Education | 1 | N/A | 2 | Self-reports of lobbying activity | Conditional |
| Smith 1984 | Education issues | 44 | 66+ | 1 | Group strength and support | Marginal |
| Wright 1990 | Superfund, farm bill | 2 | 5 | 4 | Self-reports of lobbying activity | Yes |

[a] Measures number of groups modeled in equation. Therefore "labor groups" would count as one group unless the impact of each group were modeled separately.

[b] This analysis considered the circumstances under which groups and their lobbyists were successful; some of the groups were successful and others were not.

model is to be complete. Most of the rest of the studies considered the impact of two or three groups or loose coalitions of groups. Notable exceptions are Segal et al. (1992), who included every group that testified about a Supreme Court nominee since 1955; Salamon and Siegfried (1977), who analyzed the tax burdens of 110 mining and manufacturing firms as well as four categories of petroleum industries; and Heinz and his colleagues, who collected information from eight hundred individual lobbyists representing 316 groups.

A similar pattern of limited empirical scope holds true among studies of PAC contributions. Table 7.2 presents a summary of articles published in recent years that relate PAC contributions to legislative influence. Most of the studies are based on the analysis of a single issue, and often use a single yes/no vote as the dependent variable. Only a third of the studies considered more than five issues, and only four of those consider more than a single policy area.

The PAC studies, even more than the lobbying studies, have a tendency to consider the impact of a single group in isolation, even though multiple groups may actually have been involved in the policy issue of interest. About half of the studies listed measured PAC contributions for only one group for each issue studied. A third more measured the contributions of two groups. Only Ginsberg and Green (1986) and Grenzke (1989) combine a large number of issues studied with the activities of ten or more groups. Rarely do these studies address the contributions of two or more sides to the same debate, though one might expect that a full model of contributions and their impacts should include the consideration of the behaviors of rival groups. Implicitly, by ignoring the activities of rivals, scholars assume that groups make their decisions about contributions independently of the behaviors of other groups, and that their contributions have no impact on the contributions of others. This might come as a surprise to many of those involved in the process, attentive as they are to the activities of both friend and foe. It is curious to note that despite the subsidization of research costs in the form of FEC reports and roll-call tallies, as discussed in chapter 1, studies of the impact of PACs still tend to rely on the intensive analysis of an extremely small number of observations.

Perhaps, however, it is irrelevant that individual PAC and lobbying studies are narrow. After all, taken together these studies consider hundreds and hundreds of issues and interest groups—more than enough to support broad generalizations, it would seem. There are many ways in which the issues studied in the projects mentioned in tables 7.1 and 7.2 could be well suited to give us a broad picture of the impact of interest-group lobbying when considered together. The range of issues considered is quite broad: environmental issues, trade, labor, finance, defense, education, agriculture, gun control, and welfare. Researchers have not focused on one policy domain to

**TABLE 7.2**
Studies of PAC Influence

| Citation | Topics Studied | Number of Issues | Votes | Groups[a] | PAC Influence? |
|---|---|---|---|---|---|
| Chappell 1981 | Trade: oil imports | 1 | 1 | 1 | No |
| Chappell 1982 | Various nonconflictual issues | 7 | 7 | 7 | Inconclusive/marginal effects |
| Coughlin 1985 | Trade: auto imports | 1 | 2 | 1 | Yes |
| Durden et al. 1991 | Coal mining regulations | 1 | 3 | 2 | Yes/marginal |
| Evans 1986 | Chrysler loan, windfall profits tax | 2 | 8 | 4 | Marginal effects |
| Feldstein and Melnick 1984 | Hospital cost containment | 1 | 1 | 1 | Marginal effects |
| Fleisher 1993 | Defense | 1 | 21 | 1 | Yes, strongest variable |
| Frendreis and Waterman 1985 | Trucking deregulation | 1 | 4 | 1 | Yes |
| Ginsberg and Green 1986 | Various | 100's | 100's | 14 | Yes |
| Grenzke 1989 | Various | Many | 384 | 10 | No |
| Hall and Wayman 1990 | Natural gas, dairy, job training | 3 | N/A | 3 | Yes |
| L. Johnson 1985 | Savings and loan legislation | 9 | 9 | 9 | Marginal |
| Jones and Keiser 1987 | Labor-related legislation | 20 | 20 | 1 | Yes |
| Kau et al. 1982 | Economic regulation | 8 | 8 | 4 | Marginal |
| Kau and Rubin 1982 | Economic regulation | 8 | 8 | 4 | Marginal |
| Langbein 1993 | Gun control | 1 | 6 | 3 | Yes |
| Langbein and Lotwis 1990 | Gun control | 1 | 6 | 3 | Yes |
| McArthur and Marks 1988 | Trade: auto imports | 1 | 1 | 1 | Marginal |
| Neustadtl 1990 | Labor-related legislation | 41 | 41 | 2 | Yes, varies by issue |
| Peltzman 1984 | Various | Many | 331 | 1 | Marginal |
| Quinn and Shapiro 1991 | Corporate taxation | 1 | N/A | 1 | Yes |
| Rothenberg 1992 | MX missile | 1 | 8 | 2 | No |
| Saltzman 1987 | Labor-related legislation | [b] | [b] | 2 | Yes |
| Schroedel 1986 | Finance legislation | 3 | 2 | 3 | Yes |
| Silberman and Durden 1976 | Minimum wage | 1 | 2 | 2 | Yes |
| Stratman 1991 | Farm policy | 10 | 10 | 6 | Yes for 8/10 issues |
| Vesenka 1989 | Farm bill | 1 | 14 | 1 | No |
| Wayman 1985 | Defense | 1 | 11 | 1 | Marginal, varies over time |

**TABLE 7.2** (*cont.*)

| Citation | Topics Studied | Number of Issues | Number of Votes | Number of Groups[a] | PAC Influence? |
|---|---|---|---|---|---|
| Welch 1982 | Dairy price supports | 1 | 1 | 1 | Marginal |
| Wilhite 1988 | Labor-related legislation | [b] | [b] | 1 | Mixed |
| Wilhite and Thielman 1987 | Labor-related legislation | [b] | [b] | 1 | Yes |
| Wright 1985 | Various | 5 | 5 | 5 | No |
| Wright 1990 | Superfund, farm bill | 2 | 5 | 4 | No |

[a] Measures number of groups modeled in equation. Therefore "labor groups" would count as one group unless the impact of each group was modeled separately.

[b] Uses COPE scores, which are usually based on about 20 votes.

the exclusion of others, a situation that should help anyone attempting to draw far-reaching conclusions. In other ways, however, the range of issues studied is limited. Nearly all of the studies analyze large, conflictual issues that would attract opposing groups and media attention. Any conclusions that we can draw from an analysis of these studies would be limited to issues with similar characteristics. These studies also are not designed to address the roles interest groups play in political agenda setting; instead the focus is on the final outcomes of issues that have already been defined. Most importantly, as we will note in greater detail the next section, the studies are not designed to be comparable even on the topics that they do address. Each finding stands in isolation rather than as part of a cumulative literature.

### Drawing Conclusions from a Maze of Contradictions

Looking at the studies of lobbying presented in table 7.1, we can see that the conclusions about whether direct lobbying affects congressional behavior are mixed, but that a majority of studies finds lobbying is positively associated with interest-group success. Half of the studies concluded that lobbying does have an effect, five of the studies concluded that lobbying has a marginal effect, and two concluded that lobbying has no effect. (The study by Heinz et al. differs from the others in that these scholars made a point of not asking whether lobbyists are influential, but under what circumstances are they influential. That is, they asked which variables were associated with success. This study is discussed in further detail in chapter 8.) Still, there is quite a range of findings presented in these studies.

The range is even greater among the PAC studies, a body of research infamous for its contradictory findings. Virtually every review of this literature spends time discussing how it is that some researchers have found PACs to be influential, while other researchers have found the opposite, before suggesting a revision that might point us toward a more accurate answer. (Some of the best reviews are contained in Evans 1986; Grenzke 1989; Wright 1990; Cigler 1991; and especially Smith 1995.) Of the studies presented in table 7.2, six concluded that PACs make no difference in roll call voting, fourteen said the influence of PACs was marginal or at least strongly limited by other variables such as constituency, ideology, or visibility, and thirteen found that PACs were highly influential. The final column of table 7.2 shows the mix of findings in studies of PAC contributions on congressional behavior.

Unless one attributes the contradictions within these collections of studies to sloppy scholarship (which we do not), it seems that the unavoidable conclusion is that PACs and direct lobbying sometimes strongly influence congressional voting, sometimes have marginal influence, and sometimes fail to exert influence. This in itself is a valuable finding, since it contradicts common journalistic insinuations about PACs constantly exerting their influence over all issues. Still, it begs the question: why? One thing we should have learned from these studies is that we were asking the wrong question. It should not be whether interest groups are ever influential, but when, why, and to what extent they are powerful on what types of issues. Which variables across these studies are responsible for determining whether interest groups are successful or unsuccessful in attaining their legislative goals?

Smith (1995, 94–95) lists twelve explanations that have been suggested in the literature for the conflicting findings of PAC studies. These potential variables involve differences in issue visibility, issue technicality, the concentration of costs and benefits, the degree of partisanship, public salience, amount of organized opposition, presence of lobbying activity other than contributions, how soon a senator faces reelection, the closeness of a past or upcoming election, whether the senator or representative is ideologically extreme or moderate, and whether public opinion favors the group on the given issue. Most of the same variables could conceivably be at the root of the variation we see in research involving direct lobbying.

The problem is, most of these potential explanatory variables are not measured within the studies considered here. Even within the studies that proposed these explanatory variables in the first place, Smith finds that most make their claims with very little direct evidence (1995, 94). After all, these are, for the most part, case studies of particular votes. Case studies of particular issues by definition cannot provide variation on such issue-related points as salience, costs and benefits, degree of conflict, or public opinion. Since these issue-related characteristics are constants in any given study, they are generally not measured. Thus we lack quantitative measures of these variables across the studies, precluding a systematic test.

These quantitative studies of groups in particular contexts ironically have little systematic information about context. Only thirteen of the thirty-three PAC studies (but nine of the fifteen lobbying studies) modeled into the study whether or not intergroup conflict was involved, and only two of all the studies had direct measures of how salient the issue was (Jones and Keiser 1987 and Neustadtl 1990, although Evans 1986 compared the outcomes of a high-salience case and a low-salience case). Considering that the studies including these contextual variables found that they were important in explaining variations in interest-group success, it certainly seems as though it would be important to have such variables measured across the studies.

One other possible reason for variation across the studies has nothing to do with interest-group behavior itself but rather with the way in which it was studied. As Evans (1986) points out in her review of the PAC literature, several different statistical techniques are used in these studies. About half of the PAC studies, for instance, use single-equation models, while the other half use simultaneous equations, since the ways members of Congress tend to vote can affect the campaign contributions they attract, as well as the other way around. In addition, variables are often not measured in exactly the same way. Even the dependent variables are not consistent across the studies: Among the lobbying studies, for instance, two of the articles look at changes in an outcome measure rather than changes in congressional voting. Quinn and Shapiro (1991) use change in tax policy as a dependent variable; Skocpol et al. (1993) use adoption of mothers' pensions as their dependent variable. Two other lobbying studies (Smith 1993; J. Wright 1990) also have dependent variables that are not perfectly equivalent to the others, since the first uses a series of head counts rather than actual votes, and the second uses committee votes rather than floor votes. While most of the PAC studies use congressional roll call votes as their dependent variable, Hall and Wayman (1990) use a scale of participation in committee, Quinn and Shapiro (1991) use changes in tax policy, and Wright (1990) uses committee-level votes. A related but slightly different issue is the tendency (with the notable exception of Hall and Wayman) to model interest group influence as a dichotomous variable: either the vote or outcome is affected or it is not. Even if this were not a misrepresentation of the lobbying process (an issue we will discuss later in this chapter), it increases the chance for findings that differ based on nothing but random variation if only a few issues are considered.

The primary independent variable often differs as well. In the studies of direct lobbying this difference is sobering. Nearly half of these quantitative studies of the effects of lobbying contain no direct measure of lobbying. Even in the studies that did contain a direct measure of lobbying, that measure varied. Self reports of lobbying activity (interview or survey data) were used in five of the cases, while one study used a measure based on hearing testimony (Segal et al. 1992). The most often used proxy (four uses) was the strength of the group in a given congressional district, a measure that is hardly guaranteed to correspond to actual lobbying efforts and which leaves any analysis wide open to spurious findings. Also used as proxies were the number of registered lobbyists and the COPE score of the member of Congress. It is curious that two of these proxy independent variables—group strength and COPE scores—have been used in other lobbying studies as both control variables (Austen-Smith and Wright 1994 use group strength as a control variable) and as a dependent variable (Jones and Keiser 1987 and Saltzman 1987 both use COPE scores as their dependent variable in studies of PAC influence). Clearly these measures are far from precise and open to a wide variety of interpretations and potential misinterpretations.

Since each of these studies was designed independently and used different measures, it becomes difficult to assess whether the differences in findings are the result of some substantive variable such as salience, conflict, or issue type, or whether the differences are the artifacts of variations in research methods. Smith (1995, 93) attempted to answer this question in the PAC literature, and noted that differences in the method used to measure the dependent variable and the primary independent variable do not seem to explain the variation in findings within those studies. Findings are contradictory regardless of how contributions were measured and regardless of whether the researcher looked at single votes or indexes of votes, a single interest group or many.

Likewise, within the studies of direct lobbying there is no discernible pattern in findings related to how lobbying was measured. Studies using groups' own reports of their lobbying activities arrive at mixed conclusions just as have studies using group strength as a proxy; studies looking at outcome measures rather than votes also come to contradictory conclusions. We will discuss some of the reasons why this might be in the next section.

## ISOLATED MODELS OF LOBBYING BEHAVIOR

Perhaps the most important problem with most of these studies of the influence of PACs and direct lobbying is not so much in the narrowness of their data as in the narrowness of their conception of the lobbying process. After all, two studies that were not empirically narrow—each looked at hundreds of cases involving ten or more groups (Ginsberg and Green 1986 and Grenzke 1989)—came to opposite conclusions about the influence of PACs. But as we saw in the previous section, many important variables have typically been omitted from recent studies of interest-group influence, variables that might help explain the contradictory results of those studies. Even more basically than that, however, the designs of most of the PAC and lobbying studies suggest a theoretical view of interest-group behavior at odds with empirical reality. Specifically, most of the studies are modeled as if most lobbying takes place immediately before a highly salient floor vote, in a world populated by two lobbyists and a legislator, where influence is dichotomous, and where behavior at one point in time does not affect later behavior. We will address each of these points in turn, suggesting along the way what more reasonable assumptions about interest groups might be.

### What Is the Nature of Most Group Influence?

Most quantitative assessments of group influence tend to overlook a well-documented truth about policymaking: most action takes place long before the floor vote. Descriptive case studies of interest-group efforts often show that the most difficult feat for an interest is simply to get its point of view taken seriously by Congress and the public. Bosso's (1987) study of pesticide policy showed that regulation of pesticides did not become part of the congressional agenda until the issue was redefined from one of agricultural progress to one of environmental degradation. Likewise, Nelson (1984) argued that child abuse had to be redefined from a family issue to a public-health issue before lawmakers became involved. Antismoking interests were successful in regulating cigarette advertising only after health-related aspects of smoking became more prominent than the economic aspects of tobacco farming (Fritschler 1975; Baumgartner and Jones 1993).

Legislators can be convinced to view a particular vote or issue in any of a number of ways. Groups lobbying Congress, therefore, would not need so much to change any member's mind about anything, but simply change the degree to which they associate a given issue with a given dimension: change the terms of the debate (see Jones 1994). Richard Smith (1984) analyzed education issues before the 94th Congress and showed how changes in the way a bill was interpreted by members of Congress affected votes on the issues. The debate over the Clinton health-care plan and its rivals involved several different dimensions: the potential economic impact, the unfairness of denying certain people basic medical care, and questions about the proper role of government in such matters. Numerous noncontradictory arguments were being made, each tapping a different dimension. The outcome in such debates may be determined by who is most successful at focusing attention on their preferred dimension. Attention to the use of argumentation in lobbying studies has been low. Cases are often chosen for study because they offer minimal possibilities for such changes in dimensionality, but this would make them especially uncommon.

Once an issue has been defined and has attracted governmental attention, the locus of activity still is not roll call votes. The classic policy studies described interest-group power as existing within subsystems, that is, within long-term relationships forged with agency personnel and members of congressional committees. Books aimed at instructing would-be lobbyists (e.g., Wittenberg and Wittenberg 1994; Wolpe 1990) emphasize the importance of focusing on committee action. "What happens in committee is the single most important determinant of success or failure" for a lobbyist, according to Wolpe (1990, 20). Bills are drafted in committee and committee votes influence floor votes (Fenno 1973; Davidson 1989; Kingdon 1989). Likewise, legislation can be weakened or strengthened by the way in which an agency implements it; the drafting of regulations is therefore crucial to the final outcome.

The focus on votes also makes it easy for scholars mistakenly to begin thinking about influence as a dichotomous, rather than continuous, variable. After all, an interest group either wins the vote or it does not. But in politics influence can be much more subtle than that. Imagine that Group X, which opposes Bill A, manages to get Bill A rewritten into a shadow of its former self but is unable to get the bill defeated entirely. Is this a case illustrating interest-group impotence? Vote-based measures of interest-group impact would make it seem so, but in fact the group has been relatively successful in reaching its goals.

Considering these problems, why then have most quantitative studies of interest-group influence focused on roll call votes? With a few exceptions, the emphasis has been on lobbying campaigns that take place after the issue has already been defined, placed on a formal agenda, and passed a congressional committee. Lobbying is often fierce at this stage, and groups sometimes wield great influence on roll call votes just as they do earlier in the process. But an overreliance on roll call votes gives us a distorted view of the ways groups go about lobbying and the reasons why they succeed or fail, since lobbying strategies and success rates are likely to be different depending on the stage of the process.

Certainly not all quantitative studies of interest groups have adopted unreasonable assumptions about the lobbying process. John Wright (1990) and Hall and Wayman (1990), for example, assume that interest groups are more likely to be successful in committee and so analyze lobbying efforts (including PAC contributions) before committees. John Bacheller, in a rarely cited but insightful study published in the *American Political Science Review* in 1977, develops a theory of when interest groups will focus their efforts in committee and when they will focus on floor votes. Bacheller surveyed 118 lobbyists, asking them to discuss a particular piece of legislation that they were involved with during the past year. Lobbyists dealing with noncontroversial issues reported that their lobbying activities were concentrated in committee. Lobbyists dealing with controversial issues that had been mentioned by candidates for president reported that most of their efforts took place on the House and Senate floors. Lobbyists dealing with controversial issues that were less well known (where the controversy was confined to specialized interest groups) fell between the two extremes. Hojnacki and Kimball (1996) help clarify this issue by pointing out that interest groups have two primary tasks once their issue is added to the congressional agenda. The first is to expand the size of their supportive coalition, the second is to try to shape the content of the bill as it is drafted in committee. They therefore predict that interest groups will focus on their allies when a bill is in committee, expanding to opponents and fence sitters as their resources allow when the bill reaches the floor. Considering the importance of predebate deliberations, it is indeed curious that interest-group scholars should collectively lavish so much attention to lobbying activity on the floor. It may be easier to gather such information, and the activities of groups at that stage may be more visible, but to focus on floor debates is to ignore most of what lobbyists and legislators do. Further, it is to ignore the parts of the policy process where lobbyists may be most influential in order to focus on that part where they may be merely spectacular.

## The Context of Lobbying

To create a model, one must simplify. The trick is to simplify in such a way that the model distills reality rather than distorts it. Unfortunately, the models used in most quantitative studies of interest-group influence fail to capture the essence of the nature of lobbying. In these studies, lobbying is typically portrayed as a direct, one-on-one interaction that involves only the legislator and a lobbyist from each side of the issue. The project then attempts to determine whether the direct lobbying contacts had a discernible effect on the vote of that legislator.

Certainly lobbyists do engage in such direct contacts, and surveys of interest groups have indicated that this is one of the most commonly used lobbying tactics (see chapter 8). But much of lobbying is also indirect. This makes sense if we consider that several studies have shown that legislators often prefer to take voting cues from each other rather than from lobbyists (see McFarland 1984; Schlozman and Tierney 1986; Kingdon 1989; Walker 1991). Therefore many interest groups spend time convincing congressional allies and potential allies to convince other members of Congress to support their cause. Lobbying also often takes place within coalitions, making it important to measure the efforts of all allied groups rather than that of any single group. Any model that does not take into consideration the effects of indirect lobbying and coalitional behavior is likely to be underspecified. It is convenient to assume that direct and indirect strategies will be linked, but groups are more likely to tailor their strategies more precisely than this.

The behaviors and strengths of government officials and political parties affect groups just as groups affect these actors. For example, studies of interest groups in the states have focused considerable attention on the effects of variation in the strengths of the governor and of political parties on interest-group strength (see, e.g., Zeigler and Van Dalen 1976; Morehouse 1981; Wiggins, Hamm, and Bell 1992). Such variables are of course constants in cross-sectional studies of national-level institutions but can fruitfully be studied in the states. Even at the national level, the relative mobilization and effort of government officials can have a great impact on interest-group success (see Hall and Wayman 1990; Hall 1996).

Lobbying resembles in many ways an assurance game. Often, the most crucial point that lobbyists must get across is that their issue is worth paying attention to, that their side has a chance for victory, that effort spent working on a given issue will not be for naught because of a lack of other supporters. Both legislators and potential allies in the group system must be convinced that an issue has enough chance of success that their time will not be wasted. (See Chong 1991, who argues that the civil rights movement can be understood in this way; see also Browne 1995 and Browne and Paik 1993, who analyze how members of Congress choose the issues in which to invest their time, staff, and resources.) Because of the importance of the expected behaviors of others, and because no single legislator typically controls unilaterally what the lobbyist hopes to obtain, both lobbying behavior and congressional reactions to lobbying behavior are sensitive to context. Groups choose to lobby on those issues where they have a chance of winning. Members of Congress listen to organizations when they think the organizations may end up putting together a coalition that cannot be ignored. The social nature of lobbying, with its sensitivity to context, can therefore be characterized by mimicry, cue-taking, and bandwagon effects. If lobbyists and government officials all are spending their time monitoring the activities of each other, as some studies suggest (Heinz et al. 1993), then their actions often will not be determined independently but in rapid response to commonly perceived threats and opportunities. Decisions to lobby, like decisions to listen to lobbyists, depend on one's perception of the chances of success. Since this depends on the context, it is a curious modeling strategy indeed to view lobbyists and legislators making decisions with reference only to each other.

Unfortunately, the accumulated mass of quantitative and qualitative studies of lobbying behavior has generated a great number of contradictions, with few consistent findings. Many of the reasons for this have to do with a willingness to apply a narrow set of definitions of lobbying to an even narrower empirical base. While each of the individual studies may have its merits, collectively the literature has generated more confusion than clarity.

## INTEREST GROUPS IN NONLEGISLATIVE SETTINGS

We have focused in this chapter on studies examining the role of interest groups in influencing the outcome of legislative votes. While these are perhaps the most frequently conducted type of empirical study of interest-group policy influence, there are also large bodies of literature examining the role of interest groups before the courts and within the bureaucracy. Many of the points we have brought up in this chapter have their parallel in the literatures involving the courts and the bureaucracy, but these areas also pose some unique opportunities and problems for researchers.

### Litigation and Amicus Curiae

One benefit of studying interest group involvement in the court system is that involvement in the courts is regularized and regulated. The primary avenues of direct group influence in the courts—filing suits and amicus briefs—are relatively easy to measure, and good longitudinal data are available for those willing to take the time to collect them. Suits and amicus briefs are preserved on file, listing the names of the plaintiffs and respondents and the arguments they presented. Compare such direct "lobbying" of the courts through suits and amici to direct lobbying of the legislature through personal contacts. No one keeps track of the number of legislative contacts, their content is not preserved on file, and even finding out which groups were involved in the issue can be difficult. Collecting data about group involvement in the courts is certainly not problem-free. The study of indirect influence on the courts, such as attempts to influence appointments, faces the same problems as all studies of legislative lobbying (regarding interest groups and judicial appointments see, e.g., Shapiro 1990; Segal, Cameron, and Cover 1992; Overby et al. 1992; Austen-Smith and Wright 1994; De-Gregorio and Rossotti 1995). Epstein (1991) notes that even within the realm of group-sponsored litigation, data can be a problem. Many lawyers fail to list their institutional affiliations on their legal briefs, and it can be difficult to identify secondary groups that financially or otherwise assisted the lead counsel on the suit. Still, for the most part, compared to studies of interest groups before the legislature, data on group involvement in the courts are there for the taking.

As a result, some of the largest empirical studies of interest groups have been those focusing on interest-group activities before the court, especially the role of groups in influencing the Supreme Court's choice of cases. Caldeira and Wright (1988), for example, analyzed more than two thousand petitions before the Supreme Court, looking at whether interest-group amicus briefs and a host of other potential factors increased the likelihood that the court would agree to hear the case (see also Caldeira and Wright 1990, McGuire and Caldeira 1993). An early study of this type (Hakman 1966) recorded all suits and all amicus briefs considered by the Supreme Court between 1958 and 1965, noting the amount of group involvement in filing and financially supporting these cases. Although Hakman found that group involvment in the court was minimal, O'Connor and Epstein (1982) reanalyzed his data and added eleven more recent years, finding group involvement in 49 percent of the cases before the court. (For other studies dealing with the extent of group involvment in the courts, see Casper 1972; Orren 1976; O'Connor and Epstein 1983; S. Olson 1990.) These studies are admirable for their breadth of scope and convincing in their conclusion that interest groups do help influence the agendas of the courts.

If we turn, however, to the question of whether interest groups are successful, not only in helping shape legal agendas but also in influencing outcomes, case studies are the most common research design, just as they were in the legislative arena. Unlike the studies of individual legislative votes, most of the court case studies are longitudinal in design. Still, they tend to focus on a single policy issue or a single group. Beginning with Vose's studies in the late 1950s, there has been a long list of such studies: Manwaring (1962) on mandatory flag salutes; Birkby and Murphy (1964), Cortner (1968), and Kluger (1976) on the NAACP; Barker (1967) on desegregation and reapportionment; Vose (1972) on several constitutional issues; Sorauf (1976) on the separation of church and state; Handler (1978) on the legal strategies of social movements; O'Connor (1980) on women's issues; S. Olson (1984) on the disabled; O'Neill (1985) on affirmative action; Kobylka (1987) on obscenity litigation, and Epstein and Kobylka's (1992) study of abortion and the death penalty.

The benefit, of course, to looking at issues over time, is that it makes it possible to compare different issue contexts and develop hypotheses about what circumstances lead to success before the court. This type of theory building is evident especially in the studies by Kobylka (1987) and Epstein and Kobylka (1992). Still, they remain case studies, and questions remain about whether their conclusions will hold in other issue areas. This is especially a problem since there is a strong tendency to study liberal groups whose cases ultimately proved successful. An exception is Epstein's (1985) book focusing on conservative interest groups before the courts; in it she notes that between 1959 and 1985, fifty-one out of sixty papers published on interest-group litigation focused on the activities of liberal groups.

Just as in the case studies of interest groups before the legislature, we have the problem of many case studies being selected in part because interest-group activity had evidently been successful. How can we judge whether interest groups make a difference in the outcome of cases from such a sample? One innovative study attempts to answer this question. Epstein and Rowland (1991) selected twenty matched pairs of U.S. District Court cases. In each pair, the issue raised in the case was the same, but one of the pair was filed by an interest group and the other was filed by private counsel. The researchers then compared the won-loss rates of interest groups versus private plaintiffs and found no significant difference. They concluded that interest groups wield no magic power before the courts; they are not invincible. The study provides an imaginative attempt to pin down the sticky question of influence. It is a research design uniquely appropriate for the case of the courts; a parallel study in the legislative arena would be all but impossible. Still, when assessing interest-group influence it is important to remember that without groups, many court cases would not be filed in the first place. In many cases, the plaintiff would not even have the opportunity to win if it were not for interest-group support. Studies detailing the extent of interest-group involvement in courts at every level and the impact of interest-group amicus briefs on the Supreme Court's agenda indicate that group influence can be extensive regardless of whether their winning average is higher than that of other types of plaintiffs.

Scheppele and Walker bypass the issue of measuring influence and instead use survey data to investigate the circumstances under which interest groups will choose to use the courts for policy purposes and the ways in which they tailor their strategies. They create a model that tests for the effects of internal characteristics of groups, such as organizational resources and type of constituency, as well as external characteristics of the situation, such as legal standing and the structure of conflict. They find that despite a popular view of interest groups in the courts that suggests that the courts are a venue primarily for disadvantaged groups, in fact "it is the better endowed, active, older groups facing a highly structured, contentious policy environment that are most likely to turn to the courts to achieve their policy goals" (1991, 177). They also note that interest-group legal strategies are multidimensional. For example, the groups may sometimes choose to file amicus briefs or class action suits to influence policy outcomes, but in other situations they may file suit primarily to protect the business or professional interests of particular group members. Citizen groups are much less likely to file member suits, and much more likely to file class action suits (181).

Surveys of interest-group behavior indicate that litigation is a relatively uncommon technique when compared to other group activities (in addition to Walker 1991, see Schlozman and Tierney 1983, 1986; Heinz et al. 1993; and Nownes and Freeman forthcoming). Filing suit or submitting amicus briefs is more common than engaging in protests, but less frequently used than personal lobbying contacts (the exact percentages from the surveys are presented in chapter 8). By contrast, interest-group activity before the bureaucracy is vast. In all of the surveys cited above, more than 90 percent of groups reported lobbying agency officials or testifying in agency hearings. Heinz and his colleagues found that when they asked their respondents to name the five government officials they contacted most often, the answers were split equally between officials from the legislative and executive branches (1993, 219).

## *Interest Groups and the Bureaucracy*

The literature on interest groups before the bureaucracy is vast. Most of it is tightly linked to the literature on groups before the legislature, and we have touched on it again and again in this and in preceeding chapters. The subsystem literature, for example, describes and theorizes about the interactions between interest groups, agencies, and congressional committees in a given issue area. These studies, as mentioned above, tend to be primarily theoretical or, if data are presented, they are related to a single case. Domain studies (e.g., Hansen 1991; Browne 1995) by definition deal with all actors included in the policy domain in question. The domain studies of Laumann and Knoke (1987) and Heinz et al. (1993) are exceptional in that they analyze multiple domains within the same framework.

There is, however, a relatively small body of literature that focuses more exclusively on interest group–agency interactions. Much of this is related to a larger, more general literature on regulation and implementation. As with the subsystem literature, much of the most prominent work in this area consists of theoretical pieces and models of agency—group behavior (e.g., Herring 1936; Bernstein 1955; McConnell 1966; Lowi 1969; Stigler 1971; Posner 1974; Peltzman 1976; Bendor and Moe 1985; Wilson 1989; Banks and Weingast 1992) or case studies (e.g., Selznick 1949 on the Tennessee Valley Authority; Huntington 1952 on the Interstate Commerce Commission; Mansfield 1980 on the Federal Maritime Commission; Culhane 1981 on public lands; Chubb 1983 on energy policy; Moe 1986 on the National Labor Relations Review Board; Scholz and Wei 1986 on the Occupational Safety and Health Administration; and Rothenberg 1994 on trucking regulation). All of these case studies take a longitudinal perspective, and data collection efforts tend to be extensive. Still, the exclusive use of single case studies poses the same problems we pointed to earlier in the chapter. Each has its own theoretical perspective, and it becomes impossible to determine whether the theory holds only for the case at hand, or whether its application is broader. Wilson (1989), for example, proposes that there are four types of group—agency relationships: client politics, entrepreneurial politics, conflictual interest-group politics, and majoritarian politics. He discusses the type of agency design and group system structure that would promote each of these types, and predicts the likely types of policies that would result. But to our knowledge no one has attempted to test this on a wide range of group/agency data.

One exception to the reliance on case studies is Brudney and Hebert's (1987) use of data from a survey of thirteen hundred state agency officials regarding the relative perceived influence of the governor, legislature, clientele groups, and professional associations. The case studies, however, address a much broader and more complex range of questions than this survey is able to, and pay attention to contextual variables that may be affecting the relative influence of various actors. Ideally researchers would design studies that looked at several or many issues in some detail, or that tested the propositions of some of the theories of group-agency interaction across a number of agencies.

Heinz et al.'s (1993) project allowed them to address some of the questions that have been raised over the years within the regulatory and subsystem literatures, since their study included several regulatory "events." This study stands as an exception to most of the interest-group literature, however. Apart from individual case studies, surprisingly little empirical work has been done on the role of interest groups in administrative policymaking. This is especially surprising given that a formal role for organized interests is built into the administrative rulemaking process. By law, all federal agencies must publish a notice of proposed regulations in the Federal Register and allow a period for interest groups and the general public to submit written comments on the regulation before a final version is adopted. These comments are kept on file by the agency and are public records. Marissa Golden (1995) is one of the few scholars to take advantage of this research opportunity, analyzing all comments submitted to three agencies regarding eleven different proposed regulations. Her innovative research design enabled her not only to determine the number and type of groups tending to participate in such agency policymaking procedures but to analyze the content of their arguments. Both this research design and the rulemaking comments themselves have the potential to greatly advance this area of interest-group study.

As with the studies of interest groups in the legislative arena that we discussed above, the greatest need in studies of interest groups before the courts and within the bureaucracy are data sets that extend beyond a single case and which include contextual variables about the activities of other actors and the nature of the issues at hand. Studies of interest groups within the courts have been more successful at this because of the wealth of data provided by the formal briefs filed with the court. Analyses of comments in rulemaking procedures may in the same way provide a key to broadening our studies of interest groups before the courts. This data source is somewhat limited by the fact that informal contacts of agency personnel are also an important interest-group strategy, but the comments provide a good place to begin.

## CONCLUSION

What explains the variation we see in interest-group effectiveness? Why does interest-group lobbying sometimes make a difference and sometimes not? Why do PACs sometimes seem to affect roll call voting and other times do not? What are the critical explanatory factors? The studies reviewed in this chapter, for all their contradictions, have in fact taught us something important: they allow us to stipulate at least occasional interest-group influence and to concentrate instead on the circumstances under which groups are influential. This is an important collective finding, and one that, used correctly, can allow the interest-group literature to go forward.

Although most of the studies reviewed in this chapter spend much time describing the political contexts in which group behavior takes place, it is hard to put these particular instances of policymaking in any sort of larger framework. The one-case-study-at-a-time approach makes it nearly impossible to interpret the accumulated findings since it leaves many variables unmeasured, often because they are constants within any single case. As with the Olsonian studies of the collective action dilemma discussed in chapter 4, much recent quantitative research on lobbying and influence has been distilled into a narrow, tractable issue: Does interest-group activity X cause a change in roll-call vote Y? This question, while perhaps not trivial, is far more narrow than the underlying question about interest-group influence. If most descriptions of interest-group behavior indicate that a majority of lobbying effort takes place before an issue ever comes up for a vote, why has the focus been so heavily placed on roll-call voting? If PAC influence varies according to issue salience and the presence or absence of direct lobbying, why are these variables not included in our studies? The answer seems to be that data on roll call votes and PAC contributions are easy to obtain; the other data are not. Unfortunately the easy route has led us to few conclusive findings about the political behavior of interest groups.

Simple models using proxy variables may be adequate in some cases. The assumptions inherent in most models of group behavior are designed, as in other areas of the discipline, to limit the dimensions of consideration, making the question easier to study. But where there are many potential dimensions, the equilibrium results that stem from the simplified models can be unstable artifacts of the assumptions (see Riker 1988). When admittedly simplified models produce contradictory results that are at odds with common sense, it seems likely that important variables have been overlooked or that the model is miscast. We believe this to be the case with the contradictory findings present in studies of lobbying and PAC influence.

# CHAPTER 8

# Surveys of Interest-Group Activities

LOBBYISTS can generalize about their strategies of dealing with government officials if they are forced to, but they resist global statements. While we were preparing to write this book, one of us asked a friend who represents a public-interest group in Washington which type of lobbying tactics his group most often employed. Was it legislative lobbying with direct contacts of members of Congress and their staffs, dealings with executive and regulatory agencies, or a more indirect approach involving letter-writing and public-relations campaigns? The lobbyist paused for a moment. "Well," he finally said, "it depends on what the issue is."

When a group and its lobbyists decide to work on a particular issue, they must make decisions about which governmental targets to focus on and what type of approach to use. Although limited resources may constrain its choices, a given group's targets and tactics typically will differ dramatically from issue to issue. A group seeking to influence tax policy would most likely address its efforts at Congress not the IRS. A group seeking to influence environmental policy might split its efforts, lobbying Congress regarding major shifts in policy, lobbying executive agencies regarding regulation wording and enforcement, and taking a grassroots approach on issues of sufficient salience. A group whose interests span several policy areas, as with the public interest group our friend represents, would certainly need to employ a variety of different lobbying tactics, tailoring the tactics to the issues. A group with little public support will endeavor to keep things quiet; a group hoping to expose the power of another may choose a strategy based on publicity and confrontation. Each group may choose the opposite strategy on the next issue.

The lobbyist's answer—"it depends"—highlights two important points in the study of lobbying. The first, a point that has been supported by survey after survey of interest-group leaders and lobbyists, is that most groups use a wide variety of lobbying tactics rather than relying on a single method in their efforts to influence politics. The second point, which has seldom been the focus of systematic study, is that tactic choice depends on the characteristics of the situation just as much as it depends on the characteristics of the group. Groups do not have a single strategy determined by their internal resources or membership base. Rather, they have a range of strategies available to them. The set of tactics available to each group may differ, but no group has just one strategy. Depending on the issue, they pick different strategies. The most effective groups may not be those that are best at a given strategy but rather those that have the greatest repertory of strategies available to them and who are most skillful at choosing the right strategy for the issue at hand. Asking what lobbyists usually do is like asking Pete Sampras whether he "usually" hits backhands or forehands. It depends on the situation. The best players have all the shots, and they choose them wisely.

Chapter 7 reviewed some of the difficulties in generalizing from the literature based on narrow case studies of lobbying. Even the accumulation of dozens of these studies has not led to a clear set of conclusions because of unmeasured differences in context. In this chapter we review the lobbying literature based on large-scale surveys of interest groups. In these studies, scholars have often surveyed a large sample of interest groups, asking them about lobbying behaviors across a wide range of issues. The responses they have received have proved remarkably consistent from one survey to the next, especially if one considers the extensive differences in question wording and sampling frames used by the various surveys. These surveys have provided stable empirical bases from which to generalize, and have become one of the most prominent success stories of the interest-group literature. The surveys have their limitations, however, especially if we are trying to understand the circumstances under which interest groups choose to adopt particular lobbying tactics. Unfortunately, with few exceptions, scholars have not linked the systematic study of lobbying tactics with a discussion of the contexts in which each tactic is chosen. While we have learned a number of important lessons concerning tactics and strategies of lobbying from these general studies, the next step in the literature will be taken only when scholars combine generalizability with sensitivity to context. This has been done in a few cases, as we will note in the pages to follow, but it has been rare in the literature so far.

## THE ROBUSTNESS OF SURVEY RESULTS ABOUT
## LOBBYING TACTICS

In the late 1950s, Lester Milbrath conducted the first large-scale and systematic survey of Washington-based interest groups and their lobbyists, documenting the types of tactics used to influence public policy and how effective those tactics seemed to be. A series of researchers followed in his footsteps in the late 1970s and 1980s: Berry (1977); Walker (1983, 1991); Schlozman and Tierney (1984, 1986); and Heinz et al. (1993); and, with a sample that was not exclusively focused on Washington groups, Knoke (1990a). The 1980s in particular saw a rapid advance in our knowledge of interest-group behaviors because of these large research projects. Even though each of these authors used different questions, different sampling frames, and went to the field in different years, the vast bulk of findings from this set of surveys about lobbying activities have proven remarkably robust. This is in sharp contrast to the literature on lobbying based on narrow case studies, as we noted in the previous chapter.

## The Large Surveys of Group Lobbying Activities

These large-scale surveys of interest groups are similar in design in that all asked extensive questions about the types of external political activities in which their respondents were engaged and in that five of the surveys focused on groups lobbying in Washington. Beyond that, similarities are hard to come by. Each survey was designed with different theoretical and empirical goals in mind, and the sampling frames and questions asked diverged accordingly.

Although the surveys differ substantially from one another in important ways, it is easier to compare their findings than it was to compare the case studies described in chapter 7 because the surveys are quite explicit about their sampling frames and definitions of terms. Further, the similarities in their findings about tactic choice are so strong that they remain clear in spite of the variations in question wording and sampling frames. Consistently, surveys report general agreement that certain tactics are the most common and that most groups and lobbyists use a wide range of tactics.

A quick summary of the large-scale surveys includes:

1. Milbrath (1963), who surveyed 101 people registered with the federal government as lobbyists. His focus, like that of contemporaries Bauer, Pool, and Dexter (1963), was on the role lobbyists play in providing information to members of Congress. He believed that lobbyists played an important and beneficial part in the governmental process, contributing to a broader expression of views within government. Milbrath sampled only from professional contract lobbyists required to register with the federal government, and interviewed them in person. Unlike the surveys that followed, his did not ask *whether* groups used particular lobbying tactics, but *how effective* they judged those tactics to be.

2. Jeffrey Berry (1977) did not study all types of interest groups, only groups seeking some collective good that would not selectively benefit their members. He used newspapers, magazines, and conversations with activists to identify eighty-three public-interest groups based in Washington, and conducted in-person interviews with their leaders. Following Milbrath, Berry distinguished between tactics and strategies, and attempted to explain the determinants of various lobbying strategies. Berry asked specifically about ten particular tactics.

3. Jack Walker's (1983, 1991) two mail surveys of more than one thousand Washington-based membership groups attempted to answer some of the ques-

tions raised by the Olsonian approach to group studies. His surveys investigated the ways in which groups mobilized and maintained themselves, as well as questions about their external political activities. Walker asked about eight particular tactics of influence in his 1980 survey. He compiled his samples from groups listed in the *Washington Information Directory*, including only membership groups and excluding businesses, unions, and governmental bodies.

4. Kay Lehman Schlozman and John Tierney's (1983, 1986) sample of 175 Washington interests was weighted toward the most active organizations and focused primarily on their external political activities. They also used a published directory—the *Washington Representatives Directory*—to compile their sample, weighting it based on the number of times the group was mentioned in the National Journal's Index to Organizations. The list of 27 potential lobbying tactics included in their questionnaire was the most extensive of any of the surveys. Unlike Walker, they included business lobbyists and non-membership groups in their sample.

5. John Heinz, Edward Laumann, Robert Nelson, and Robert Salisbury (1993) completed in-person interviews with nearly eight hundred lobbyists as well as 316 representatives of organized interests in 1983–1984, again focusing on the most active political players. Rather than spread their efforts thin across the entire political spectrum, however, they focused on four policy areas (health, energy, agriculture, and labor). Their sampling method relied not only on a published directory (again, *Washington Representatives*) but included computerized searches of newspaper and magazine articles, and interviews with officials involved in the policy areas studied. The findings of their study are wide-ranging; the project's central questions stemmed from the debate over pluralism, specifically whether important national policy decisions are made within relatively insular subgovernments or relatively open networks. In contrast with the other studies, these authors asked respondents to discuss a particular issue or set of issues, rather than to simply generalize about their activities across a range of issues.

6. Sociologist David Knoke (1990a) surveyed 459 group leaders by phone and nearly nine thousand group members by mail, focusing primarily on issues of group democracy and member participation, although he also included questions about lobbying activities. His sample, drawn from the *Encyclopedia of Associations*, contains only membership organizations, including a large proportion of organizations from outside Washington, and a large number of recreational groups, which one would not be expect to be overtly political. (While the *Washington Information Directory* and the *Washington Representatives Directory* explicitly attempt to compile lists of organized interests, including businesses, known to be involved in lobbying, the *Encyclopedia of Associations* attempts to list all national membership groups in the United States, regardless of location.)

In the 1990s, two large-scale surveys of interest groups active in state capitals were also conducted. The first, by Virginia Gray and David Lowery (1996), was designed to learn about the mechanisms that drive the growth and decline of interest-group populations, and so is not closely related to the surveys dealing with interest group lobbying activities that we discuss here. (See also Hrebenar and Thomas 1987, 1992, 1993a, 1993b, who compiled reports from scholars in all fifty states about interest-group activities, and Rosenthal 1992, who gives a qualitative picture of state interest-group activity.) The second, by Nownes and Freeman (forthcoming), replicates in many ways the work done by Schlozman and Tierney more than a decade earlier, only this time using a mail survey sent to 595 lobbyists and 301 interest group leaders in three state capitals. We include this survey in our discussion of the large-scale surveys that follows.

### Reported Use of Various Lobbying Tactics

Table 8.1 gives a summary of the most relevant findings on the choice of lobbying tactics from this diverse set of studies. Twenty-three of Schlozman and Tierney's twenty seven lobbying tactics are presented here, along with the corresponding findings from the other surveys wherever possible.

In spite of vast differences in sampling frames and question wording, consistencies emerge from these six surveys regarding the types of lobbying tactics groups use and the relative popularity of those tactics. (Since Milbrath's study did not compile statistics on how many lobbyists used each tactic, it is not included in table 8.1.) Table 8.1 shows that throughout the surveys, face-to-face contacts and testimony at public hearings are two of the most common tactics used by Washington interest groups and their lobbyists. Although the overall levels of tactic use are lower, this same pattern holds true even in the survey of membership groups conducted by David Knoke (1990a), despite the large number of apolitical groups in his sample. Perhaps most surprising are the findings by Nownes and Freeman (forthcoming). Sampling lobbyists in state capitals rather than Washington, more than ten years after the Washington surveys were conducted, they compiled results that were remarkably similar to those of Schlozman and Tierney, whose questions they adopted. In thirteen of the twenty-three questions about tactics adopted from the earlier survey, the Nownes and Freeman responses came within 5 percentage points of those compiled by Schlozman and Tierney. There are differences among the responses, to be sure (these are discussed at some length by Nownes and Freeman), but the most striking aspect of these data is how similar they are to a survey conducted on such a different population. The same could be said about the other surveys

**TABLE 8.1**
Consistency of Reported Tactic Use across Six Surveys

| Tactics | Schlozman and Tierney | Walker | Heinz et al. | Berry | Knoke | Nownes and Freeman |
|---|---|---|---|---|---|---|
| | | *Reported Use in Each Study* | | | | |
| **Testimony** at legislative or agency hearings | 99 | | 95/87[a] | 88 | 49 | 99 |
| **Direct contacts** of legislators or other officials | 98 | 78/80[a] | | | 84 | 65 | 97 |
| **Informal contacts** of legislators or other officials | 95 | | 95/92[a] | | | 81 |
| **Presenting research results** | 92 | | | 69 | | |
| **Coalitions:** working with other groups | 90 | | 99[b] | | 58 | 93 |
| planning strategy with government officials | 85 | | | | | 84 |
| **Mass media:** talking to journalists | 86 | 72 | | 38[c] | 15 | 74 |
| paid advertisements | 31 | | | | | 21 |
| **Policy formation:** drafting legislation | 85 | | 80 | | | 88 |
| drafting regulations | 78 | | 76 | | | 81 |
| shaping policy implementation | 89 | | | | | 85 |
| serving on advisory commissions | 76 | | | | | 76 |
| agenda-setting | 84 | | | | | 83 |
| **Constituent influence:** letter-writing or telegram campaigns | 84 | | | 68 | 67 | 83 |
| working with influential citizens | 80 | | | 62 | | 92 |
| alerting legislators to district effects | 92 | | | | | 94 |
| **Litigation:** filing suits or amicus briefs | 72 | 56 | 64 | 51 | 11 | 40 |
| **Elections:** campaign contributions | 58 | | | 6 | | 45 |
| campaign work | 24 | 23 | | | | 29 |
| candidate endorsements | 22 | | | | 5 | 21 |
| **Protests or demonstrations** | 20 | 7 | | 23 | | 21 |
| **Other tactics:** monitoring | | | 99 | | | |
| influencing appointments | 53 | | | | | 42 |
| doing favors for officials | 56 | | | | | 36 |

*Sources*: Schlozman and Tierney 1986, 150; Walker 1991, 109; Heinz et al. 1993, 65; Berry 1977, 214; Knoke 1990a, 208; Nownes and Freeman forthcoming.

[a] The first percentage refers to legislative lobbying activities, the second to executive and agency activities.

[b] Heinz et al. asked about "maintaining contacts with other organizations" rather than "joining coalitions."

[c] Berry asked about "public relations campaigns" rather than "talking to the mass media."

as well. The populations sampled are quite different: Schlozman and Tierney and Heinz et al. focused on the most active groups in Washington, while Walker focused on membership groups. Berry included only public interest groups, groups which by definition lack a built-in selective incentive for members that can give other interest groups a competitive edge in lobbying. Many of Knoke's groups were apolitical groups located outside of Washington. Given these differences, we would expect to find few similarities among the findings presented here, but instead the overall pattern of interest group behavior that emerges is quite consistent.

Informal contacts of officials and joining coalitions of other groups were both often-cited tactics of group influence in the surveys by Schlozman and Tierney (1986), Heinz et al. (1993), and Nownes and Freeman (forthcoming); those tactics weren't included in the other surveys. Mentioned somewhat less frequently throughout the six surveys, but still quite common, were tactics involving policy formation (e.g., drafting legislation or regulations) and constituency influence (e.g., letter-writing campaigns and asking influential citizens to contact government officials). Throughout all the surveys, the least-used tactics of influence were those involving election work and protests.

Less consistency across surveys is apparent in the use of litigation as a political strategy. Schlozman and Tierney report the highest percentage of groups litigating (72 percent), while only 40 percent of Nownes and Freeman's groups and 11 percent of Knoke's groups reported using the courts. This variation across the surveys is understandable when we consider that Scheppele and Walker (1991) found that the use of litigation as a tactic of political influence was extremely sensitive to differences in group type and resources. These are exactly the variables that are likely to be systematically different across surveys with such different sampling frames.

Differences likewise occur among responses regarding the use of the mass media and advertising. While Schlozman and Tierney (1986), Walker (1991), and Nownes and Freeman (forthcoming) ask about use of "mass media" and report fairly high percentages of groups using that tactic (86 percent, 72 percent, and 74 percent, respectively), Berry (1977) asks about "public relations," and reports only 38 percent using the tactic. Only 15 percent of Knoke's respondents reported using the mass media. In the case of Berry's public interest groups, it seems likely that differences in question wording explain the disparate finding, especially since Schlozman and Tierney had found that citizen groups were more likely to cite contacting the media as an important tactic than other groups were (1986, 152). It is less clear why Knoke found so few groups using the media, although the large number of primarily apolitical groups in his sample is a likely cause.

Besides a general agreement about the types of tactics used and few strong disagreements about how often they are used, there is an even stronger message in this tally of lobbying tactics: Most groups use a wide variety of tactics. Across the board, the majority of these tactics are used by two-thirds or more of the responding groups. This finding holds true throughout the surveys, but perhaps can be seen most clearly using data from Schlozman and Tierney (1983, 1986). Of the twenty-seven different lobbying tactics they inquired about, fourteen were used by 80 percent of the groups surveyed; the same pattern holds in Nownes and Freeman (forthcoming). Reanalysis of Walker's larger data sets likewise shows that specialization by tactic is rare. Of eight possible tactics of influence, the mean number of tactics reported was six (source: 1985 Walker survey). Interest groups tend to do many things in their efforts to influence policy; specialization on a single lobbying tactic is quite uncommon.

The results of the surveys of group activity reported in table 8.1 make clear that groups engage in a wide range of lobbying activities. The biggest difference across the surveys is the length of the list of activities they chose to inquire about—this point comes through at a glance because of the large number of blank spaces in the table. To a large extent, the range of activities reported depends simply on the range of questions asked. Where Schlozman and Tierney delved deeply into a wide range of potential activities, they found that most groups responded that they engaged in most of those activities. Where Heinz and colleagues added a new question, about "keeping track of developments in federal government policies," they found 99 percent of their respondents reported that they did so. This observation raises a troubling question: are the activities covered in table 8.1 those that take up the bulk of the time of most American lobbyists? If not, what else are they doing, and how would we know it? Are the most effective and useful strategies covered in these batteries of survey questions?

One difficulty in the survey questions on lobbying is that they focus on discrete actions such as contacting officials, filing suits, or testifying in hearings. What about more continuous efforts simply to maintain relations, clearly an important tactic of group behavior? Nearly thirty years ago, Lewis Dexter noted that most of what effective Washington representatives do involves little "lobbying" per se. That is, lobbyists spend relatively little time actually buttonholing members of Congress and delivering their group's sales pitch, and much time conducting research, maintaining good relations, and monitoring what is taking place within government (Dexter 1969). This observation is brought up to date by the work done by Heinz and his colleagues (Heinz et al. 1993), the only one of the major national surveys to ask explicitly whether the group spends time monitoring government activities. (Nownes and Freeman [forthcoming] found a similar pattern in the states.)

In chapter 2 we reviewed a series of definitional problems. One of the most serious areas of difficulty is in defining exactly what we mean by lobbying. In the quantitative case-study literature, lobbying is typically defined quite narrowly; in the broad surveys just reviewed, questions typically review many elements of lobbying behavior. Even in these cases, however, it is worth questioning whether the discrete activities typically enumerated in the surveys might not miss some important other activities.

Just as general efforts at building or maintaining close relations are typically not included in surveys of lobbying behaviors, scholars find it difficult to build attention to issue-definition and agenda-setting into their studies of lobbying. Schlozman and Tierney found that more than 80 percent of the groups they surveyed reported being active in efforts to set the agenda, but other surveys have not picked up on this finding (with the exception of Nownes and Freeman forthcoming, which reported a similar percentage). One difficulty with studying the issue-definition approach to lobbying is that the strategy may be most effective when it is directed at no single target. The most effective efforts to change how issues are defined affect whole policy communities, not single legislative decision makers. Much quantitative research on lobbying, such as that reviewed in chapter 7, assumes that each lobbyist has a particular target to whom they hope to transmit certain information. The political process can be much more amorphous that this; some of the most effective strategies of policymaking may involve much more general efforts at issue-definition. Neither the surveys nor the quantitative case studies reviewed in the last chapter have succeeded in addressing this issue.

Also surprisingly absent from most of the surveys on lobbying are discussions of how groups choose the targets of their lobbying efforts. Controversies have swirled in the literature concerning the degree to which lobbyists "merely" focus on providing information to their governmental allies, allowing them to lobby their peers, or whether lobbyists focus their efforts, as one might expect, on convincing the undecided or converting those who are predisposed against the position of the group. In spite of divergent findings on this topic since Bauer, Pool, and Dexter (1963) described the importance of working with one's allies, the general surveys reviewed in table 8.1 have not addressed this question in a definitive manner. Partly, as we will discuss below, this is because of their desire to generalize about group activities across all cases rather than focusing on precise issues of lobbying activity.

All in all, the surveys reviewed in table 8.1 show a great deal of consistency in their findings. In spite of important differences in question wordings, sampling frames, and other elements of the research projects reported, the surveys paint a relatively coherent picture of the work of a lobbyist: lobbyists engage in a wide range of behavior focusing especially on direct contacts with those in government dealing with the issues that concern them. Just as striking as the similarities in the survey results are some clear omissions. Few surveys deal with questions of choice of targets, agenda-setting, issue-definition, or monitoring.

## *Tactic Effectiveness and Importance*

The list provided in table 8.1 shows how commonly many tactics are used by a variety of groups, but it does not assess the relative effectiveness of each of the tactics listed. Only Milbrath (1963) and Berry (1977) addressed this point directly. Berry asked his respondents to evaluate the effectiveness of ten tactics of influence. Personal presentations (direct lobbying) and letter writing were cited as most effective, rated highly by about half of the respondents. Testifying at public hearings was at the bottom of the list, ranked as effective by only 28 percent of the groups using that tactic. In a finding that might well be seen as a harbinger of things to come, contributing money to candidates was a tactic used by only 6 percent of the groups surveyed in these early surveys, but it was seen as effective by 100 percent of those groups.

Berry's findings are echoed in part in Milbrath's survey of lobbyists and thirty-eight members of Congress or their staff. Milbrath found that direct personal contacts were the tactic cited as most effective, scoring an average of about nine on a ten-point scale. Presentation of research results was ranked next, averaging about seven on the effectiveness scale. Unlike Berry's respondents, however, Milbrath's respondents ranked testifying at hearings fairly high—giving it a six on the effectiveness scale, higher than the scores for constituency contacts and letter-writing campaigns. Still, we can see that across surveys and across the decades, most groups view direct contacts as the most productive use of their time. Testifying at formal hearings may be a common tactic, and those who testify may also be those who make the direct contacts in other forums, but groups consistently report direct contacts to be the most effective strategy when asked.

How productive is productive? The surveys, for the most part, do not attempt to assess whether interest groups actually wield influence or are effective at achieving their goals. There are good reasons for this. Most of the surveys do not ask about specific policy cases, and therefore would have to ask groups to generalize about their effectiveness across issues. Also, self-reports of effectiveness pose serious reliability risks. An exception to this general difficulty in dealing with effectiveness is provided by Heinz et al. (1993). They asked about specific policy cases and verified lobbyists' assessments of effectiveness with government officials familiar with the case. These scholars did not ask simply whether lobbyists were effective but rather about the circumstances where they were more effective. Lobbyists were asked whether they had achieved all, most, half, few, or none of their objectives in the given case. With these data in hand, the authors conducted statistical tests to predict the effectiveness of their lobbyists. The authors note that they were less concerned with the strategies by which organized interests are effective and more interested in whether there were particular types of actors who were consistently more influential than others (1993, 8). Regression analyses found that the lobbyist's years in government, the number of important political players known by the lobbyist, and whether the lobbyist represented a professional association were associated with greater effectiveness. The economic liberalism of the group was negatively associated with effectiveness. A series of other variables, including the type of lobbying (direct contacts, litigation, mobilizing public opinion, etc.) and the degree of conflict surrounding the issue, showed no significant effect. All in all, this effort to explain effectiveness systematically on the basis of such explicit indicators fell flat: The regression equations explained only 11 percent of the variance. The researchers concluded:

> The most important point, however, is that so much of the variance in success is not explained by these analyses. This suggests that the determinants of success are usually situation specific. The outcomes appear to turn less on the presence or absence of broad variables—organizational resources, political finance activity, partisan political affiliation, lawyers' skills, or the pursuit of a congressional or an executive branch strategy—than on much more particular factors that vary from issue to issue. (Heinz et al. 1993, 351)

As the authors acknowledge, their analysis also was limited by the fact that virtually all of the issues analyzed were on the high end of the salience scale—they were relatively big, important issues involving multiple policy players and significant government decisions. Whether more variance would be found among nonsalient, quiet issues, or by looking at the agenda-setting process rather than at issues already on the government agenda, has yet to be determined.

### THE BREADTH OF INTEREST-GROUP LOBBYING EFFORTS

As the Washington policy community has become more complex over the years, many have noted the tendency for groups to specialize in increasingly narrow activities (see especially Browne 1990 and Gray and Lowery 1996). However, there is a countervailing trend at work as well: Even as groups may specialize, they must also beware of changes in other policy areas that may affect them. There is pressure simultaneously to be a specialist organization and to monitor—and potentially to act in—a broad range of issues. We can see this with reference to Jack Walker's data on group activities.

In his 1985 survey of membership organizations active in national policy-making, Walker asked about each group's degree of interest in ten policy

## TABLE 8.2
### Specialists and Generalists among Washington Interest Groups

| | Number of Policy Areas where the Group Is "Very Interested" | | | | | |
|---|---|---|---|---|---|---|
| | *0* | *1* | *2* | *3–4* | *5–10* | *Total* |
| Number of groups | 100 | 252 | 214 | 225 | 98 | 889 |
| Percent | 11.3 | 28.3 | 24.1 | 25.3 | 11.0 | 100.0 |

*Source*: Calculated from Walker 1985 dataset.

areas (see Walker 1991, 70–72). Some groups indicated that they were "very interested" in a great number of domains, while others showed a more specialized or limited range of interest. Table 8.2 shows the range of responses.

From this simple frequency distribution, we can see that a great variety of types of organizations are active in Washington. For some, public policy is not the main concern. A solid one hundred organizations stated that they were not "very interested" in any policy area mentioned in the Walker questionnaire. This could be for two reasons: either they are not active in the policy process at all or they are active in an area that Walker did not include in his list. There could be a number of groups interested in such areas as the arts, religion, or sports that found none of the Walker policy areas to correspond closely with their interests. (The list of the ten policy areas is presented in table 8.4, below; see also Walker 1991, 70, 218–19.)

Among those groups that are very interested in at least one area of policy, we can see another important distinction. Slightly more than half indicated that they were very interested in only one or two policy areas, while a little more than a third said they were very interested in three or more policy areas. Some groups are true specialists, operating within a narrow issue niche, while others appear to be generalist organizations. (Nineteen groups—2 percent of the total—indicated they were "very interested" in eight or more of the ten areas.)

If we broaden the scope of the responses, however, to include those groups reporting that they were at least "somewhat" interested in a policy area, a pattern of widespread policy monitoring emerges. Table 8.3 shows how many organizations said they were "very" or "somewhat" interested in the ten policy areas.

Fully 97 percent of the Walker groups indicate that they are at least "somewhat" interested in one of his ten policy areas, and the vast majority indicate several areas of interest. These findings fit in well with many previous findings in the literature, especially Mancur Olson's (1965) by-product theory and Heinz et al.'s (1993) monitoring idea. From Olson, we are led to expect that groups may often be formed for reasons unrelated to questions

TABLE 8.3
Broad Range of Issues Monitored by American Interest Groups

| | Number of Policy Areas where the Group Is "Very" or "Somewhat" Interested | | | | | | | | |
|---|---|---|---|---|---|---|---|---|---|
| | *0* | *1* | *2* | *3* | *4* | *5* | *6* | *7–10* | *Total* |
| Number of groups | 26 | 71 | 91 | 101 | 141 | 138 | 79 | 242 | 889 |
| Percent | 2.9 | 8.0 | 10.2 | 11.4 | 15.9 | 15.5 | 8.9 | 27.2 | 100.0 |

*Source*: Calculated from Walker 1985 dataset.

of public policy, and that, once established, they may become active in policy only as a small part of their overall activities. For some groups, policy is simply not a main concern, or even an important one. (However, it is worth keeping in mind that for many large organizations, General Motors, for example, even a small proportion of their overall attention may be large in absolute terms.) From Salisbury, Heinz, and colleagues, we are reminded of the importance of policy monitoring: with so many things going on simultaneously in government, groups need simply to have their antennae up. For these and other reasons, then, we should not be surprised by the large numbers of groups indicating they are at least "somewhat interested" in a large number of policy areas.

Among the vast majority of groups that indicated interest, and presumably activity, in at least one policy area, we again see an important distinction between specialist organizations as compared with those that might be considered generalist groups. Twenty-nine percent of the sample indicated that they were "somewhat" interested in three or fewer policy areas, and 68 percent indicated they were interested in four or more areas. (The median number of mentions is four.) Many groups are extremely general in their outlooks: More than one quarter of the groups responding to the Walker survey indicated interest in seven or more of his ten policy areas. Clearly, for the vast majority of Washington organizations, considerable resources are spent in monitoring a wide range of policy activities of the government. Few organizations are able to remain securely within a narrow issue niche. Groups never know from what direction a new policy may come that has dramatic effects on their members, and their typical reaction to this uncertainty is to cast their net widely in the search of information and warnings.

Table 8.4 shows the degree to which specialization differs by policy area. It shows the number of groups "very interested" in each policy area by the number of other policy areas in which they are also "very interested."

No broad area of American politics seems to be home to a set of interest groups that are exclusively interested in that area of policy. There are some

### TABLE 8.4
Degree of Interest-Group Specialization by Policy Area

| Policy Area in which a Group Is Very Interested | Number of Other Areas in which the Group Is Also Very Interested | | | | |
| --- | --- | --- | --- | --- | --- |
| | None | One | Two or More | Total | N |
| Defense, national security, foreign policy | 20.7 | 19.5 | 59.8 | 100.0 | 174 |
| Health and human services | 17.1 | 23.2 | 59.7 | 100.0 | 310 |
| Transportation | 15.3 | 17.2 | 67.5 | 100.0 | 163 |
| Energy and natural resources | 14.7 | 20.7 | 64.6 | 100.0 | 232 |
| Agriculture | 13.7 | 25.0 | 61.3 | 100.0 | 124 |
| Education | 12.9 | 25.5 | 61.6 | 100.0 | 263 |
| Civil rights, civil liberties | 9.0 | 16.7 | 74.3 | 100.0 | 210 |
| Housing and urban policy | 6.8 | 14.5 | 78.7 | 100.0 | 117 |
| Management of the economy | 6.5 | 22.0 | 71.5 | 100.0 | 291 |
| Structure of government | 4.1 | 18.8 | 77.1 | 100.0 | 170 |

*Source*: Calculated from Walker 1985 dataset.

areas with greater specialization than others, to be sure. However, even such areas as national defense include a large majority of groups that are simultaneously interested in several other areas of policy. Whether we look at the question from the perspective of the group, as in tables 8.2 and 8.3, or from the perspective of the policy area, as in table 8.4, we can see that interest groups active in the Washington policy community are rarely able to specialize completely. The complications of policymaking force the majority of them to attend simultaneously to several different policy areas at once.

One might conjecture that the various levels of issue specialization shown in tables 8.2 and 8.3 could be due to the different sizes of the organizations represented in the Walker survey. After all, some of the groups included in these tables are huge membership organizations with budgets in the millions of dollars annually, while others are small groups with no paid staff whatsoever. There is only a meager and statistically insignificant relationship between the size of a group's staff and its degree of issue-specialization, however. Among those groups with no paid staff, the mean number of areas where the group is very interested is 1.8; this number increases to 2.8 for the largest organizations, those with fifty or more paid staff. However there is great variability within categories of staff size: Many large groups specialize, and many small ones are active in many policy areas. Apparently, many organizations feel the need to be active, or at least to show interest, in a great number of policy areas, whether or not they have the manpower to do as much as they might like. There is little wonder, given these findings, that coalitions are attractive to groups: if group leaders feel the need to remain active in so many different policy areas simultaneously and if this need is unrelated to the size of their staffs, then the leaders must be active in seeking out low-cost mechanisms to remain informed and to show some signs of activity.

These findings from the Walker survey correspond closely to those of Heinz et al. (1993) and to those of Salisbury (1990), in spite of some important differences in how these studies were designed. According to Heinz and his colleagues,

> When we presented respondents with a list of twenty policy events that had occurred in their domain the preceding four years, they indicated at least "some" interest in eleven events, on average. We found that no fewer than 53 respondents and an average of more than 100 respondents had been interested in each event. . . . [R]epresentatives do not usually focus on a particular committee or administrative agency; they report regular contact with four or five separate government agencies on average, typically including both executive and legislative branch agencies. Moreover, the average representative spends time in more than half the subfields within his or her policy domain and, in addition, in some four other major policy fields. (1993, 379)

This last finding corresponds almost exactly to that of Walker just described. Salisbury (1990) points out that broad monitoring of governmental activities is the rule among Washington interest groups; further, Heinz et al. point to the range of interests that are typically mobilized in many policy controversies. "These examples underscore two aspects of the modern interest representation system: That major policy decisions are not made by closed circles of interest groups and, the necessary corollary, that numerous interest groups monitor any given policy question and consider taking a more active role in the debate" (Heinz et al. 1993, 380). As groups monitor broadly, of course they often find out that their activities should be focused in some area outside their normal "niche," or core area of interest, and they do not hesitate to become active. The net result of this broad monitoring, then, is a broader range of action, leading to a cumulatively more complex and uncontrollable system of interest representation. "The efforts of individual interest groups to reduce uncertainty, then, may have the opposite effect in the aggregate" (Heinz et al. 1993, 381).

Two of the largest and most influential studies of interest groups conducted in the 1980s reach an identical conclusion: even while groups are proliferating in the nation's capital, and even while each may have an incentive to specialize and to create a distinct identity separate from those of its rivals, even more powerful incentives exist for groups to spread their gaze widely, to monitor a number of policy areas within the government, to be active in many areas, to avoid reliance only on a key set of contacts within the government, and to cultivate a broad range of contacts. In a Washington policy community marked by thousands of competing interests, lobbying is a game of information, of cooperation, and of anticipation of the actions of others. The typical American interest group is involved in such a wide range of policy areas and such a diverse set of issues that they cannot follow a "one size fits all" policy in choosing their lobbying tactics.

### STRATEGIES AND TACTICS OF LOBBYING

The surveys discussed in this chapter so far have done a good job of enumerating various tactics of lobbying but have not gone far in explaining how lobbyists devise their strategies. Considering the broad range of issues in which the typical group is active, as our review of the Walker data and Salisbury's findings make clear, it would be unrealistic to assume that groups behave similarly in all those different areas. This brings us to the distinction that Lester Milbrath made between tactics and strategies (1963, 41; see also Berry 1977, 212). Tactics describe the individual external activities in which groups engage: meeting with legislators, filing suit, or mounting an advertising campaign. Strategies involve some particular combination of tactics and imply a mechanism by which influence is believed to be achieved. Strategies are combinations of tactics used in particular situations. Groups may have similar repertoires of tactics available for use, but their strategies of lobbying will vary depending on such factors as the issue at hand, the predispositions of those making the decision, and the strategies of others attempting to influence the same policymakers.

The large-scale surveys of interest groups have contributed a general agreement that groups make use of a wide range of tactics to influence policy, and they have shown that the types of tactics used have remained surprisingly constant over the years. Still, we are far from able to resolve the fiercely fought debates over interest-group strategies laid out in the previous chapter. Do interest groups use these tactics to inform their friends or pressure their enemies? What makes a group turn to attempts to influence the public rather than keeping its fight within its beltway issue network? Thanks to the surveys, we know much about how groups use particular tactics, but little about how they choose their strategies.

Jeffrey Berry identified four different types of interest-group strategies, which he defined as a "general, long-term approach to lobbying" (1977, 253). His definition is slightly different than the one we use here, but there are important similarities. The four strategies of lobbying he focused on were (1) law, which includes the tactics of litigation and administrative interventions; (2) confrontation, which includes protests, whistle-blowing, share-holders' actions, releasing research results, and public relations; (3) information, which includes such tactics as releasing research results, engaging in public relations campaigns, making personal presentations to government decision makers (direct lobbying), and congressional testimony; and (4) constituency influence, which covers such tactics as organizing letter-writing campaigns, setting up contacts by influential group members, publicizing voting records, and making campaign contributions (1977, 263). According to Berry, the choice of these strategies of lobbying would depend both on internal group characteristics and on the external political context (see also and Schlozman and Tierney 1986). Examples of organizational characteristics that would be expected to affect the choice of strategies would be such things as resource availability (does the group have a legal staff?) and the personal predispositions of staff members. Political context would include the salience of the issue, the degree of conflict involved, and the receptiveness of government officials to the group's position. Berry argued that groups would tailor their lobbying strategies on the basis of their internal capabilities and to fit the nature of the issue at hand. His notion of strategies thus includes the key distinction that we make between general tendencies and applications to particular issues. Strategies are the application of sets of tactics to particular issues. They are a result of both internal organizational variables and the political context. They differ from group to group but also from issue to issue.

Data from surveys of interest groups have often been used to support the idea that group resources and organizational structure are important influences on lobbying strategies and tactic choice (Berry 1977; Schlozman and Tierney 1986; Knoke 1990a; Walker 1991; also see J. Wilson 1973 for a theoretical discussion). Schlozman and Tierney find, for example, that citizen groups are much less likely to make campaign contributions to candidates than are corporations, unions, and trade groups; unions and citizen groups are more likely to publicize voting records and use direct-mail fund raising. They note, however, that the similarities among the groups are more striking than the differences. As we discussed earlier, most interest groups make use of a wide variety of tactics, so most groups report using the majority of listed tactics.

While surveys of interest groups have paid a good deal of attention to testing the idea that internal organizational characteristics affect the choice of strategies, for the most part their data do not allow direct tests of the effects of external explanatory variables. An analysis conducted by Gais and Walker (1991), however, did test the importance of one external variable as well as several internal variables in determining tactic choice. Using factor analysis, Gais and Walker divide the tactics groups used into "inside strategies" and "outside strategies" depending on whether the strategy would be used by groups that are insiders to the political process or groups that are outside the dominant political subsystem (1991, 110). Insider tactics included legislative lobbying, administrative lobbying, litigating, and electioneering. Outside tactics included protesting, providing speakers, and sponsoring lay conferences. Working with the media loaded as both an inside and outside tactic.

Gais and Walker predicted that groups' choice of whether to use an "inside" strategy of direct lobbying or an "outside" strategy of grass-roots lobbying would be determined by internal resources, the character of the group's membership, the group's sources of financial support, and the degree of conflict faced, as measured by a question asking whether the group "usually" faced conflict in its policy arena. They found that groups highly reliant on patrons tended to use outside strategies more often, as did citizen groups. Profit groups tended to use inside strategies; mixed and nonprofit sector groups hovered around the median (1991, 114–15). High reported levels of conflict were strongly associated with reported use of inside lobbying tactics among all group types, and citizen and nonprofit groups were more likely to turn to outside lobbying tactics if they reported high levels of conflict. The more conflict, the more lobbying reported.

Explanations of lobbying strategies based on group resources are an important first step, but a complete model obviously must consider the context of the lobbying situation. In the model presented by Gais and Walker (1991), regression analysis produced a statistical explanation of only 30 percent of the variation in strategies. Three sources of noise can potentially explain this low predictive power: aggregation across the different tactics groups use; aggregation across the different policy domains where they are active; and aggregation from the issue to the issue-area. In the first case, since survey data show that most groups use many types of tactics, "insider" groups also sometimes use "outsider" tactics and vice versa. Secondly, if most groups are active in multiple policy arenas, as we showed above they are, the groups may face conflict in some areas but not in others. Even if a group was only active in a single policy area, it would likely still be involved in a number of different issues and would tailor its lobbying strategies to the issue at hand. Since the same groups may use both inside and outside strategies and operate in both conflictual and nonconflictual domains, any analysis that uses the group rather than the issue as the unit of analysis will find much of its explanatory value devoured by these problems of aggregation.

Why are surveys so bad at teaching us about group strategies? Our argument in this chapter is that it is because most surveys ask groups to generalize across issues, thus obscuring a great deal of information. This is a serious problem only if most groups face a variety of different political contexts in their work. If most groups deal in only one policy area and that area is relatively homogeneous, then there is no reason to think that asking them to generalize across issues will cause a significant loss of information. Our review of the evidence concerning the number of issue-areas that American groups regularly are involved in makes it clear, however, that lobbyists cannot rely on a single strategy. While they are constrained by their internal resources, they must adopt their plans to the situation at hand. The large percentage of unexplained variance in the Gais and Walker analysis suggests that there is still much to be learned about lobbying strategies, despite the progress of the large-scale surveys of the 1980s.

## CONCLUSION

Our review of the large-scale surveys of lobbying convinces us of two things: groups engage in a wide variety of lobbying tactics, and scholars have yet to explain how they choose among those tactics. The surveys have allowed significant progress in many areas, and their findings have been remarkably robust in spite of differences in methodology. The next step in understanding lobbying strategies must include choosing the best from the contextually rich but confusing literature on case studies we reviewed in chapter 7 and the broad surveys we reviewed in this chapter.

While none of the studies we have reviewed argues that we should ignore the context of lobbying, we still have relatively little data about the choice and effectiveness of particular lobbying strategies. Relatively few people have made it a point to study a wide variety of cases of policymaking to assess these decisions or their implications. Past research on interest-group lobbying behavior has for the most part been based either on case studies or on surveys in which respondents were asked to generalize over a large number of cases. Both methods of research have taught us much about the behavior of lobbyists and organized interests, but a methodological hurdle prevents them from successfully testing theories about group strategies. While one type of study—the broad-based surveys—lacks data about specific issues on which to test such theories, the other type—policy case studies—typically includes such a limited number of issues that generalization to the interest-group system is all but impossible.

The detailed description of political circumstances provided by case studies has suggested that contextual variables—including salience, conflict, and the behavior of other actors—are of great importance in influencing the choice of tactics by interest groups. Unlike most surveys of interest groups, policy case studies use the issue, not the group, as the unit of analysis. Comparing across cases is difficult, however, since research questions and methods vary as widely as the substance of the cases studied, as we reviewed in chapter 7. Broad-based surveys of interest groups solve the problem of generalizability and have done an excellent job of assessing the importance of group structure and resources to strategies of lobbying. There is a limit, however, to what we can know through a focus only on internal characteristics of groups rather than also including information on the context of their lobbying efforts. By averaging across issues, many theoretically important variables are aggregated away. Groups are asked to generalize about their behavior across issues, despite indications that most groups are involved in multiple issue-areas and use different tactics depending on the circumstances. As a result, the predictive power of models of interest-group behavior has been low.

The problem is that both types of studies lack variance on the policy dimension. They often look either at a single case of policymaking or consider no specific cases of policymaking. As a result, many potentially important explanatory variables are held constant within each study. Critical variables are designed into the project as constants or remain unmeasured. Most of the recent large-scale studies of interest groups have concerned themselves with questions of bias in the group system, and have thus focused primarily on which types of groups are more likely to be active and to use which types of tactics. All of the survey researchers agree that the external political context is an important determinant of interest-group decision-making, and yet the surveys for the most part do not systematically collect information about that context.

If interest groups must cope with a variety of political contexts, then their answers regarding which lobbying strategies they adopt will certainly depend on that context. As scholars designed a series of broad surveys of group activities in the 1980s, they knew that behaviors depended on context, but they were so concerned with broad issues of how groups mobilize and what types of tactics are most common overall that they failed to link their questions on group activities to any precise cases of policymaking (with the notable exception of Heinz et al. 1993, as mentioned above). Generalizing from the case-study literature was impossible because of the wide and unmeasured variation in context. Generalizing from the survey literature about the choice of strategies is impossible as well because there is typically no variation in context. Somehow, scholars must solve the problem of how to build in sensitivity to the contexts of policymaking with broad surveys of group behavior.

Although past survey questions for the most part have asked interest-group leaders to generalize across issues, thus obscuring any contextual information, there is no reason why this must be the case. John Kingdon's well-known study of congressional decision making (1989) was based on fieldwork in which he asked members of Congress to answer questions about their decision making in the context of particular issues. Could we not do the same with interest groups? In fact is has been done: the interviews conducted by Heinz et al. (1993) posed questions in relation to eighty different specific issues, and other interest-group research (e.g., Browne 1995, Laumann and Knoke 1987) has taken a similar approach. For the most part, however, surveys have tended to ask groups what they "usually" do, not what they did in a particular case.

# CHAPTER 9

# Learning from Experience

IN THIS BOOK, we have reviewed a wide range of literature on the activities and importance of interest groups in American politics during the past century, with particular emphasis on the period since 1945. Interest groups have been a central feature of American politics since the founding of the republic. Since George Washington, political leaders and commentators of all types have consistently argued that no full understanding of the political system can be had without a full understanding of the roles, motivations, and effectiveness of organized interests. The framers of the Constitution expressly considered the problem of how to handle "factions," as indicated by their discussions of the problem, especially in *Federalist* No. 10. Groups have been central to our conception of how the government operates, and indeed to how our government was designed, since the beginning. Politicians and political commentators have never wavered from this view of the importance of groups in politics.

Political scientists have generally agreed with the politicians about the importance of groups. However, throughout the preceding chapters, we have reviewed a great ambivalence on the part of scholars for the study of groups. At times, political scientists, sociologists, and others have put groups at the core of their theories and analytical frameworks. At other times, however, groups have received scant attention; political scientists have focused on other institutions or on the mass public in general, ignoring the roles of groups or relegating them to a marginal role.

Why should political scientists put groups at the center of their analytical frameworks and theories of politics during some periods but allot groups scarce space on the scholarly agenda at other times? The answer clearly does not lie in the importance of groups in politics. This has been a constant throughout history, whereas scholarly attention has waxed and waned. The answer seems to be related to the abilities of scholars to design research projects that address important questions about the roles of groups in politics and provide convincing evidence. The study of groups harbors many analytical pitfalls; many of the most important activities and characteristics of groups have proven extremely difficult to study in a systematic manner. Without good evidence about what groups do and why, scholars have often moved on to other topics. In this concluding chapter, we review our findings about the state of the literature on groups, discussing its development, problems, and prospects. We review some of the reasons for our discipline's ambivalent stance toward the study of groups, then focus our attention on what scholars must do to make the study of groups as important in political science as groups are widely acknowledged to be in politics.

## LEARNING FROM SUCCESS

We began our book with a discussion in chapter 1 about areas of advance, areas of avoidance, and areas of confusion. The individual accomplishments of scholars investigating the roles of groups are considerable. Five particular areas of advance deserve consideration: Mobilization studies; the large-scale surveys; domain studies; studies of social movements; and comparative studies of the policy roles of groups. This is certainly not an exhaustive list, but in these areas we have considerably better understandings of the roles of groups now than two generations ago.

Perhaps the greatest advances have come in our collective knowledge about interest mobilization. Since Olson laid out his theory of collective action three decades ago, scholars have outlined and tested theories related to differential propensities to mobilize to attain political goals. Political scientists can say with much greater certainty today than a generation ago that the entry of the American public into the interest-group system is biased in important ways. We know about these biases from studies of the memberships of particular groups discussed in chapter 4, from the surveys of individual participation in groups that were discussed in chapter 5, and from the studies and surveys of the group system discussed in chapters 6 and 8. We know about the type of people who tend to join groups, we know what groups do to attract those people, and we know which types of groups tend to be more successful and represented in greater numbers than others. The group system is differentially populated by the well-to-do and the well educated, and the groups represented in the system are far more likely to be related to occupations and concentrated monetary interests than to intangible or diffuse interests.

The large-scale surveys of interest groups also have taught us much about the various tactics groups use in their attempts to influence policy. As we saw in chapter 8, these findings about tactics have proved quite robust. Despite significant differences in sampling methods, sampling universes, and question wording, the use of various tactics is paralleled throughout a wide range of interest-group surveys conducted over the past twenty years. Direct lobbying and testimony at hearings are among the most commonly used tactics, for example, whether the lobbyists are in Washington or in state capitals, and whether they represent businesses or public interest groups. While there are differences among the different types of groups—

and among the various surveys—the similarities are more striking than the differences.

Particular domains within the interest-group universe have also been well documented. For instance, within the agricultural policy domain, studies have shown not only how interest groups and legislators usually interact but how those interactions have varied over time and across circumstances. Agricultural policy in Washington has been known among political scientists as a classic policy subsystem, with plenty of reciprocal backscratching among bureaucrats, legislators, and interest groups, but the domain studies have shown us how these relationships have varied. Interest groups involved in agricultural policy have fared worse when they were seen as lacking electoral clout (Hansen 1991), when they were interested in food stamps rather than grain price supports (Berry 1984b), or when nonagricultural committees claimed jurisdiction over issues that affected agricultural interest groups (Browne 1995, 142–48; for a more limited test see Jones, Baumgartner, and Talbert 1993). Health policy, energy policy, and labor policy have also been extensively studied. Where these studies have been most successful, they have integrated information about the behavior of governmental actors with information about interest-group actors, and either explicitly or implicitly considered the nature of the issues involved, how those issues were presented, and the electoral implications of those presentations.

Comparative studies of social movements remain a vibrant and active area in political science and sociology. A recent edited volume (McAdam, McCarthy, and Zald 1996) presents a variety of studies focusing on three elements of sociological explanations: the political opportunity structure afforded by the actions and institutions of the state; the mobilizing structures or the organizations that attempt to channel the efforts of the social movement; and the concept of cultural framings, or the ways in which ideas are presented to support the social movement and/or to discredit the regime against which the movement is struggling. Social movements face serious problems of mobilization but also a wide variety of solutions to their dilemmas.

Comparative studies of the roles of groups have similarly integrated the study of group activities with an analysis of their relations with government agencies. Indeed, the literature on corporatism, pluralism, statism, and group-state relations in general in comparative politics has focused almost exclusively on documenting the range of relations between government agencies and groups as they make policy. Groups in comparative politics are typically not studied in isolation; they are discussed insofar as their relations with government authorities help explain the constraints on government policies in various countries. In a comparative perspective, groups are part of a context that structures the behaviors of governments, and government agencies are part of a context that structures the actions of groups. Groups are studied as part of a broader context, rarely in isolation. This analytic strategy stands in sharp contrast to much of what we have observed in American politics. While the comparative literature on groups is not without its flaws, one positive element is its attention to the context of group behaviors.

Noting these examples of advance in interest-group research does not imply that good individual studies are not common outside those areas or that all studies within those areas are worthy of emulation. Rather, considering the studies as a group, these areas have provided a much more fruitful research agenda than many other areas of interest-group research, taken collectively. Why is this? What do these studies have in common that scholars might learn from or try to emulate? There are three important parts to such an explanation: theoretical coherence, scope, and attention to context.

The mobilization studies have made as much progress as they have because they share a unifying paradigm, the collective-action logic laid out by Olson. It has not been the vastness of their data sets or the cleverness of their research designs that has brought advance, but rather the fact that they share a common theoretical outlook. A great diversity of scholars have used a wide range of methods to investigate various elements of the puzzle of group mobilization. As we reviewed in chapters 4, 5, and 6, these scholars do not agree on all elements of their findings or even how to interpret each of their findings. But they share a common set of questions so that the implications of the conclusions from one study are typically apparent to the authors of the next. No single study has been organized to investigate all elements of the collective-action dilemma. The studies in this area are not particularly noteworthy for their large scope, though some of the large surveys have important evidence on parts of the collective-action question. Rather, the distinguishing feature of this part of the literature is its conceptual framework. This situation stands in sharp contrast to other areas, where scholars have worked in relative theoretical isolation from each other, not just using a different set of tools but indeed asking different questions. So one route to advance is theoretical coherence. This coherence does not imply rigidity or unswerving devotion to a given explanation but simply that scholars are investigating parts of the same puzzle.

To say that an area of the literature has benefited from the relative coherence of its theoretical perspective is little help to those working in areas where no single perspective merits such domination. Of course theoretical clarity is better than anarchy, but integrating theories cannot be wished into existence; paradigms do not unify by decree. When we noted the problems in much of the literature on lobbying in chapter 7, we noted the range of theoretical questions that various scholars investigated. This by itself is not a fatal flaw. There are many different questions of interest in the study of lobbying, and there is no reason to expect a single perspective to be useful in investigating all of them. In those areas of the study of groups where many different research questions require the use of many different theoretical perspectives, there remain some important lessons. First, we need to avoid the false hope that findings from a myriad of small studies will accumulate in these areas as they do in areas such as collective action. Without a common theory, the number of studies may grow indefinitely without ever accumulating into a coherent set of conclusions. So studies in these areas should be large enough to support a solid set of conclusions on their own rather than aspiring only to fill a small gap in the literature, hoping that other studies will successively fill the others. In areas with less theoretical coherence, small-scale studies are not guaranteed to add up to anything in particular, even as hundreds of them accumulate. Second, considering the importance of context in determining group behaviors, studies in these areas need to pay careful attention to the environmental determinants of group behaviors. Studies of large scope with attention to context will help the literature develop greater theoretical coherence.

The surveys of interest groups have been successful in large part simply because of their great size. By gathering a wide variety of data from a wide range of groups, they have shown us a great deal about the memberships and activities of groups. These data not only provide us with a description of the interest-group system, they have been used to test theories about the nature of groups and could provide the basis of some of the assumptions made in formal models of group behavior. Without these surveys, most of our baseline information about the size and activities of organized interests would not exist. The relatively large samples and careful sampling techniques of these surveys have contributed to the reliability of these data, as discussed in chapter 8. Most importantly, the interpretation of the results of the large surveys of group activities does not depend on the comparison of the findings of one study with those of others. This stands in contrast to the quantitative case-study literature on lobbying behaviors, for example, where a finding that certain groups used outside lobbying strategies would have to be put in context with other studies based on other cases in order to be interpreted most effectively. The large surveys, by contrast, have provided a set of important findings partly because they are large enough to stand alone. In the absence of a strong and widely shared theoretical perspective, this is especially important.

The domain studies, the social movement studies, and the comparative research projects have been successful for a different reason. While most of these studies are fairly large in scale, at least in comparison to many of the PAC and lobbying studies discussed in chapter 7, their relative success has been due in large part to their attention to the political context in which groups operate. Rather than focusing narrowly on the interest group or groups in question at a single point in time, these studies have tended to include a wide range of actors involved in the policy process, and often to consider their actions over time. This allows them to study the dynamics of the interactions of these actors over time and across situations. This has enormous implications for theory-building, as it pushes authors to investigate hypotheses about the dynamics of the relations among interest groups and governmental officials. Most of the important questions in the study of lobbying have to do with how groups relate to government officials, what determines the structure of these relations, and what effects these relations have on policy outputs and representation. Studies that have been most successful have integrated the study of groups with the study of their partners in the policy process.

Our review of some particular areas of success should certainly convince no one that these areas harbor no important unanswered questions. Indeed they do. Some consideration of what remains to be done even within the areas of relative success shows the importance of our three factors: context, scope, and theory. For example, within the general area of group mobilization, Olson's logic and set of questions only take the literature so far. This perspective helps to predict who will organize and who will lobby, but not what the effects of those efforts will be. We have pointed out that the studies of collective action have imposed an opportunity cost that has hurt studies of the external activities of groups over the decades. And even within the collective action research paradigm, questions remain unanswered. Why, for instance, do some disadvantaged groups manage to organize while others do not? We have many partial theories and many case studies here, but no conclusive evidence or convincing overall demonstrations. Why do some potential members with a strong interest in an organization's collective goal join, while others do not? To answer these questions requires more than a simple model, more than a small-scale study with one or two groups. To answer these questions requires information about the political contexts in which the groups and individuals find themselves. Many researchers are beginning to conclude that understanding individual motivations is not enough. Being provided the opportunity to participate matters greatly (see, e.g., Schlozman, Verba, and Brady 1995; Huckfeldt and Sprague 1992, 1995). The simple fact of being asked to join is enough to move many people out of their lethargy (Walsh and Warland 1983; Johnson 1995). The political environment, not only individual motivations, is a primary determinant of which groups fail and which thrive (Hunter et al. 1991; Gray and Lowery 1996). Olson provided us with a theory of how individual-level motivations affect the group system; the next step is to consider the contextual and macro-level forces that help shape those motivations and the system itself.

The large-scale surveys of interest groups have done an excellent job of providing us with answers about what groups do, but they tell us little about when and how and why they do these things. The reason, as we laid out in chapter 8, is that the surveys are for the most part not linked to issues. Again, they lack information about the political context, about the institutions and environments that shape interest-group choices. The domain studies discussed in chapter 7 successfully integrate information about other political institutions and the political context into their research, but generalizations often prove difficult. Although the domain studies may have information about many issues and often cover many years, the nagging questions will remain: Is agricultural policy just different from other types of policy? Does what we learned about energy policy hold true in other areas? Why or why not?

Scholars after 1970 have often defined lobbying activities quite narrowly. In the search for analytic tractability, the behaviors of groups have often been studied in isolation from the complexities of the policy process. Studies have tended either to focus narrowly on a single issue at a single point in the policy process, or have taken an opposite approach, using surveys to ask groups to generalize about their experiences across time and over many issues. The first approach creates a case study in which many potentially important variables—issue type, policy domain, public opinion, conflict, scope, salience—are held constant. The second approach aggregates across these same important variables. The next generation of studies should combine the sensitivity to context of the case study and the generalizability of the survey. As it stands, neither approach so far has succeeded in creating a broad view of group lobbying activities with sensitivity to political context.

## AVOIDANCE AND CONFUSION

The literature on interest groups has taught us much about the tactics groups use and how many groups of various kinds there are. It has encouraged scholars to become much more systematic in the ways in which they study groups. But despite the advances reviewed in the previous section, there remain significant areas of avoidance and confusion within the literature on groups. We are more systematic in our studies, but our knowledge is narrow, leaving many important gaps. In particular, though we have many studies of lobbying, we have few strong conclusions about effectiveness or the conditions of group power. The few studies that have attempted to draw such conclusions have been circumscribed efforts to measure the effect of direct lobbying or campaign contributions on a few congressional votes. It is unsurprising that this area of the literature should be the source of the greatest confusion and the most contradictions. The empirical base is narrow and most scholars have avoided adding to it other than one case at a time. The large-scale surveys of the 1980s are notable in part because they stand alone;

few have followed in this tradition in spite of the visibility and influence that these large projects have had.

Having reviewed these sources of avoidance and confusion throughout this book, what conclusions can we draw from them? In the previous section we discussed reasons for some of the successes in the interest-group literature; in this section, we address some of the explanations for avoidance and confusion. Difficulties within the literature seem to stem primarily from two sources, one technical and one conceptual. The technical problem is that studies tend to be too small; the conceptual problem is that they are too isolated. The problems are related.

### The Small Scale of Interest-Group Research

One striking feature of the literature, and one that could easily be rectified, is the modest scope of most empirical studies. To illustrate this feature of the literature, we consider every article on interest groups published in the *APSR* since 1950. Of the 123 articles (see appendix), forty-one were qualitative essays and thirteen presented a formal theory offering no systematic treatment of data. Excluding those studies leaves us with sixty-nine studies, each of which tests some theoretical propositions of the group system. Limiting ourselves only to these studies, we ask three simple questions: How many issues were analyzed; how many domains; and how many groups? The results are presented in table 9.1.

**TABLE 9.1**
Limited Empirical Scope of *APSR* Articles on Interest Groups

|  | None | One | 2–5 | >5 |
| --- | --- | --- | --- | --- |
| Number of issues analyzed | 27 | 24 | 6 | 12 |
| Number of domains analyzed | 19 | 36 | 8 | 6 |
| Number of groups analyzed | 7 | 14 | 16 | 32 |

Studies on groups published in the discipline's top journal during the postwar years reflect the nature of the literature in an important way. Whereas many of the essays and reviews may have been broad, the quantitative studies have typically featured extremely narrow empirical bases. Forty percent of the quantitative studies discuss no particular policy issue at all; of those forty-two studies that do consider specific issues, twenty-four are based on only one issue. Only twelve studies base their conclusions on a study of more than five issues. Looking at the number of policy domains discussed shows a similar trend: Only six studies consider issues in more than five domains. Even the number of groups analyzed is surprisingly small. Only thirty-two articles have been published in the *APSR* during almost a half-century that report in a quantitative manner on the activities of more than five groups.

We have also noted the research designs used in these sixty-nine articles in order to see if the narrow empirical scope of these projects might be justified somehow by a complicated experimental design, or perhaps a longitudinal approach that would require the intensive analysis of a small number of groups. This is not the case. The single most common design, used in forty of the articles, was a cross-sectional comparison at a single point in time. Longitudinal designs covering less than ten years were used in twelve articles; longitudinal designs covering more than ten years were used in thirteen articles; the other articles used a combination of designs.

According to this analysis, then, the modal type of interest-group study in the premier journal of political science over the postwar period is a cross-sectional comparison of a few groups working on a single issue at one point in time. Such a research approach seems a perfect strategy for producing unexplained variation between studies. It is a recipe for the creation of a contradictory and noncumulative literature. Each study provides such a narrow base from which to generalize, with so little contextual information provided to link the studies, that confusion is inevitable. Each study may stand on its own, but how are they to be compared? We can trace confusion in this literature, therefore, not only to the ambiguities of measurement and of definition that we discussed in chapter 2 but also to the emphasis on the intensive and small-scale analysis of an extremely limited data set. Each study may individually be designed to answer its particular question, but, given the choice, no scholar would probably choose to organize an entire literature on the basis of such a set of studies as we see in table 9.1. Indeed, if given the assignment to organize a literature and a collective set of research projects best suited to produce no common conclusions, one could scarcely imagine a better way to do it than what we observe here.

The bright side to our analysis of published work in the *APSR* is that trends seem to be favoring the larger, empirically more substantial studies. Although one-shot, cross-sectional studies remain as common as ever, eight of the twelve studies analyzing more than five issues were published after 1980. Likewise, twenty-five of the thirty-two studies analyzing more than five groups were published after 1980. This pattern is an encouraging move in the right direction. We expect that technological innovation should make it easier for scholars to engage in larger-scale projects. Our analysis here should help convince scholars that we need to take advantage of these possibilities to improve the empirical base on which our theories must ultimately rest.

## *Attention to Context*

The second source of problems within the literature is conceptual and has to do with studying interest groups in isolation. This is related to the problem of studies resting on too narrow an empirical base, in that studying a single interest group at a single point in time will certainly not teach us anything about dynamics, but the issue extends beyond the mere size of the data set. Increasing the scope of study is important not simply for reasons of reliability, but for reasons of validity. That is, we increase the size of our data sets so that we can say with assurance that our findings are generalizable. But we must increase the breadth of our data sets—adding in variables for the actions of other interest groups, for the actions of government officials, for the degrees of conflict and public salience represented by the issues in question—because we know that group activities are likely to be decided in large part on the basis of contextual factors. We can ignore the context and hope that our findings will prove robust on average, but the more sophisticated strategy is to build contextual factors into our studies. This strategy stands in contrast to some prominent trends. Scholars have often been careful to isolate their studies, narrowly defining them around a particular aspect of group behavior. Larger studies, with greater attention to context, are likely to be more fruitful.

One example of the temptation for restrictive models of group behavior is in the deduction of hypotheses concerning group behavior in a one-shot game, whereas group behavior in the real world is almost always part of an ongoing and often long-term relationship. Isolating a single movement out of an iterated process is likely to lead to dramatically different equilibrium outcomes than that which would result from studying that process over time (see Trivers 1971; Axelrod 1981, 1984; Goodin 1984; Ostrom 1990; Hansen 1991). This is essentially what scholars are doing when they attempt to study the effects of lobbying by looking at the results of a single roll-call vote. Many important elements of the policy process, such as cue-taking, agenda-setting, and manipulation of issue definitions, cannot be explained without explicit attention to the social and temporal context of lobbying. These behaviors make no sense in the one-shot case, but they are known to be fundamental to what groups do. Heinz et al. (1993), Browne and Paik (1993), Browne (1995), and Nownes and Freeman (forthcoming) all describe policy communities where most actors spend large proportions of their time monitoring the activities of others. If all the policymakers are spending so much time monitoring the environment, and if they are all monitoring the same events, then their actions will be determined not independently, but often in rapid response to commonly perceived threats and opportunities. The importance of expectations of the behaviors of others in determining group behaviors can be seen in such works as Chong's (1991) description of the civil rights movement, Marwell and Oliver's (1993) description of the role of social groups in overcoming the collective-action dilemma, or in Rothenberg's (1992) description of how Common Cause chose to focus its lobbying efforts on the MX missile program after concluding that its traditional priority of campaign reform had little hope of passage at the time. Rather than fight a losing battle with few allies, groups and individuals often prefer to join a winning coalition. Similarly, models and studies of lobbying that limit their attention to the actions of interest groups ignore that legislators often prefer to take voting cues from each other (see McFarland 1984; Schlozman and Tierney 1986; Kingdon 1989; Walker 1991). In sum, there are a number of factors related to the contexts of group behavior that make it especially unlikely for significant improvements in our collective knowledge to come from studies that design the context out of the study.

In studies of policymaking and lobbying, attention to the substance of the policy debate can be essential. Policies are made in government through a process of argumentation. Groups are most influential when they can be effective in promoting a particular issue-definition. In their primer for lobbyists entitled *How to Win in Washington*, explaining how the Washington policy process works, the first piece of advice that Ernest and Elisabeth Wittenberg give is "Define the issue" (1994, 13). Increasingly, scholars are coming to note the importance of argumentation, issue-definition, and agenda-setting in public policy. Without attention to the behaviors of other actors and the changing nature of the issue itself, lobbying may look like a pressure game or simple transfer of information, as it once was modeled. But lobbying, especially in today's crowded arena, is dedicated in large part to directing limited attention to particular pieces of information or particular aspects of an issue. These efforts at agenda-setting, issue definition, and framing do more to determine winners and losers in politics than any arm-twisting before the final roll-call vote.

Many of the most influential recent books on groups and the policy process share a contextually rich view of the policy process, such as Hansen's (1991) work on access and influence among farmers, McFarland's (1993) review of cooperation between environmental and business interests in making decisions about mining policy, Heinz and colleagues' (1993) survey of lobbyists and group leaders in a variety of areas, or Browne's (1995) study of congressional decision making on agriculture issues. Each of these works is notable for the combination of theoretically important findings and an ability to integrate variation in the political context into a discussion of group behaviors and influence.

A more recent literature has begun to attempt to build explicit models of issue-definition, framing, and argumentation into studies of lobbying. From

Stone's *Policy Paradox and Political Reason* (1988) or Majone's *Evidence, Argument, and Persuasion in the Policy Process* (1989), we have moved to a new set of studies that attempt to note the importance of argumentation in particular policy debates (also see McKissick 1995). Bryan Jones's 1994 book on decision making, with its attention to the multidimensional nature of most public policy debates, builds on Riker's numerous arguments about the incentives for strategic policymakers to manipulate elements of the public debate to their advantage (see Riker 1983, 1984, 1986, 1990, 1996). These theoretical and case-study efforts to deal with the dimensional structure of politics by paying attention to how policymakers attempt to affect attention to various dimensional elements need to be followed by larger scale and systematic treatments of such issues in a great range of contexts. This will make the literature on lobbying recognizable to a lobbyist. They spend much of their time, after all, attempting to promote certain understandings of their issues. Models of their behavior should recognize this.

The questions raised by this set of scholars are clear. Is it possible to organize large-scale research projects that would illuminate the type of strategies of policymaking that Riker, Jones, and others have argued to be fundamental to politics? Can we generate testable theories about the motivations and abilities of lobbyists to raise new dimensions of issues or otherwise to affect the understanding of a debate? Can we trace efforts at venue-shopping quantitatively? The answer is yes. The empirical literature on lobbying and interest-group relations with government has suffered from a gap between the intensive analysis of lobbying in a single or a few cases on the one hand and the broad generalizations of lobbying behaviors in surveys on the other. There is little justification for the continued dichotomy of context-sensitive case studies and context-insensitive surveys. By collecting information from a generalizable sample of groups about their behaviors across a range of issues, we can solve some fundamental issues in this literature.

Case studies and theoretical work have shown important elements of lobbying to be related to questions of issue-definition and political context. These important topics can be studied only in the context of a particular policy issue. But for each scholar to discuss them only for a single issue leaves the literature open to the accumulation of more incomparable case studies. The solution must lie either in the development of a set of norms and indicators that would make case studies comparable or in the design of context-sensitive studies that cover not only many groups, but many issues and many policy domains as well.

Our review of the literature shows a great number of contradictions and difficulties. It should be clear that the explanation for this has very little to do with the quality of individual studies and very much to do with the lack of a shared general paradigm, a tendency to try to isolate interest-group behavior rather than integrate it into the rest of politics, and the extremely narrow empirical base on which so many studies are based. The lack of a central paradigm is not unusual within the social sciences, and although we may work toward the development of such a paradigm, there are no easy fixes. We can, however, change the way we study interest groups to make our research broader and more sensitive to context. In the next section we will lay out several research designs—all of which have been used at least once—that would allow scholars to make this change.

## BUILDING A NEW LITERATURE ON INTEREST GROUPS, AGAIN

The research designs laid out here are not meant to be exhaustive, but rather suggestive. All are designs that others could emulate, and although some of them represent well-funded efforts by senior scholars, others are dissertation projects. The designs have in common a combination of attention to the behavior of groups and to their political contexts, and samples that span multiple issue areas.

### *Doing It All*

Heinz, Laumann, Nelson, and Salisbury (1993) have put together the largest and one of the most painstakingly designed interest-group projects ever to be undertaken. Their project is admirable because it combines many of the benefits of domain studies—attention to issues and to the behaviors of multiple policy actors—with the study of four different policy domains, allowing their conclusions to be more reliably generalizable. The project did take more than a decade of work by four senior scholars, and it received significant funding both from the American Bar Association and the National Science Foundation. The scale of the project is certainly not one that everyone could replicate, but aspects of the project may be emulated relatively simply, especially its use of multiple types of policy actors and the way in which it ties information about lobbying to information about particular issues.

The ways in which these scholars selected their respondents were complex and multilayered, and we will not detail them here. What is important for this discussion is that their sample included not only a random sample of more than three hundred organized interests, weighted toward the most politically active, but also included nearly eight hundred of the lobbyists they retained and about three hundred government officials with whom they had dealings. The project did not assume that lobbyists worked in a vacuum, or that the behavior of other actors would be unimportant, but systematically took account of those other actors. A second way in which the research design of this project is worth emulating is in its use of specific issues on which to base its questions. The researchers selected twenty issues in each of the four policy areas they studied, and based many of their questions about lobbying on those issues. This allowed them to combine information about the issue with information about what the lobbyists did.

This combination of data allowed these scholars to demonstrate that there is no central core of interest-group decision makers ruling the policy process. Interest groups of all types were characterized as battling uncertainty in Washington, spending most of their time monitoring the activities of other policy actors rather than actively lobbying officials. Only a design this broad would have allowed them to state convincingly that "major policy decisions are not made by closed circles of interest groups and . . . numerous interest groups monitor any given policy question and consider taking a more active role in the debate" (Heinz et al. 1993, 380). Basing their study on a set of eighty particular issues across four domains allowed the interviews to focus not on generalizations and central tendencies, but on activities in a particular context familiar to the respondent. The broad empirical scope of the project ensures that it will continue to be used as a point of reference for years to come.

### Network Analysis

The Heinz et al. project is of course part of a broader research paradigm more common in sociology than in political science, but it merits greater attention in our discipline. Network analysis offers the possibility of expanding our understandings of how policymakers relate to each other within established policy subsystems. These studies begin with an enumeration of the set of participants in a given public policy issue or domain, typically taken from publicly available records such as lists of committee witnesses, newspaper accounts, judicial filings, and agency testimony. Interviews are then conducted with a sample of those involved, generally focusing on those who appear on more than one list and who are therefore assumed to be the more central players. Questions can focus on many elements, but typically include substantial coverage of paths of communications. Network analysts then are able to construct a map of communications within a policy domain, noting which actors tend to have relatively central positions within the structure of flow of information and which ones are peripheral or only occasional participants. Further, these studies allow for measures of the density of communication within the domain or issue. Some domains, for example, have relatively dense structures, where a high proportion of participants are in contact with each other; others involve much looser structures where any given participant may be in contact only with a few others. Similarly, some issues involve wide communications and participation by great proportions of those in the domain, whereas other issues attract the participation only of a small set of core participants. These patterns of communications have

implications for levels of conflict, for the diversity of interests able to participate, and for the ease with which policymakers can forge a consensus on
given policy disputes. Properly done, network analyses can be compared
either across issue-domains, showing the relative cohesiveness of various
domains, or across issues, showing the degree to which different issues
within a domain attract the attention of various constellations of network
actors.

Network analysis provides an established set of research methodologies
not only for sampling and interviewing but also for data analysis and presentation, since sociologists have been using the technique for decades. It
avoids the issue of power and influence by focusing on questions of communication patterns; it benefits substantially from its focus in interviews on
particular issues rather than only on general patterns. Analysts can therefore
reach conclusions about how patterns of participation differ across different
types of issues. Political scientists have rarely adopted the methodologies of
network analysis, with the notable exception of Heinz and colleagues (1993).
Partly, this may be because of the large scope of many of the network projects and their attendant costs and time frames. Many of the methods of
network analysis are adaptable for use by political scientists interested in
mapping out patterns of participation on particular issues. Further, use of
these methods would greatly facilitate the comparison of results from one
issue to the next. (For an introduction to the concepts and methods of network analysis, see Knoke 1990b, esp. 163–74; other examples include Laumann and Knoke 1987; Knoke et al. 1996; Laumann, Knoke, and Kim 1985;
Heinz et al. 1993; Knoke and Kuklinski 1982.)


### Context on a Smaller Scale

Leech (1998) also used a design that provided information about particular
issues, their political contexts, and the activities of hundreds of interest
groups, although on a much more modest scale than that undertaken by
Heinz and his colleagues. Leech's project involved a mail survey of nearly
eight hundred interest groups with offices in Washington. Rather than asking groups which lobbying tactics they "usually used" or selecting the issues
beforehand, Leech asked her respondents to identify the issue with which
they had most recently been involved and then to answer a series of questions based on that issue. In addition to questions about the organization and
the lobbying tactics they used in connection with that issue, respondents
were asked a series of questions about the nature of the issue, including
questions about conflict, salience, and the activities of other groups and government officials on that issue. The resulting data set allows the testing of
hypotheses about the circumstances under which interest groups choose

one lobbying strategy over another. Although the sample of issues in the study cannot be said to accurately reflect the universe of all issues, the range of issues involved was quite broad, including many of the most publicized bills of 1996 and many issues that received no outside attention. A sample of issues chosen only from newspapers, Congressional Quarterly, or a list of statutes would not be so broad because such a sample would not include small, quiet issues that no one but the group in question cared about, or issues that were handled through agency rulemaking procedures. Many of the issues cited by respondents were not the primary focus of the bill or rule in question, and some of them never succeeded in reaching the formal agenda.

Scholars may avoid the study of policy issues because no such sample can be guaranteed to be generalizable, but it is worth remembering that perfection is the enemy of progress. In this case it is also logically impossible to attain. The literature stands to gain considerably from a set of research projects building up from the study of the behaviors of many groups operating in many contexts. Kingdon's (1995) study of agenda-setting in health-care and transportation focused on such a design; his study of congressional voting decisions (1989) adopted a similar approach. Baumgartner's study of agenda-setting and strategic policymaking in France (1989) similarly adopted the approach of selecting a range of issues and comparing group behaviors in particular contexts. He noted more variation in behavior by type and salience of the issue than by type of organization involved. Kollman (1998) based his study of groups' decisions to go "outside" in their lobbying efforts on a survey of groups, but he asked each group about their behavior in a range of cases. His design allowed the comparison of hundreds of "group-issue pairs," rather than being limited to generalizations about group decisions in general or in a "typical" case. Each of these examples shows how attention to context can be built into an interview-based study, often for dissertation-scale projects. Leech shows how the technique can be adopted for a much larger mail survey; Heinz and colleagues show the value of the design on a grander scale.

### Working Back from Issues

Marissa Golden (1995) provides another example of the value of studying lobbying behavior in the context of particular decisions. She examined interest-group participation in the federal rulemaking process, collecting data about the groups that submitted written comments during the notice and comment period of the process. Rather than selecting well-known examples of rulemaking or relying on survey responses to assess participation in the process, Golden used the Federal Register to compile a list of eleven issues from three agencies. She then examined the actual comments filed with the agencies for each of those issues. Using the actual comments provides a more reliable indicator of participation than self-reported participation from surveys, but Golden notes that more importantly, "reported participation tells us whether or not groups engage in this behavior but little about who submits comments in specific cases." In other words, most survey research (with some notable exceptions listed above) asks about what the respondent usually does, but not how different cases might attract different sets of interest-group participants. In this research design, the behaviors are studied directly as they relate to a particular case.

Golden's design requires the compilation of a fair amount of contextual information about each issue, which of course puts a limit on the number of issues to be analyzed in a single project. For each case, on the other hand, one can see the range of interest-group participation. In addition, even with this case-intensive collection of data, she was able to analyze several different issues across three disparate agencies (the Environmental Protection Agency, the National Highway Traffic Safety Administration, and the Department of Housing and Urban Development). The results of her study demonstrated a heavy bias toward business participation in the federal rulemaking process, as others had shown before. On the other hand, Golden's approach allowed a greater range of businesses and organizations to come into the project, and there was no doubt that her finding of business advantage could have been an artifact of sampling only organizations listed in directories of lobbyists and interest organizations. Different organizations were active in each of the rules she studied, painting a picture of participation that looked more like an issue network than a rigid subsystem. Many individual businesses became involved in the process, even those without Washington offices. Further, the role of technical experts within the business community was made clear. An innovative research approach led to a number of new findings.

### Qualitative Designs

Of course, quantitative designs are not the only way to assess interest-group participation and influence in the policy process. Mucciaroni (1995) described policymaking in four areas—taxation, business regulation, trade protection, and agricultural subsidies—over several decades to see whether history confirmed his predictions about the conditions under which interest groups would be successful before government. Mucciaroni considered what legislation had passed, read reports in political media like Congressional Quarterly about the general reception groups received, and noted changes in the types and levels of regulations, taxes, duties, and subsidies over time. The policies he considered all had in common concentrated benefits and diffuse costs, as well as strong interest-group support. What then, could account for differences in how successful the supportive groups were over time? Why were farm groups more successful in getting and maintaining subsidies in the 1980s; why did businesses fare worse in controlling regulatory issues after 1970?

Mucciaroni considered the salience of the issue, the way in which it was defined, the institutional context (including the degree of agency autonomy and the rules and procedures governing congressional committees), and group-level variables such as degree of mobilization, level of resources, membership composition, degree of organized opposition, and effectiveness at coalition building. He found limited support for group-level variables. While higher levels of mobilization did coincide with rising fortunes, mobilization itself did not seem to be determinative. The definition of the issue mattered greatly; for example, concentrated producer benefits were sometimes understood to be serving the public good but at other times were not seen in this way. Similarly, the institutional context mattered. The strength of political leadership and the relative insulation of powerful committees from electoral concerns were especially important. In addition, he found that "the main source of countervailing power vis-à-vis entrenched economic interests has been actors in government rather than in society. The policy changes that have come about are not primarily the result of the pushing and hauling of organized interests" (181). While Mucciaroni's findings do not address the roles that interest groups may play in helping redefine issues (only in the effects that existing issue definitions have on group fortunes), his research design does allow him to support mid-level generalizations about the relationships among interest groups, government officials, government institutions that help further our understanding of how the group system operates.

### Scope, Theory, and Context

We have no magic solutions to the difficulties of studying how interest groups behave in the complex environments of national politics. However, we can support a set of simple recommendations based on our review. Areas of the literature that have avoided attention to the context of group behaviors, those that have been home to scores of isolated and small-scale studies but to few larger ones, and areas without any widely shared set of theoretical questions have not developed as well as those areas where one or more of these elements have been present. The solution is more work, but not just any type of work. The work that will rejuvenate the field is that which combines sensitivity to context, is large in its empirical scope, and addresses important theoretical questions. Easier said than done? Certainly. But we have given several examples of works that correspond to a profile that would be recognizable to a lobbyist.

The examples that we have provided are small in number and are designed merely to illustrate that innovative and successful projects likely to move the field forward will follow no rigid rules of design. Some of those we have mentioned are qualitative, others are highly quantified; some are longitudinal, others are cross-sectional designs; some are multiyear, large-scale collaborations between senior scholars, others are dissertation-sized projects. The route to innovation and improvement in the literature does not come from adopting any particular design. On the contrary, progress comes from the accumulation of studies that can be compared with each other. The eclecticism that many have noted in the study of interest groups is indeed a value. The trick is to organize a literature that allows many diverse designs and different approaches to be integrated with each other rather than to stand in elegant isolation.

Three items might be considered before a new research project is undertaken. First, what is the scope of the theoretical conclusions that one would like to support? Typically, we want to be grand in our conclusions. But if we want to be large in our generalizations, we should not be narrow in our gathering of evidence. Reviewing table 9.1 from earlier in this chapter, it seems clear that if scholars had first asked themselves about the breadth of conclusions they would like to support, they would not have decided on the cross-sectional analysis of a single case as the dominant research strategy in the area. Broad conclusions should rest on broad empirical support.

The second item is to consider the adage that a particularly tempting data source may well be "too good to be true." The areas of the literature that have been home to the most confusing collection of contradictory findings have been those where scholars have attempted to make use of data collected by others for a different purpose. Data that come for free are often worth exactly their cost. This is not always the case, but our collective experience with a wealth of studies analyzing the consequences of PAC contributions should clearly demonstrate that the mere availability of data on a small number of variables will not lead to any particular advances unless these data are combined with equally impressive data on the other theoretically important variables. Careful consideration of this item would likely lead to much more significant investments in data gathering. Typically, publicly available data sources give information only on a small fraction of the variables that would be necessary to test a model of group behavior. They are a first step not a panacea.

Finally, the third item for consideration is the degree to which a research project can be made to fit in with, rather than stand out from, a body of theoretically related literature. Studies that fill gaps within a coherent intellectual body of knowledge may safely be smaller in scope and narrower in focus than studies that have the ambition to propose a new theoretical approach. In sum, the literature demonstrates that successful projects and successful parts of the literature have benefited from a coherent set of research questions; from studies large in scope; and from studies with considerable attention to the context of group behavior.

## CONCLUSION

Why should political scientists care about interest-group studies? What about organized interests is relevant to our understanding of the political system? Once the need to pose such questions would have been inconceivable. Politics was virtually defined as the struggle between groups; the study of groups equaled the study of politics. This came to be true in large part because of the pivotal questions being posed by interest-group scholars of a generation ago: Who wields power in a democracy? How are people represented before government? How does the policy process work? The answers to these questions had important implications for all areas of political science, and interest-group studies thus were unarguably of central relevance.

Although studies of interest groups once routinely succeeded in posing important questions, they were often far less successful in answering those questions. The measurement of power, in particular, stymied researchers and led to hotly debated and contradictory conclusions. The group approach to politics was criticized as unsystematic, unscientific, and grounded in discredited pluralistic assumptions. Modern-day scholars have attempted to take a more systematic approach to studying groups, and narrowed their focus in an attempt to answer at least some small questions incontrovertibly. Perhaps the topics are less central to political science than the research agenda set out by the old group approach, but at least we get clear answers, or so the argument seems to go.

Unfortunately, the turn toward tractability has not rescued the group literature. Tightly circumscribed and statistically advanced investigations of group power, such as the studies of PAC influence on congressional roll-call votes discussed in chapter 7, have proven to be at least as contradictory and inconclusive as the descriptive community power studies of the previous generation. In addition, rather than solving the problems of measuring power and influence, most scholars have simply ignored the problem, choosing instead to study the internal workings of groups. These internal workings are certainly theoretically interesting, and have important implications for the external political behaviors of groups (although those implications are too seldom studied), but at base they are a side issue. Unless groups play important roles in politics and policymaking, then their internal workings are irrelevant—a curiosity, nothing more. We of course argue, without much fear of contradiction, that groups are important to politics and policymaking. But then should our central focus not be to investigate those roles directly?

We seem faced with a collective action problem for the literature on groups: how can scholars organize their individual projects in a way that not only allows them to reach strong conclusions based on good evidence but also that will allow the literature as a whole to be cumulative rather than contradictory, an ensemble of related findings rather than a cacophony of discordant sounds? The literature on interest groups will have a great impact only if it can combine a focus on important questions of democratic representation with the evidence needed to answer those questions. So far, this has not occurred because scholars have failed either to answer the important questions, or have focused so much on providing convincing evidence that they have been willing to focus on questions that are less than central to the democratic process. Our review of the literature has been designed to illustrate the patterns of progress and to suggest some general guidelines for future improvement that stem logically from experience.

Groups are at the heart of the political process; they are central to the process of representation just as they are key elements of how democratic representation can be distorted through influence and one-sided mobilization. They motivate people in elections; they channel participation through neighborhoods, schools, ethnic groups, and in professions; they disseminate information from political elites to the mass public; they are active at every level of government in providing information, in speaking for affected constituencies, and in debating the merits of proposed policy changes; they work in almost every conceivable way to affect the government, sometimes for the better, often for the worse. Groups are a difficult set of institutions to study in a systematic way because their activities are so varied and their implications so broad. It is this very breadth, however, that makes it important for political science to pay more attention to groups. Group interests are basic to the practice of politics; interest groups must be basic to the study of politics as well.

# Appendix

## Articles on Interest Groups Published in
## the *American Political Science Review*, 1950–1995

The list below includes all articles or commentaries of greater than five pages in length published in the *American Political Science Review* between 1950 and 1995 on the topics of interest groups in American politics or interest-group theory. Articles are included in this list if one of the primary variables discussed is an interest group or groups, or if pluralism or collective action was a central theme of the article. Articles dealing primarily with interest groups in other countries are not included. All published work greater than five pages in length is included. Accordingly, this list includes some book-review essays and commentaries as well as regular research articles. Because we include any article that uses groups as a primary independent variable, this list includes a wide range of studies. Entries are presented in reverse chronological order.

### 1995

Nature or Nurture? Sources of Firm Preference for National Health Reform, by Cathie Jo Martin, 898–913.

The Enactment of Mothers' Pensions: Civic Mobilization and Agenda Setting or Benefits of the Ballot? by Cheryl Logan Sparks and Peter R. Walniuk, with response by Theda Skocpol, 710–30.

Campaign Contributions and Access, by David Austen-Smith, 566–81.

Social Construction (continued), by Robert C. Lieberman, with response by Helen Ingram and Anne L. Schneider, 437–46.

### 1994

The Determinants of Industry Political Activity, 1978–1986, by Kevin B. Grier, Michael C. Munger, and Brian E. Roberts, 911–26.

Limits of Political Strategy: A Systemic View of the African American Experience, by Lucius J. Baker, 1–13.

### 1993

Lawyers, Organized Interests, and the Law of Obscenity: Agenda Setting in the Supreme Court, by Kevin T. McGuire and Gregory A. Caldeira, 717–26.

Women's Associations and the Enactment of Mothers' Pensions in the United States, by Theda Skocpol, Christopher Howard, Susan Goodrich Lehmann, and Marjorie Abend-Wein, 686–701.

The Destruction of Issue Monopolies in Congress, by Bryan D. Jones, Frank R. Baumgartner, and Jeffery C. Talbert, 657–71.

Social Construction of Target Populations: Implications for Politics and Policy, by Anne Schneider and Helen Ingram, 334–47.

A Signaling Model of Informative and Manipulative Political Action, by Susanne Lohmann, 319–33.

## 1992

Courting Constituents? An Analysis of the Senate Confirmation Vote on Justice Clarence Thomas, by Marvin L. Overby, Beth M. Henschen, Michael H. Walsh, and Julie Strauss, 997–1003.

The Presidency and Organized Interests: White House Patterns of Interest Group Liaison, by Mark A. Peterson, 612–25.

## 1991

Business Political Power: The Case of Taxation, by Dennis P. Quinn and Robert Y. Shapiro, 851–74.

Debunking the Myth of Interest Group Invincibility in the Courts, by Lee Epstein and C. K. Rowland, 205–17.

Do Endorsements Matter? Group Influence in the 1984 Democratic Caucuses, by Ronald B. Rapoport, Walter J. Stone, and Alan I. Abramowitz, 193–203.

## 1990

Explaining New Deal Labor Policy, by Theda Skocpol, Kenneth Finegold, and Michael Goldfield, 1297–1315.

Buying Time: Moneyed Interests and the Mobilization of Bias in Congressional Committees, by Richard L. Hall and Frank W. Wayman, 797–820.

The Continuing Significance of Race: The Transformation of American Politics, by Dale Rogers Marshall, 611–16.

Contributions, Lobbying, and Committee Voting in the U.S. House of Representatives, by John R. Wright, 417–38.

Cooperation by Design: Leadership, Structure, and Collective Dilemmas, by William T. Bianco and Robert Bates, 133–47.

The International Trade Commission and the Politics of Protectionism, by Wendy L. Hansen, 21–46.

## 1989

How Much Do Interest Groups Influence State Economic Growth? by Paul Brace, Youssef Cohen, Virginia Gray, and David Lowery, 1297–1308.

Worker Insurgency, Radical Organization, and New Deal Labor Legislation, by Michael Goldfield, 1257–82.

The Cooperative Resolution of Policy Conflict, by Paul J. Quirk, 905–22.

Personal Influence, Collective Rationality, and Mass Political Action, by Steven E. Finkel, Edward N. Muller, and Karl-Dieter Opp, 885–903.

Union Organization in Advanced Industrial Democracies, by Michael Wallerstein, 481–501.

## 1988

The Political Economy of State Medicaid Policy, by Charles J. Barrileaux and Mark E. Miller, 1089–1107.
Organizational Maintenance and the Retention Decision in Groups, by Lawrence S. Rothenberg, 1129–52.
Organized Interests and Agenda Setting in the U.S. Supreme Court, by Gregory A. Caldeira and John R. Wright, 1109–27.
Churches as Political Communities, by Kenneth D. Wald, Dennis E. Owen, and Samuel S. Hill Jr., 531–48.
Interest Group Politics and Economic Growth in the U.S. States, by Virginia Gray and David Lowery, 109–31.

## 1987

Who Works with Whom? Interest Group Alliances and Opposition, by Robert H. Salisbury, John P. Heinz, Edward O. Laumann, and Robert L. Nelson, 1217–34.
Rebellious Collective Action Revisited, by George Klosko, with a response by Edward N. Miller and Karl-Dieter Opp, 557–64.
Institutional Structure and the Logic of Ongoing Collective Action, by Jonathan Bendor and Dilip Mookherjee, 129–54.
What Moves Public Opinion? by Benjamin I. Page, Robert Y. Shapiro, and Glenn R. Dempsey, 23–44.

## 1986

Regulatory Enforcement in a Federalist System, by John T. Scholz and Feng Heng Wei, 1249–70.
Organizing Groups for Collective Action, by Robyn M. Dawes, John M. Orbell, Randy T. Simmons, and Alphons J. C. van de Kragt, 1171–85.
Control and Feedback in Economic Regulation: The Case of the NLRB, by Terry M. Moe, 1094–1116.
The Political Economy of the Tariff Cycle, by James Cassing, Timothy J. McKeown, and Jack Ochs, 843–62.
Rational Choice and Rebellious Collective Action, by Edward N. Muller and Karl-Dieter Opp, 471–87.
The Political Economy of Trade: Institutions of Protection, by Judith Goldstein, 162–84.
Legislators and Interest Groups: How Unorganized Interests Get Represented, by Arthur T. Denzau and Michael C. Munger, 89–106.

## 1985

Control and Feedback in Economic Regulation: The Case of the NLRB, by Terry M. Moe, 1094–1116.

An Adaptive Model of Bureaucratic Politics, by Jonathan Bendor and Terry M. Moe, 755–74.

A Politico-Economic Theory of Income Redistribution, by Robert D. Plotnick and Richard F. Winters, 458–73.

PACs, Contributions, and Roll Calls: An Organizational Perspective, by John R. Wright, 400–414.

Provision of Public Goods and the CMS Experimental Paradigm, by Amnion Rapport, 148–55.

A Theoretical Analysis of the "Green Lobby," by V. Kerry Smith, 132–47.

The Political Economy of Group Membership, by John Mark Hansen, 79–96.

## 1984

Individual Participation in Collective Racial Violence: A Rational Choice Synthesis, by T. David Mason, 1040–56.

Interest Representation: The Dominance of Institutions, by Robert H. Salisbury, 64–76.

Advocacy, Interpretation, and Influence in the U.S. Congress, by Richard A. Smith, 44–63.

## 1983

Potential Responsiveness in the Bureaucracy: Views of Public Utility Regulation, by William Gormley, John Hoadley, and Charles Williams, 704–17.

Religious Marginality and the Free Exercise Clause, by Frank Way and Barbara J. Burt, 652–65.

Pluralism and Social Choice, by Nicholas R. Miller, 734–47.

The Origins and Maintenance of Interest Groups in America, by Jack L. Walker, 390–406.

Neo-Pluralism: A Class Analysis of Pluralism I and Pluralism II, by John F. Manley, with responses by Charles E. Lindblom and Robert Dahl, 368–86.

The Minimal Contributing Set as a Solution to Public Goods Problems, by Alphons J. C. van de Kragt, John M. Orbell, and Robyn M. Dawes, 112–22.

Radicalism or Reformism: The Sources of Working-Class Politics, by Seymour Martin Lipset, 1–18.

## 1981

Research Frontier Essay: When Are Interests Interesting? The Problem of Political Representation of Women, by Virginia Sapiro, with comment by Irene Diamond and Nancy Hartsock, 701–21.

Party and Bureaucracy: The Influence of Intermediary Groups on Urban Public Service Delivery, by Bryan D. Jones, 688–700.

Elite Integration in the United States and Australia, by John Higley and Gwen Moore, 581–97.

## 1977

Economic Power and Political Influence: The Impact of Industry Structure on Public Policy, by Lester M. Salamon and John J. Siegfried, 1026–43.

Lobbyists and the Legislative Process: The Impact of Environmental Constraints, by John M. Bacheller, 252–63.

## 1976

The Future of Community Control, by Norman I. Fainstein and Susan S. Fainstein, 905–23.

Standing to Sue: Interest Group Conflict in the Federal Courts, by Karen Orren, 723–41.

Agenda Building as a Comparative Political Process, by Roger Cobb, Jennie-Keith Ross, and Marc Howard Ross, 126–38.

## 1975

Nondecisions and Power: The Two Faces of Bachrach and Baratz, by Geoffrey Debnam, with response from Peter Bachrach and Morton S. Baratz and a rejoinder, 889–907.

## 1974

On the Origins of Interest-Group Theory: A Critique of a Process, by G. David Garson, 1505–19.

Provision of Collective Goods as a Function of Group Size, by John Chamberlin, 707–16.

## 1973

The Conditions of Protest Behavior in American Cities, by Peter K. Eisinger, 11–28.

## 1971

Nondecisions and the Study of Local Politics, by Raymond E. Wolfinger, with comment by Frederick W. Frey and a rejoinder, 1063–1104.

## 1970

Forms of Representation: Participation of the Poor in the Community Action Program, by Paul E. Peterson, 491–507.

Emotional Experiences in Political Groups: The Case of the McCarthy Phenomenon, by Steven R. Brown and John D. Ellithorp, 349–66.

## 1969

Social Structure and Political Participation: Developmental Relationships, Part II, by Norman H. Nie, G. Bingham Powell Jr., and Kenneth Prewitt, 808–32.

Social Structure and Political Participation: Developmental Relationships, Part I, by Norman H. Nie, G. Bingham Powell Jr., and Kenneth Prewitt, 361–78.

## 1968

Sources of Local Political Involvement, by Robert R. Alford and Harry M. Scoble, 1192–1206.

Protest as a Political Resource, by Michael Lipsky, 1144–58.

On the Neo-Elitist Critique of Community Power, by Richard M. Merelman, 451–60.

## 1967

Ethnic Politics and the Persistence of Ethnic Identification, by Michael Parenti, 717–26.

Protest Participation among Southern Negro College Students, by John M. Orbell, 446–56.

Bar Politics, Judicial Selection, and the Representation of Social Interests, by Richard A. Watson, Rondal G. Downing, and Frederick C. Spiegel, 54–71.

The Public Philosophy: Interest-Group Liberalism, by Theodore Lowi, 5–24.

## 1966

Some Effects of Interest Group Strength in State Politics, by Lewis A. Froman, Jr., 952–62.

Attitude Consensus and Conflict in an Interest Group: An Assessment of Cohesion, by Norman R. Luttbeg and Harmon Zeigler, 655–66.

Political Attitudes and the Local Community, by Robert D. Putnam, 640–54.

Further Reflections on "The Elitist Theory of Democracy," by Robert A. Dahl, 296–305.

A Critique of the Elitist Theory of Democracy, by Jack L. Walker, 285–95.

## 1965

Scientists and the Policy Process, by Avery Leiserson, 408–29.

## 1964

Pragmatism and the Group Theory of Politics, by David G. Smith, 600–610.

## 1962

Two Faces of Power, by Peter Bachrach and Morton S. Baratz, 947–52.

The Threat of Violence and Social Change, by H. L. Nieburg, 865–73.

Agricultural Subsidies in England and the United States, by J. Roland Pennock, 621–33.

## 1961

In the Footsteps of Community Power, by Lawrence J. R. Herson, 817–30.

TVA and Power Politics, by Aaron Wildavsky, 576–90.

Representation in Congress: The Case of the House Agriculture Committee, by Charles O. Jones, 358–67.

Political Recruitment and Party Structure: A Case Study, by Lester G. Seligman, 77–86.

## 1960

"The Group Basis of Politics": Notes on Analysis and Development, by Robert T. Golembiewski, 962–71.

The Cosmology of Arthur F. Bentley, by Myron Q. Hale, 955–61.

Pressure Group Theory: Its Methodological Range, by R. E. Dowling, 944–54.

The Political Attitudes and Preferences of Union Members: The Case of the Detroit Auto Workers, by Harold L. Sheppard and Nicholas A. Masters, 437–47.

Systemic Political Theory: Observations on the Group Approach, by Stanly Rothman, 15–33.

## 1959

Toward an Understanding of Public School Politics, by Thomas H. Eliot, 1032–51.

Business and Politics: A Critical Appraisal of Political Science, by Robert A. Dahl, 1–34.

## 1958

The Spirit of Private Government, by Grant McConnell, 754–70.

Foreign Aid and the Policy Process, 1957, by H. Field Haviland, Jr., 689–724.

The Supreme Court and Group Conflict: Thoughts on Seeing Burke Put Through the Mill, by Alan F. Westin, 665–77.

From Lochner to Brown v. Topeka: The Court and the Conflicting Concepts of the Political Process, by Albert A. Mavrinac, 641–64.

A Critique of the Ruling Elite Model, by Robert A. Dahl, 463–69.

A Comparative Study of Interest Groups and the Political Process, by Gabriel A. Almond, 270–82.

## 1957

"The Public Interest" in Administrative Decision-Making, by Glendon A. Schubert, Jr., 346–68.

## 1954

The Protection of the Public Interest with Special Reference to Administrative Regulation, by Emmette S. Redford, 1103–13.

The Politics of Collective Bargaining: the Postwar Record in Steel, by Frederick H. Harbison and Robert C. Spencer, 705–20.

Extra-Legal Political Parties in Wisconsin, by Frank J. Sorauf, 692–704.

A Pressure Group and the Pressured, by Oliver Garceau and Corinne Silverman, 672–91.

## 1952

The Group Basis of Politics: Notes for a Theory, by Earl Latham, 376–97.
The American Tradition of Empirical Collectivism, by Currin V. Shields, 104–20.

## 1951

New Party Associations in the West, by Hugh A. Bone, 1115–25.
The Public Interest in Emergency Labor Disputes, by Robert B. Dishman, 1100–1114.

## 1950

Shipping Quotas and the Military Assistance Program, by Marshall Knappen, 933–41.
Review of Arthur Bentley: *The Process of Government: A Study of Social Pressures*, by Bertram M. Gross, 742–48.
Congress and Water Resources, by Arthur A. Maass, 576–93.

# References

Aberbach, Joel D., Robert D. Putnam, and Bert A. Rockman. 1981. *Bureaucrats and Politicians in Western Europe*. Cambridge: Harvard University Press.

Ainsworth, Scott. 1993. Regulating Lobbyists and Interest Group Influence. *Journal of Politics* 55: 41–56.

Ainsworth, Scott, and Itai Sened. 1993. The Role of Lobbyists: Entrepreneurs with Two Audiences. *American Journal of Political Science* 37: 834–66.

Almond, Gabriel A. 1958. Comparative Study of Interest Groups. *American Political Science Review* 52: 270–82.

———. 1983. Corporatism, Pluralism, and Professional Memory. *World Politics* 35: 245–60.

Almond, Gabriel A., and Sidney Verba. 1965. *The Civic Culture*. Boston: Little, Brown.

Anton, Thomas J. 1980. *Administered Politics: Elite Political Culture in Sweden*. Boston: Martinus Nijhoff.

Arnold, R. Douglas. 1982. Overtilled and Undertilled Fields in American Politics. *Political Science Quarterly* 97: 91–103.

———. 1990. *The Logic of Congressional Action*. New Haven, Conn.: Yale University Press.

Austen-Smith, David. 1993. Information and Influence: Lobbying for Agendas and Votes. *American Journal of Political Science* 37: 799–833.

Austen-Smith, David, and John R. Wright. 1994. Counteractive Lobbying. *American Journal of Political Science* 38: 25–44.

Axelrod, Robert. 1981. The Emergence of Cooperation among Egoists. *American Political Science Review* 75: 306–18.

———. 1984. *The Evolution of Cooperation*. New York: Basic Books.

———. 1986. An Evolutionary Approach to Norms. *American Political Science Review* 80: 1097–1111.

Babchuck, Nicholas, and Alan Booth. 1969. Voluntary Association Membership: A Longitudinal Analysis. *American Sociological Review* 34: 31–45.

Bacheller, John M. 1977. Lobbyists and the Legislative Process: The Impact of Environmental Constraints. *American Political Science Review* 71: 252–63.

Bachrach, Peter, and Morton Baratz. 1962. The Two Faces of Power. *American Political Science Review* 56: 947–52.

Bailey, Stephen Kemp. 1950. *Congress Makes a Law: The Story behind the Employment Act of 1946*. New York: Columbia University Press.

Banks, Jeffrey S., and Barry R. Weingast. 1992. The Political Control of Bureaucracies under Asymmetric Information. *American Journal of Political Science* 36: 509–24.

Barker, Lucius. 1967. Third Parties in Litigation: A Systematic View of the Judicial Function. *Journal of Politics* 24: 41–69.

Bauer, Raymond A., Ithiel de Sola Pool, and Lewis A. Dexter. 1963. *American Business and Public Policy: The Politics of Foreign Trade*. New York: Atherton Press.

Baumgartner, Frank R. 1989. *Conflict and Rhetoric in French Policymaking*. Pittsburgh: University of Pittsburgh Press.

Baumgartner, Frank R., and Bryan D. Jones. 1991. Agenda Dynamics and Policy Subsystems. *Journal of Politics* 53: 1044–74.

———. 1993. *Agendas and Instability in American Politics*. Chicago: University of Chicago Press.

Baumgartner, Frank R., and Beth L. Leech. 1996a. The Multiple Ambiguities of "Counteractive Lobbying." *American Journal of Political Science* 40: 521–42.

———. 1996b. Good Theories Deserve Good Data. *American Journal of Political Science* 40: 565–69.

Baumgartner, Frank R., and Jeffery C. Talbert. 1995. Interest Groups and Political Change. In *New Directions in American Politics*, ed. Bryan D. Jones. Boulder, Westview Press.

Baumgartner, Frank R., and Jack L. Walker, Jr. 1988. Survey Research and Membership in Voluntary Associations. *American Journal of Political Science* 32: 908–28.

———. 1989. Educational Policy Making and the Interest Group Structure in France and the United States. *Comparative Politics* 21: 273–88.

———. 1990. Response to Smith's "Trends in Voluntary Group Membership: Comments on Baumgartner and Walker": Measurement Validity and the Continuity of Results in Survey Research. *American Journal of Political Science* 34: 662–70.

Becker, Gary S. 1983. A Theory of Competition among Pressure Groups for Political Influence. *Quarterly Journal of Economics* 98: 371–400.

———. 1985. Public Policies, Pressure Groups, and Dead Weight Costs. *Journal of Public Economics* 28: 330–47.

Bendor, Jonathan, and Terry M. Moe. 1985. An Adaptive Model of Bureaucratic Politics. *American Political Science Review* 79: 755–74.

Bentley, Arthur F. 1908. *The Process of Government*. Chicago: University of Chicago Press.

Bernstein, Marver H. 1955. *Regulating Business by Independent Commission*. Princeton, N.J.: Princeton University Press.

Berry, Jeffrey M. 1977. *Lobbying for the People: The Political Behavior of Public Interest Groups*. Princeton, N.J.: Princeton University Press.

———. 1984a. *The Interest Group Society*. Boston: Little, Brown.

———. 1984b. *Feeding Hungry People: Rulemaking in the Food Stamp Program*. New Brunswick, N.J.: Rutgers University Press.

———. 1989a. *The Interest Group Society*. 2d ed. New York: HarperCollins.

———. 1989b. Subgovernments, Issue Networks, and Political Conflict. In *Remaking American Politics*, ed. Richard Harris and Sidney Milkis. Boulder, Colo.: Westview Press.

———. 1994a. An Agenda for Research on Interest Groups. In *Representing Interests and Interest Group Representation* ed. William Crotty, Mildred A. Schwartz, and John C. Green. Lanham, Md.: University Press of America.

———. 1994b. The Dynamic Qualities of Issue Networks. Paper presented at the annual meetings of the American Political Science Association, New York.

———. 1997. *The Interest Group Society*. 3d ed. New York: HarperCollins.

Bikhchandani, Sushil, David Hirshleifer, and Ivo Welch. 1992. A Theory of Fads,

Fashion, Custom, and Cultural Change as Informational Cascades. *Journal of Political Economy* 100: 992–1026.

Birkby, Robert, and Walter Murphy. 1964. Interest Group Conflict in the Judicial Arena: The First Amendment and Group Access to the Courts. *Texas Law Review* 42: 1018–48.

Blaisdell, Donald C. 1941. *Economic Power and Political Pressures.* Washington, D.C.: Government Printing Office.

———. 1949. *Economic Power and Political Pressures.* Washington, D.C.: Temporary National Economic Committee Monograph no. 26.

Blaisdell, Donald. C. 1957. *American Democracy under Pressure.* New York: Ronald.

Blum, Debra E. 1996. Mapping out the State of Giving. *Chronicle of Philanthropy,* Aug. 8.

Bosso, Christopher J. 1987. *Pesticides and Politics: The Life Cycle of a Public Issue.* Pittsburgh: University of Pittsburgh Press.

Bosso, Christopher J. 1995. The Color of Money: Environmental Interest Groups and the Pathologies of Fund Rasing. In *Interest Group Politics*, 4th ed., ed. Allan J. Cigler and Burdett A. Loomis. Washington: Congressional Quarterly.

Bradsher, Keith. 1995. Sugar Price Supports Survive Political Shift. *New York Times,* Sept. 29.

Brown, Bernard E. 1963. Pressure Politics in the Fifth Republic. *Journal of Politics* 25: 509–25.

Brown, Kirk F. 1983. Campaign Contributions and Congressional Voting. Paper presented at the annual meeting of the American Political Science Association, Chicago.

Browne, William P. 1988. *Private Interests, Public Policy, and American Agriculture.* Lawrence: University Press of Kansas.

———. 1990. Organized Interests and Their Issue Niches: A Search for Pluralism in a Policy Domain. *Journal of Politics* 52: 477–509.

———. 1995. *Cultivating Congress: Constituents, Issues, and Interests in Agricultural Policymaking.* Lawrence: University Press of Kansas.

Browne, William P., and Won K. Paik. 1993. Beyond the Domain: Recasting Network Politics in the Postreform Congress. *American Journal of Political Science* 37: 1054–78.

Brudney, Jeffrey L., and F. Ted Hebert. 1987. State Agencies and Their Environments: Examining the Influence of Important External Actors. *Journal of Politics* 49: 186–206.

Buchanan, James, and Gordon Tullock. 1962. *The Calculus of Consent.* Ann Arbor: University of Michigan Press.

Burns, James MacGregor. 1963. *The Deadlock of Democracy.* Englewood Cliffs, N.J.: Prentice-Hall.

Caldeira, Gregory A. and John R. Wright. 1988. Organized Interests and Agenda-Setting in the U.S. Supreme Court. *American Political Science Review* 82: 1109–27.

———. 1990. Amici Curiae before the Supreme Court: Who Participates, When, and How Much? *Journal of Politics* 52: 782–806.

Casper, Jonathan. 1972. *The Politics of Civil Liberties.* New York: Harper and Row.

Cater, Douglass. 1964. *Power in Washington.* New York: Random House.

Chamberlin, John. 1974. Provision of Collective Goods as a Function of Group Size. *American Political Science Review* 68: 707–16.

Chappell, Henry W. Jr. 1981. Campaign Contributions and Voting on the Cargo Preference Bill: A Comparison of Simultaneous Models. *Public Choice* 36: 301–12.

———. Campaign Contributions and Congressional Voting: A Simultaneous Probit-Tobit Model. *Review of Economics and Statistics* 62: 77–83.

Chong, Dennis. 1991. *Collective Action and the Civil Rights Movement.* Chicago: University of Chicago Press.

Chubb, John E. 1983. *Interest Groups and the Bureaucracy: The Politics of Energy.* Stanford, Calif.: Stanford University Press.

Chubb, John E., and Paul E. Peterson, eds. 1989. *Can the Government Govern?* Washington, D.C.: Brookings.

Cigler, Allan J. 1991. Interest Groups: A Subfield in Search of an Identity. In *Political Science: Looking to the Future*, ed. William Crotty, vol. 4. Evanston, Ill.: Northwestern University Press.

———. 1994. Research Gaps in the Study of Interest Group Representation. In *Representing Interests and Interest Group Representation*, ed. William Crotty, Mildred A. Schwartz, and John C. Green. Lanham, Md.: University Press of America.

Cigler, Allan J., and Burdett A. Loomis, eds. 1995. *Interest Group Politics.* 4th ed. Washington, D.C.: Congressional Quarterly.

Clark, Peter B., and James Q. Wilson. 1961. Incentive Systems: A Theory of Organizations. *Administrative Science Quarterly* 6: 129–66.

Cleiber, Dennis, James King, and H. R. Mahood. 1987. PAC Contributions, Constituency Interest and Legislative Voting: Gun Control Legislation in the U.S. Senate. Paper presented at the annual meeting of the Midwest Political Science Association, Chicago.

Cleveland, Frederick A. 1913. *Organized Democracy.* New York: Longmans, Green.

Clymer, Adam. 1996. Senate Kills Bill to Limit Spending in Congress Races. *New York Times*, June 26.

Commisa, Anne Marie. 1995. *Governments as Interest Groups: Intergovernmental Lobbying and the Federal System.* Westport, Conn.: Praeger.

Cortner, Richard C. 1968. Strategies and Tactics of Litigants in Constitutional Cases. *Journal of Public Law* 17: 287–307.

Coughlin, Cletus G. 1985. Domestic Content Legislation: House Voting and the Economic Theory of Regulation. *Economic Inquiry* 23: 437–48.

Crawford, Kenneth Gale. 1939. *The Pressure Boys: The Inside Story of Lobbying in America.* New York: J. Messner.

Crenson, Matthew A. 1971. *The Unpolitics of Air Pollution.* Baltimore, Md.: Johns Hopkins University Press.

———. 1987. The Private Stake in Public Goods: Overcoming the Illogic of Collective Action. *Policy Sciences* 20: 259–76.

Croly, Herbert. 1915. *Progressive Democracy.* New York: Macmillan.

Crotty, William, Mildred A. Schwartz, and John C. Green, eds. 1994. *Representing Interests and Interest Group Representation.* Lanham, Md.: University Press of America.

Culhane, Paul J. 1981. *Public Lands Politics: Interest Group Influence on the Forest*

*Service and the Bureau of Land Management*. Baltimore, Md.: Johns Hopkins University Press.

Curtis, James. 1971. Voluntary Association Joining: A Cross-National Comparative Note. *American Sociological Review* 36: 872–80.

Curtis, James E., Edward G. Grabb, and Douglas E. Baer. 1992. Voluntary Association Membership in Fifteen Countries: A Comparative Analysis. *American Sociological Review* 57: 129–52.

Dahl, Robert A. 1957. The Concept of Power. *Behavioral Science* 2: 201–15.

———. 1961. *Who Governs?* New Haven, Conn.: Yale University Press.

———. 1966a. Further Reflections on "The Elitist Theory of Democracy." *American Political Science Review* 60: 296–305.

———, ed. 1966b. *Political Oppositions in Western Democracies*. New Haven, Conn.: Yale University Press.

Danielian, Lucig H., and Benjamin I. Page. 1994. The Heavenly Chorus: Interest Group Voices on TV News. *American Journal of Political Science* 38: 1056–78.

Davidson, Roger H. 1989. Multiple Referral of Legislation in the U.S. Senate. *Legislative Studies Quarterly* 14: 375–92.

Davis, James Allan, and Tom W. Smith. 1994. *General Social Surveys, 1972–1994: Cumulative Codebook*. Chicago: National Opinion Research Center.

Dawes, Robyn M., John M. Orbell, Randy T. Simmons, and Alphons J. C. van de Kragt. 1986. Organizing Groups for Collective Action. *American Political Science Review* 80: 117–85.

DeGregorio, Christine, and Jack E. Rossotti. 1995. Campaigning for the Court: Interest Group Participation in the Bork and Thomas Confirmation Precesses. In *Interest Group Politics*, 4th ed., ed. Allan J. Cigler and Burdette A. Loomis. Washington, D.C.: CQ Press.

DeNardo, James. 1985. *Power in Numbers: The Political Strategy of Protest and Rebellion*. Princeton, N.J.: Princeton University Press.

Dexter, Lewis Anthony. 1969. *How Organizations Are Represented in Washington*. Indianapolis: Bobbs-Merrill.

Dogan, Mattei, ed. 1975. *The Mandarins of Western Europe*. New York: Halsted Press.

Domhoff, G. William. 1967. *Who Rules America?* Englewood Cliffs, N. J.: Prentice-Hall.

Durden, Garey C., Jason F. Shogren, and Jonathan I. Silberman. 1991. The Effects of Interest Group Pressure on Coal Strip-Mining Legislation. *Social Science Quarterly* 72: 237–50.

Eckstein, Harry. 1960. *Pressure Group Politics*. Princeton, N.J.: Princeton University Press.

———. 1966. *Division and Cohesion in Democracy*. Princeton, N.J.: Princeton University Press.

Edles, L. Peter. 1993. *Fundraising: Hands-On Tactics for Nonprofit Groups*. New York: McGraw-Hill.

Ehrmann, Henry. 1957. *Organized Business in France*. Princeton, N.J.: Princeton University Press.

———. 1958. *Interest Groups on Four Continents*. Pittsburgh: University of Pittsburgh Press.

Epstein, Lee. 1985. *Conservatives in Court*. Knoxville: University of Tennessee Press.

Epstein, Lee. 1991. Courts and Interest Groups. In *American Courts*, ed. John B. Gates and Charles A. Johnson. Washington, D.C.: CQ Press.

Epstein, Lee, and Joseph F. Kobylka. 1992. *The Supreme Court and Legal Change*. Chapel Hill: University of North Carolina Press.

Epstein, Lee, and C. K. Rowland. 1991. Debunking the Myth of Interest Group Invincibility in the Courts. *American Political Science Review* 85: 205–17.

Evans, Diana M. 1986. PAC Contributions and Roll-call Voting: Conditional Power. In *Interest Group Politics*. 2d ed., ed. Allan J. Cigler and Burdett A. Loomis. Washington, D.C.: Congressional Quarterly.

Farkas, Suzanne. 1971. *Urban Lobbying: Mayors in the Federal Arena*. New York: New York University Press.

Feldstein, Paul J., and Glenn Melnick. 1984. Congressional Voting Behavior on Hospital Legislation: An Exploratory Study. *Journal of Health Politics, Policy and Law* 8: 686–701.

Fenno, Richard F., Jr. 1973. *Congressmen in Committees*. Boston: Little, Brown.

Finifter, Ada, ed. 1983. *Political Science: The State of the Discipline*. Washington, D.C.: American Political Science Association.

———, ed. 1993. *Political Science: The State of the Discipline II*. Washington, D.C.: American Political Science Association.

Finkel, Seven E., Edward N. Muller, and Karl-Dieter Opp. 1989. Personal Influence, Collective Rationality, and Mass Political Action. *American Political Science Review* 83: 885–903.

Fleisher, Richard. 1993. PAC Contributions and Congressional Voting on National Defense. *Legislative Studies Quarterly* 18: 391–409.

Fowler, Linda L., and Ronald G. Shaiko. 1987. The Grass Roots Connection: Environmental Activists and Senate Roll Calls. *American Journal of Political Science* 31: 484–510.

Freeman, J. Leiper. 1955. *The Political Process*. Garden City: Doubleday.

———. 1965. *The Political Process: Executive Bureau-Legislative Committee Relations*. Rev. ed. New York: Random House.

Frendreis, John P., and Richard W. Waterman. 1985. PAC Contributions and Legislative Behavior: Senate Voting on Trucking Deregulation. *Social Science Quarterly* 66: 401–12.

Fritschler, A. Lee. 1975. *Smoking and Politics*. 2d ed. Englewood Cliffs, N.J.: Prentice-Hall.

Gais, Thomas L. 1996. *Improper Influence: Campaign Finance Law, Political Interest Groups, and the Problem of Equity*. Ann Arbor: University of Michigan Press.

Gais, Thomas L., and Jack L. Walker, Jr. 1991. Pathways to Influence in American Politics. *In Mobilizing Interest Groups in America*, by Jack L. Walker, Jr. Ann Arbor: University of Michigan Press.

Gamson, William. 1990. *The Strategy of Social Protest*. 2d ed. Belmont, Calif.: Wadsworth.

Garson, G. David. 1974. On the Origins of Interest-Group Theory: A Critique of a Process. *American Political Science Review* 68: 1505–19.

———. 1978. *Group Theories of Politics*. Beverly Hills, Calif.: Sage.

Gaventa, John. 1980. *Power and Powerlessness: Quiescence and Rebellion in an Appalachian Valley*. Urbana: University of Illinois Press.

Ginsberg, Benjamin, and John C. Green. 1986. The Best Congress Money Can Buy: Campaign Contributions and Congressional Behavior. In *Do Elections Matter?* ed. Benjamin Ginsberg and Alan Stone. Armonk, N.Y.: M.E. Sharpe.

Golden, Marissa Martino. 1995. Interest Groups in the Rulemaking Process: Who Participates? Whose Voices Get Heard? Paper presented at the Third National Public Management Conference, Lawrence, Kansas, October 5–7.

Goldstein, Kenneth M. 1995. Seeding the Grass Roots: Mobilization and Contacting Congress. Paper presented at the annual meeting of the Midwest Political Science Association, Chicago.

Goodin, Robert E. 1984. Itinerants, Iterations and Something in-Between. *British Journal of Political Science* 14: 129–32.

Granovetter, Mark. 1978. Threshold Models of Collective Behavior. *American Journal of Sociology* 83: 1420–43.

Gray, Virginia, and David Lowery. 1993a. The Diversity of State Interest Group Systems. *Political Research Quarterly* 46: 81–97.

———. 1993b. Stability and Change in State Interest Group Systems: 1975 to 1990. *State and Local Government Review* 25: 87–96.

———. 1994. Interest Group System Density and Diversity: A Research Update. *International Political Science Review* 15: 5–14.

———. 1995. The Demography of Interest Organization Communities: Institutions, Associations, and Membership Groups. *American Politics Quarterly* 23: 3–32.

———. 1996. *The Population Ecology of Interest Representation*. Ann Arbor: University of Michigan Press.

Green, Donald P., and Ian Shapiro. 1994. *Pathologies of Rational Choice Theory*. New Haven, Conn.: Yale University Press.

Greenberg, George D., Jeffrey A. Miller, Lawrence B. Mohr, and Bruce C. Vladeck. 1977. Developing Public Policy Theory: Perspectives from Empirical Research. *American Political Science Review* 71: 1532–43.

Greenstein, Fred I., and Nelson W. Polsby, eds. 1975. *Handbook of Political Science*. Reading, Mass.: Addison-Wesley.

Greenstone, J. David. 1975. Group Theories. In *Micropolitical Theory*, Vol. 2 of *Handbook of Political Science*, ed. Fred I. Greenstein and Nelson W. Polsby. Reading, Mass.: Addison-Wesley.

Grenzke, Janet M. 1989. PACs and the Congressional Supermarket: The Currency Is Complex. *American Journal of Political Science* 33: 1–24.

Griffith, Ernest S. 1939. *The Impasse of Democracy*. New York: Harrison-Hilton.

Gurr, Ted Robert. 1970. *Why Men Rebel*. Princeton, N.J.: Princeton University Press.

Haider, Donald H. 1974. *When Governments Come to Washington: Governors, Mayors, and Intergovernmental Lobbying*. New York: Free Press.

Hakman, Nathan. 1966. Lobbying the Supreme Court: An Appraisal of "Political Science Folklore." *Fordham Law Review* 35: 15–50.

Hall, Peter. 1986. *Governing the Economy: The Politics of State Intervention in Britain and France*. New York: Oxford University Press.

Hall, Richard L. 1996. *Participation in Congress*. New Haven, Conn.: Yale University Press.

Hall, Richard L., and Frank W. Wayman. 1990. Buying Time: Moneyed Interests and the Mobilization of Bias in Congressional Committees. *American Political Science Review* 84: 797–820.

Handler, Joel. 1978. *Social Movements and the Legal System.* New York: Academic Press.

Hansen, John Mark. 1985. The Political Economy of Group Membership. *American Political Science Review* 79: 79–96.

———. 1991. *Gaining Access: Congress and the Farm Lobby, 1919–1981.* Chicago: University of Chicago Press.

Hardin, Charles M. 1952. *The Politics of Agriculture.* Glencoe, Ill.: Free Press.

Hardin, Russell. 1982. *Collective Action.* Baltimore, Md.: Johns Hopkins University Press.

Hart, Albert B. 1907. Growth of American Theories of Popular Government. *American Political Science Review* 1: 531–60.

Hayes, Michael T. 1978. The Semi-Sovereign Pressure Groups. *Journal of Politics* 40: 134–61.

Heclo, Hugh. 1974. *Modern Social Policies in Britain and Sweden: From Relief to Income Maintenance.* New Haven, Conn.: Yale University Press.

———. 1978. Issue Networks and the Executive Establishment. In *The New American Political System,* ed. Anthony King. Washington, D.C.: American Enterprise Institute.

Heinz, John P., Edward O. Laumann, Robert L. Nelson, and Robert H. Salisbury. 1993. *The Hollow Core: Private Interests in National Policymaking.* Cambridge: Harvard University Press.

Herring, E. Pendleton. 1929. *Group Representation before Congress.* Washington, D.C.: Brookings.

———. 1936. *Public Administration and the Public Interest.* New York: McGraw-Hill.

———. 1967. *Group Representation before Congress.* New York: Russell and Russell.

Hojnacki, Marie. 1997. Interest Groups' Decisions to Join Alliances or Work Alone. *American Journal of Political Science* 41: 61–87.

Hojnacki, Marie, and David Kimball. 1996. Organized Interests and the Decision of Whom to Lobby in Congress. Paper presented at the annual meeting of the American Political Science Association, San Francisco.

Hrebenar, Ronald J., and Clive S. Thomas, eds. 1987. *Interest Group Politics in the American West.* Salt Lake City: University of Utah Press.

———, eds. 1992. *Interest Group Politics in the Southern States.* Tuscaloosa, Ala.: University of Alabama Press.

———, eds. 1993a. *Interest Group Politics in the Midwestern States.* Ames, Iowa: Iowa State University Press.

———, eds. 1993b. *Interest Group Politics in the Northeastern States.* College Park, Pa.: Penn State University Press.

Huckfeldt, Robert, and John D. Sprague. 1992. Political Parties and Electoral Mobilization: Political Structure, Social Structure and the Party Canvass. *American Political Science Review* 86: 70–86.

———. 1995. *Citizens, Politics, and Social Communication.* New York: Cambridge University Press.

Hunter, Floyd. 1953. *Community Power Structure*. Chapel Hill: University of North Carolina Press. (Also published in 1963 by Anchor Books, Garden City, N.Y.)

Hunter, Kennith G., Laura Ann Wilson, and Gregory G. Brunk. 1991. Societal Complexity and Interest-Group Lobbying in the American States. *Journal of Politics* 53: 488–503.

Huntington, Samuel P. 1952. The Marasmus of the ICC: The Commission, the Railroads, and the Public Interest. *Yale Law Review* 61: 467–509.

Hyman, Herbert H., and Charles R. Wright. 1971. Trends in Voluntary Association Membership of American Adults: Replication Based on Secondary Analysis of National Sample Surveys. *American Sociological Review* 36: 191–206.

Isaac, R. Mark, James M. Walker, and Susan H. Thomas. 1984. Divergent Evidence on Free Riding: An Experimental Examination of Possible Explanations. *Public Choice* 43: 113–49.

Jenkins, J. Craig. 1985. *The Politics of Insurgency*. New York: Columbia University Press.

Jenkins, J. Craig, and Craig M. Eckert. 1986. Channeling Black Insurgency: Elite Patronage and Professional Social Movement Organizations in the Development of the Black Power Movement. *American Sociological Review* 79: 79–96.

Jenkins, J. Craig, and Charles Perrow. 1977. Insurgency of the Powerless: Farm Workers Movements, 1946–1972. *American Sociological Review* 42: 248–68.

Jenkins-Smith, Hank C., Gilbert K. St. Clair, and Brian Woods. 1991. Explaining Change in Policy Subsystems: Analysis of Coalition Stability and Defection over Time. *American Journal of Political Science* 35: 851–80.

Johnson, Linda L. 1985. The Effectiveness of Savings and Loan Political Action Committees. *Public Choice* 46: 289–304.

Johnson, Paul E. 1995. How Environmental Groups Recruit Members: Does the Logic Still Hold Up? Paper presented at the annual meeting of the Midwest Political Science Association, Chicago.

Jones, Bryan D. 1994. *Reconceiving Decision Making in Democratic Politics*. Chicago: University of Chicago Press.

Jones, Bryan D., Frank R. Baumgartner, and Jeffery C. Talbert. 1993. The Destruction of Issue Monopolies in Congress. *American Political Science Review* 87: 657–71.

Jones, Woodrow Jr., and K. Robert Keiser. 1987. Issue Visibility and the Effects of PAC Money. *Social Science Quarterly* 68: 170–76.

Jordan, Grant, and William A. Maloney. 1996. How Bumble-bees Fly: Accounting for Public Interest Participation. *Political Studies* 44: 668–85.

Kabashima, Ikuo, and Hideo Sato. 1986. Local Content and Congressional Politics: Interest Group Theory and Foreign Policy Implications. *International Studies Quarterly* 30: 295–314.

Kalt, Joseph P., and Mark A. Zupan. 1984. Capture and Ideology in the Economic Theory of Politics. *American Economic Review* 74: 279–300.

Kariel, Henry. 1961. *The Decline of American Pluralism*. Stanford, Calif.: Stanford University Press.

Katzenstein, Peter J. 1985. *Small States in World Markets*. Ithaca, N.Y.: Cornell University Press.

Kau, James B., and Paul H. Rubin. 1982. *Congressmen, Constituents, and Contributors: Determinants of Roll Call Voting in the House of Representatives*. Boston: Martinus Nijhoff.

Kau, James B., Donald Keenan, and Paul H. Rubin. 1982. A General Equilibrium Model of Congressional Voting. *Quarterly Journal of Economics* 97: 271–93.

Keeler, John T. S. 1987. *The Politics of Neocorporatism in France*. New York: Oxford University Press.

Key, V. O., Jr. 1964. *Politics, Parties, and Pressure Groups*. 5th ed. New York: Crowell.

Kingdon, John W. 1984. *Agendas, Alternatives, and Public Policies*. Boston: Little, Brown.

————. 1989. *Congressmen's Voting Decisions*. 3d ed. Ann Arbor: University of Michigan Press.

————. 1995. *Agendas, Alternatives, and Public Policies*. 2d. ed. New York: Harper-Collins.

Kitschelt, Herbert B. 1986. Political Opportunity Structures and Political Protest: Anti-Nuclear Movements in Four Democracies. *British Journal of Political Science* 16: 57–85.

Klandermans, Bert, and Dirk Oegama. 1987. Potentials, Networks, Motivations, and Barriers: Steps Towards Participation in Social Movements. *American Sociological Review* 52: 519–31.

Kluger, Richard. 1976. *Simple Justice*. New York: Alfred A. Knopf.

Knappen, M. 1950. Shipping Quotas and the Military Assistance Program. *American Political Science Review* 44: 933–41.

Knoke, David. 1986. Associations and Interest Groups. *Annual Review of Sociology* 12: 1–21.

————. 1988. Incentives in Collective Action Organizations. *American Sociological Review* 53: 311–29.

————. 1990a. *Organizing for Collective Action: The Political Economies of Associations*. Hawthorne, N.Y.: Aldine de Gruyter.

————. 1990b. *Political Networks: The Structural Perspective*. New York: Cambridge University Press.

Knoke, David, and James H. Kuklinski. 1982. *Network Analysis*. Beverly Hills: Sage.

Knoke, David, Franz Urban Pappi, Jeffrey Broadbent, Yutaka Tsujinaka. 1996. *Comparing Policy Networks: Labor Politics in the U.S., Germany, and Japan*. New York: Cambridge University Press.

Kobylka, Joseph F. 1987. A Court-Created Context for Group Litigation: Libertarian Groups and Obscenity. *Journal of Politics* 49: 1061–78.

————. 1991. *The Politics of Obscenity*. Westport, Conn: Greenwood Press.

Kollman, Ken. 1997. Inviting Friends to Lobby: Interest Groups, Ideological Bias, and Congressional Committees. *American Journal of Political Science* 41: 519–44.

————. 1998. *Outside Lobbying: Public Opinion and Interest Group Strategies*. Princeton, N.J.: Princeton University Press.

Landé, Karl H. 1973. Networks and Groups in Southeast Asia: Some Observations on the Group Theory of Politics. *American Political Science Review* 67: 103–27.

Landes, William M., and Richard A. Posner. 1975. The Independent Judiciary in Interest Group Perspective. *The Journal of Law and Economics* 18: 875-901.

Lane, Edgar. 1964. *Lobbying and the Law*. Berkeley: University of California Press.

Langbein, Laura. 1993. PACs, Lobbies, and Political Conflict: The Case of Gun Control. *Public Choice* 75: 254–71.

Langbein, Laura, and Mark. Lotwis. 1990. The Political Efficacy of Lobbying and Money: Gun Control in the U.S. House, 1986. *Legislative Studies Quarterly* 15: 413–40.

LaPolombara, Joseph. 1960. The Utility and Limitations of Interest Group Theory in Non-American Field Settings. *Journal of Politics* 22: 29–49.

———. 1964. *Interest Groups in Italian Politics*. Princeton, N.J.: Princeton University Press.

Laumann, Edward O., and David Knoke. 1986. Social Network Theory. In *Approaches to Social Theory*, ed. Siegwart Lindenberg, James S. Coleman, and Stefan Nowak. New York: Russell Sage Foundation.

———. 1987. *The Organizational State: Social Choice in National Policy Domains*. Madison: University of Wisconsin Press.

Laumann, Edward O., David Knoke, and Yong-Kak Kim. 1985. An Organizational Approach to State Policymaking: A Comparative Study of Energy and Health Domains. *American Sociological Review* 50: 1–19.

Leech, Beth L. 1998. Lobbying Strategies of American Interest Groups. Ph.D. diss., Texas A&M University.

Lehmbruch, Gerhard, and Philippe C. Schmitter, eds. 1982. *Patterns of Corporatist Policy Making*. London: Sage.

Leighley, Jan E. 1995. Attitudes, Opportunities, and Incentives: A Review Essay on Political Participation. *Political Research Quarterly* 48: 181–209.

Lewis, Neal A. 1995. Patent-Extension Loophole Creates Drug-maker Battle. *New York Times*, Sept. 28.

Lichbach, Mark Irving. 1995. *The Rebel's Dilemma*. Ann Arbor: University of Michigan Press.

———. 1996. *The Cooperator's Dilemma*. Ann Arbor: University of Michigan Press.

Lijphart, Arend. 1968. *The Politics of Accomodation: Pluralism and Democracy in the Netherlands*. Berkeley: University of California Press.

———. 1969. Consociational Democracy. *World Politics* 21: 207–25.

Lipsky, Michael. 1968. Protest as a Political Resource. *American Political Science Review* 62: 1144–58.

Lowenstein, Daniel H. 1982. Campaign Spending and Ballot Propositions: Recent Experience, Public Choice Theory, and the First Amendment. *UCLA Law Review* 29: 505–641.

Lowi, Theodore J. 1969. *The End of Liberalism*. New York: Norton.

Maass, Arthur. 1951. *Muddy Waters: Army Engineers and the Nation's Rivers*. Cambridge: Harvard University Press.

Macridis, Roy C. 1961. Interest Groups in Comparative Analysis. *Journal of Politics* 23: 25–46.

Mahood, H. R. 1967. Pressure Groups: A Threat to Democracy? In *Pressure Groups in American Politics*, ed. H. R. Mahood. New York: Charles Scribner's Sons.

Majone, Giandomenico. 1989. *Evidence, Argument, and Persuasion in the Policy Process*. New Haven: Yale University Press.

Mansbridge, Jane J. 1992. A Deliberative Theory of Interest Representation. In *The Politics of Interests*, ed. Mark P. Petracca. Boulder: Westview Press.

Mansfield, Edward. 1980. Federal Maritime Commission. In *The Politics of Regulation*, ed. James Q. Wilson. New York: Basic Books.

Manwaring, David. 1962. *Render unto Caesar: The Flag Salute Controversy*. Chicago: University of Chicago Press.

Marwell, Gerald, and Ruth E. Ames. 1979. Experiments on the Provision of Public Goods. I. Resources, Interest, Group Size, and the Free Rider Problem. *American Journal of Sociology* 84: 1335–60.

———. 1980. Experiments on the Provision of Public Goods. II. Provision Points, Stakes, Experiences, and the Free Rider Problem. *American Journal of Sociology* 85: 926–37.

———. 1981. Economists Free Ride, Does Anyone Else? Experiments on the Provision of Public Goods IV. *Journal of Public Economics* 15: 295–310.

Marwell, Gerarld, and Pamela Oliver. 1993. *The Critical Mass in Collective Action*. New York: Cambridge University Press.

Marwell, Gerald, Pamela E. Oliver, and Ralph Prahl. 1988. Social Networks and Collective Action: A Theory of the Critical Mass. III. *American Journal of Sociology* 94: 502–34.

Mason, A. T. 1950. Business Organized as Power: The New Imperium in Imperio. *American Political Science Review* 44: 323–42.

McAdam, Doug. 1982. *Political Process and the Development of Black Insurgency: 1930–1970*. Chicago: University of Chicago Press.

———. 1983. Tactical Innovation and the Pace of Insurgency. *American Sociological Review* 48: 735–54.

———. 1986. Recruitment to High Risk Activism: The Case of Freedom Summer. *American Journal of Sociology* 92: 64–90.

———. 1988. *Freedom Summer*. New York: Oxford University Press.

McAdam, Doug, John D. McCarthy, and Mayer N. Zald, eds. 1996. *Comparative Perspectives on Social Movements: Political Opportunities, Mobilizing Structures, and Cultural Framings*. New York: Cambridge University Press.

McArthur, John, and Steven V. Marks. 1988. Constitutent Interest vs. Legislator Ideology: The Role of Political Opportunity Cost. *Economic Inquiry*, July, 461–70.

McCarthy, John D., and Mayer N. Zald. 1978. Resource Mobilization and Social Movements: A Partial Theory. *American Journal of Sociology* 82: 1212–41.

McConnell, Grant. 1966. *Private Power and American Democracy*. New York: Alfred A. Knopf.

McFarland, Andrew S. 1966. Power, Critical Decisions, and Leadership: An Analysis of Empirical Pluralist Theory. Ph.D. dissertation, University of California, Berkeley.

———. 1969. *Power and Leadership in Pluralist Systems*. Stanford, Calif.: Stanford University Press.

———. 1984. *Common Cause: Lobbying in the Public Interest*. Chatham, NJ: Chatham House.

———. 1987. Interest Groups and Theories of Power in America. *British Journal of Political Science* 17: 129–47.

———. 1991. Interest Groups and Political Time: Cycles in America. *British Journal of Political Science* 21: 257–84.

———. 1993. *Cooperative Pluralism*. Lawrence: University Press of Kansas.

McGuire, Kevin T., and Gregory A. Caldeira. 1993. Lawyers, Organized Interests, and the Law of Obscenity: Agenda Setting in the Supreme Court. *American Political Science Review* 87: 746–55.

McKissick, Gary J. 1995. Interests, Issues, and Emphases: Lobbying Congress and the Strategic Manipulation of Issue Dimensions. Paper presented at the annual meeting of the Midwest Political Science Association, Chicago.

Milbrath, Lester W. 1963. *The Washington Lobbyists*. Chicago: Rand McNally.

Mills, C. Wright. 1956. *The Power Elite*. New York: Oxford University Press.

Mitchell, Robert C. 1979. National Environmental Lobbies and the Apparent Illogic of Collective Action. In *Collective Decision Making: Applications from Public Choice Theory*. ed. Clifford S. Russell. Baltimore, Md.: Johns Hopkins University Press.

———. 1981. From Elite Quarrel to Mass Movement. *Society* 18: 76–84.

Mitchell, William C., and Michael C. Munger. 1991. Economic Models of Interest Groups: An Introductory Survey. *American Journal of Political Science* 35: 512–46.

Moe, Terry M. 1980a. *The Organization of Interests: Incentives and the Internal Dynamics of Political Interest Groups*. Chicago: University of Chicago Press.

———. 1980b. A Calculus of Group Membership. *American Journal of Political Science* 24: 593–632.

———. 1981. Toward a Broader View of Interest Groups. *Journal of Politics* 43: 531–43.

———. 1986. Control and Feedback in Economic Regulation: The Case of the NLRB. *American Political Science Review* 79: 1094–1116.

Morehouse, Sarah McCally. 1981. *State Politics, Parties and Policy*. New York: Holt, Rinehart and Winston.

Morris, Aldon D. 1984. *The Origins of the Civil Rights Movement*. New York: Free Press.

Morris, Aldon D., and Carol McClurg Mueller, eds. 1992. *Frontiers in Social Movement Theory*. New Haven, Conn.: Yale University Press.

Morton, Rebecca B. 1987. A Group Majority Voting Model of Public Good Provision. *Social Choice and Welfare* 4: 117–31.

———. 1991. Groups in Rational Turnout Models. *American Journal of Political Science* 35: 758–76.

Mucciaroni, Gary. 1995. *Reversals of Fortune: Public Policy and Private Interests*. Washington, D.C.: Brookings.

Mueller, Dennis G., and Peter Murrell. 1986. Interest Groups and the Size of Government. *Public Choice* 48: 125–45.

Muller, Edward, and Karl-Dieter Opp. 1986. Rational Choice and Rebellious Collective Action. *American Political Science Review* 80: 471–89.

Muller, Edward, and Karl-Dieter Opp. 1987. Rebellious Collective Action Revisted. *American Political Science Review* 81: 561–64.

Murawski, John. 1996. A Banner Year for Giving. *Chronicle of Philanthropy*. May 30.

Nelson, Barbara J. 1984. *Making an Issue of Child Abuse*. Chicago: University of Chicago Press.

Neustadtl, Alan. 1990. Interest Group PACsmanship: An Analysis of Campaign Contributions, Issue Visibility, and Legislative Impact. *Social Forces* 69: 549–64.

Niskanen, William. 1971. *Bureaucracy and Representative Government*. Chicago: Aldine.

Nownes, Anthony J., and Patricia Freeman. Forthcoming. Interest Group Activity in the States. *Journal of Politics*.

O'Connor, Karen. 1980. *Women's Organizations' Use of the Courts*. Lexington, Mass.: Lexington Books.

O'Connor, Karen, and Lee Epstein. 1982. Amicus Curiae Participation in U.S. Supreme Court Litigation: An Appraisal of Hakman's "Folklore." *Law and Society Review* 16: 311–20.

———. 1983. The Rise of Conservative Interest Group Litigation. *Journal of Politics* 45: 479–89.

O'Neill, Timothy. 1985. *Bakke and the Politics of Equality: Friends and Foes in the Classroom of Litigation*. Middletown, Conn.: Wesleyan University Press.

Odegard, Peter H. 1928. *Pressure Politics: The Story of the Anti-Saloon League*. New York: Columbia University Press.

Oliver, Pamela E., Gerald Marwell, and Ruy Teixeira. 1985. A Theory of the Critical Mass. I. Interdependence, Group Heterogeneity, and the Production of Collective Goods. *American Journal of Sociology* 91: 522–56.

Olsen, Johan P. 1983. *Organized Democracy*. Bergen: Universitetsforlaget.

Olson, Mancur, Jr. 1965. *The Logic of Collective Action*. Cambridge: Harvard University Press.

———. 1979. Group Size and Contributions to Collective Action: A Response. *Research in Social Movements, Conflicts and Change* 2: 149–50.

———. 1982. *The Rise and Decline of Nations*. New Haven, Conn.: Yale University Press.

———. 1986. A Theory of the Incentives Facing Political Organizations: Neo-Corporatism and the Hegemonic State. *International Political Science Review* 7: 165–89.

Olson, Susan. 1984. *Clients and Lawyers: Securing the Rights of Disabled Persons*. Westport, Conn.: Greenwood Press.

———. 1990. Interest Group Litigation in Federal District Court: Beyond the Political Disadvantage Theory. *Journal of Politics* 52: 854–82.

Orren, Karen. 1976. Standing to Sue: Interest Group Conflict in the Federal Courts. *American Political Science Review* 70: 723–41.

Ostrom, Elinor. 1990. *Governing the Commons: The Evolution of Institutions for Collective Action*. New York: Cambridge University Press.

Overby, L. Marvin, Beth M. Henschen, Michael H. Walsh, and Julie Strauss. 1992. Courting Constituents? An Analysis of the Senate Confirmation Vote on Justice Clarence Thomas. *American Political Science Review* 86: 997–1003.

Paige, Jeffrey M. 1975. *Agrarian Revolution: Social Movements and Export Agriculture in the Underdeveloped World*. New York: Free Press.

Paolino, Phillip. 1995. Group-Salient Issues and Group Repesentation: Support for Women in the 1992 Senate Elections. *American Journal of Political Science* 39: 294–313.

Peltzman, Sam. 1976. Toward a More General Theory of Regulation. *Journal of Law and Economics* 19: 211–40.

———. 1984. Constituent Interest and Congressional Voting. *Journal of Law and Economics* 27: 181–210.

Peterson, Paul E. 1970. Forms of Representation: Participation of the Poor in the Community Action Program. *American Political Science Review* 64: 491–507.

Petracca, Mark P., ed. 1992a. *The Politics of Interests.* Boulder: Westview Press.

———. 1992b. The Rediscovery of Interest Group Politics. In *The Politics of Interests*, ed. Mark P. Petracca. Boulder: Westview Press.

———. 1992c. The Changing State of Interest Group Research: A Review and Commentary. In *The Politics of Interests*, ed. Mark P. Petracca. Boulder: Westview Press.

Pollack, James K. 1927. Regulation of Lobbying. *American Political Science Review* 21: 335–41.

Pollack, James K., Edward B. Logan, and Edward P. Costigan. 1933. *Lobbying.* Chicago: University of Chicago Press.

Polsby, Nelson W. 1963. *Community Power and Political Theory.* New Haven, Conn.: Yale University Press.

Posner, Richard A. 1974. Theories of Economic Regulation. *Bell Journal of Economics and Management Science* 5: 335–58.

Putnam, Robert D. 1993. *Making Democracy Work.* Princeton, N.J.: Princeton University Press.

———. 1994. Bowling Alone: Democracy in America at the End of the Twentieth Century. Paper presented at the Nobel Symposium "Democracy's Victory and Crisis," Uppsala, Sweden, August 27–30.

———. 1995. Tuning In, Tuning Out: The Strange Disappearance of Social Capital in America. *PS* 28: 664–83.

Quinn, Dennis P., and Robert Y. Shapiro. 1991. Business Political Power: The Case of Taxation. *American Political Science Review* 85: 851–74.

Rauch, Jonathan. 1994. *Demosclerosis: The Silent Killer of American Government.* New York: Random House.

Redford, Emmette S. 1969. *Democracy in the Administrative State.* New York: Oxford University Press.

Richardson, Jeremy J., ed. 1982. *Policy Styles in Western Europe.* Boston: Allen and Unwin.

———, ed. 1993. *Pressure Groups.* New York: Oxford University Press.

Richardson, Jeremy J., and A. G. Jordon. 1979. *Governing under Pressure.* Oxford: Martin.

Riker, William H. 1964. Some Ambiguities in the Notion of Power. *American Political Science Review* 58: 341–49.

———. 1983. Political Theory and the Art of Heresthetics. In *Political Science: The State of the Discipline*, ed. Ada Finifter. Washington, D.C.: American Political Science Association.

———. 1984. The Heresthetics of Constitution-Making: The Presidency in 1787, with Comments on Determinism and Rational Choice. *American Political Science Review* 78: 1–16.

———. 1986. *The Art of Political Manipulation.* New Haven, Conn.: Yale University Press.

———. 1988. *Liberalism against Populism.* Prospect Heights, Ill.: Waveland Press.

———. 1990. Heresthetic and Rhetoric in the Spatial Model. In *Advances in the Spatial Theory of Voting*, ed. James M. Enelow and Melvin J. Hinich. New York: Cambridge University Press.

Riker, William H. 1996. *The Strategy of Rhetoric*. New Haven, Conn.: Yale University Press.

Riley, Dennis D. 1990. Of Subgovernments and Issue Networks: Just One More Time. Paper presented at the annual meeting of the Southern Political Science Association, Atlanta.

Rokkan, Stein. 1966. Norway: Numerical Democracy and Corporate Pluralism. In *Political Oppositions in Western Democracies*, ed. Robert A. Dahl. New Haven, Conn.: Yale University Press.

Rosenstone, Steven J., and John Mark Hansen. 1993. *Mobilization, Participation, and Democracy in America*. New York: Macmillan.

Rosenthal, Alan. 1992. *The Third House: Lobbyists and Lobbying in the States*. Washington, D.C.: Congressional Quarterly.

Rothenberg, Lawrence S. 1988. Organizational Maintenance and the Retention Decision in Groups. *American Political Science Review* 82: 1129–52.

———. 1992. *Linking Citizens to Government: Interest Group Politics at Common Cause*. New York: Cambridge University Press.

———. 1993. Review of Petracca, *The Politics of Interests*. *Journal of Politics* 55: 1165–7.

———1994. *Regulation, Organizations, and Politics: Motor Freight Policy at the Interstate Commerce Commission*. Ann Arbor: University of Michigan Press.

Sabatier, Paul A. 1988. An Advocacy Coalition Framework of Policy Change and the Role of Policy-Oriented Learning Therein. *Policy Sciences* 21: 129–68.

———. 1992. Interest Group Membership and Organization: Multiple Theories. In *The Politics of Interests*, ed. Mark P. Petracca. Boulder, Colo.: Westview.

Sabatier, Paul A., and Hank C. Jenkins-Smith. 1993. *Policy Change and Learning*. Boulder, Colo.: Westview Press.

Sabatier, Paul A., and Susan McLaughlin. 1990. Belief Congruence between Interest Group Leaders and Members: An Empirical Analysis of Three Theories and a Suggested Synthesis. *Journal of Politics* 52: 914–35.

Salamon, Lester M., and John J. Siegfried. 1977. Economic Power and Political Influence: The Impact of Industry Structure on Public Policy. *American Political Science Review* 71: 1026–43.

Salisbury, Robert H. 1969. An Exchange Theory of Interest Groups. *Midwest Journal of Political Science* 13: 1–32.

———, ed. 1970. *Interest Group Politics in America*. New York: Harper and Row.

———. 1975. Interest Groups. In *Nongovernmental Politics*. Vol. 4 of *Handbook of Political Science*, ed. Fred I. Greenstein and Nelson W. Polsby. Reading, Mass.: Addison-Wesley.

———. 1983. Interest Groups: Toward a New Understanding. In *Interest Group Politics*. 1st ed., ed. Allan J. Ciglar and Burdett A. Loomis. Washington, D.C.: Congressional Quarterly.

———. 1984. Interest Representation: The Dominance of Institutions. *American Political Science Review* 78: 64–76.

———. 1990. The Paradox of Interests in Washington D.C.: More Groups and Less Clout. In *The New American Political System*. 2d ed., ed. Anthony S. King. Washington: American Enterprise Institute.

———. 1994. Interest Structures and Policy Domains: A Focus for Research. In

*Representing Interests and Interest Group Representation*, ed. William Crotty, Mildred A. Schwartz, and John C. Green. Washington, D.C.: University Press of America.

———. 1995. On the Concept of Interest Group Member. Paper presented at the annual meeting of the Midwest Political Science Association, Chicago.

Saltzman, Gregory M. 1987. Congressional Voting on Labor Issues: The Role of PACs. *Industrial and Labor Relations Review* 40: 163–79.

Sandler, Todd. 1992. *Collective Action: Theory and Applications*. Ann Arbor: University of Michigan Press.

Schattschneider, E. E. 1935. *Politics, Pressures, and the Tariff*. New York: Prentice-Hall.

———. 1960. *The Semi-Sovereign People*. New York: Holt, Rinehart and Winston.

Scheppele, Kim Lane, and Jack L. Walker, Jr. 1991. The Litigation Strategies of Interest Groups. In *Mobilizing Interest Groups in America* by Jack L. Walker, Jr. Ann Arbor: University of Michigan Press.

Schlozman, Kay Lehman. 1984. What Accent the Heavenly Chorus? Political Equality and the American Pressure System. *Journal of Politics* 46: 1006–32.

Schlozman, Kay Lehman, and John T. Tierney. 1983. More of the Same: Washington Pressure Group Activity in a Decade of Change. *Journal of Politics* 45: 351–77.

———. 1986. *Organized Interests and American Democracy*. New York: Harper and Row.

Schlozman, Kay Lehman, and Sidney Verba. 1979. *Injury to Insult: Unemployment, Class, and Political Response*. Cambridge: Harvard University Press.

Schlozman, Kay Lehman, Sidney Verba, and Henry E. Brady. 1995. Participation's Not a Paradox: The View from American Activists. *British Journal of Political Science* 25: 1–36.

Schmidt, Vivien A. 1996. *From State to Market? The Transformation of French Business and Government*. New York: Cambridge University Press.

Schmitter, Philippe C. 1974. Still the Century of Corporatism? *Review of Politics* 36: 85–131.

Schmitter, Philippe C., and Gerhard Lehmbruch, eds. 1979. *Trends Towards Corporatist Intermediation*. Beverly Hills, Calif.: Sage.

Scholz, John T., and Feng Heng Wei. 1986. Regulatory Enforcement in a Federalist System. *American Political Science Review* 80: 1249–70.

Schriftgiesser, Karl. 1951. *The Lobbyists: The Art and Business of Influencing Lawmakers*. Boston: Little, Brown.

Schroedel, Jean Reith. 1986. Campaign Contributions and Legislative Outcomes. *Western Political Quarterly* 40: 371–89.

Scott, Andrew M., and Margaret A. Hunt. 1965. *Congress and Lobbies: Image and Reality*. Chapel Hill: University of North Carolina Press.

Segal, Jeffrey A., Charles M. Cameron, and Albert D. Cover. 1992. A Spatial Model of Roll Call Voting: Senators, Constituents, Presidents, and Interest Groups in Supreme Court Confirmations. *American Journal of Political Science* 36: 96–121.

Selznick, Philip. 1949. *TVA and the Grass Roots*. Berkeley: University of California Press.

Shapiro, Martin. 1990. Interest Groups and Supreme Court Appointments. *Northwestern University Law Review* 84: 935–61.

Shott, John G. 1950. *The Railroad Monopoly: An Instrument of Banker Control of the American Economy*. Washington, D.C.: Public Affairs Institute.

Silberman, Jonathan I., and Garey C. Durden. 1976. Determining Legislative Preferences on the Minimum Wage: An Economic Approach. *Journal of Political Economy* 84: 317–29.

Skocpol, Theda, Marjorie Abend-Wein, Christopher Howard, and Susan Goodrich Lehmann. 1993. Women's Associations and the Enactment of Mothers' Pensions in the United States. *American Political Science Review* 87: 686–701.

Smith, Richard A. 1984. Advocacy, Interpretation, and Influence in the U.S. Congress. *American Political Science Review* 78: 44–63.

———. 1993. Agreement, Defection, and Interest-Group Influence in the U.S. Congress. In *Agenda Formation*, ed. William H. Riker. Ann Arbor: University of Michigan Press.

———. 1995. Interest Group Influence in the U.S. Congress. *Legislative Studies Quarterly* 20: 89–139.

Sorauf, Frank J. 1976. *The Wall of Separation: Constitutional Politics of Church and State*. Princeton, N.J.: Princeton University Press.

———. 1992. *Inside Campaign Finance*. New Haven, Conn.: Yale University Press.

Stehle, Vince. 1995. European Volunteerism Trails U.S. *Chronicle of Philanthropy*, 27 July, 14–15.

Stigler, George. 1971. The Theory of Economic Regulation. *Bell Journal of Economics and Management Science* 2: 3–21.

———. 1972. Economic Competition and Political Competition. *Public Choice* 13: 91–106.

———. 1974. Free Riders and Collective Action. *Bell Journal of Economics and Management Science* 5: 359–65.

Stone, Deborah A. 1988. *Policy Paradox and Political Reason*. Glenview, Ill.: Scott, Foresman.

Stratmann, Thomas. 1991. What do Campaign Contributions Buy? Deciphering Causal Effects of Money and Votes. *Southern Economic Journal* 57: 606–20.

Suleiman, Ezra N. 1974. *Politics, Power, and the Bureaucracy in France*. Princeton, N.J.: Princeton University Press.

Tarrow, Sidney. 1994. *Power in Movement: Social Movements, Collective Action, and Politics*. New York: Cambridge University Press.

Taylor, Michael. 1987. *The Possibility of Cooperation*. New York: Cambridge University Press.

———, ed. 1988. *Rationality and Revolution*. New York: Oxford University Press.

Tillock, Harriet, and Denton E. Morrison. 1979. Group Size and Contribution to Collective Action: A Test of Mancur Olson's Theory on Zero Population Growth, Inc. *Research in Social Movements, Conflict, and Change* 2: 131–58.

Tilly, Charles. 1978. *From Mobilization to Revolution*. Reading, Mass.: Addison-Wesley.

———. 1986. *The Contentious French*. Cambridge: Harvard University Press.

Trivers, Robert L. 1971. The Evolution of Reciprocal Altruism. *Quarterly Review of Biology* 46: 35–57.

Truman, David B. 1951. *The Governmental Process: Political Interests and Public Opinion*. New York: Alfred A. Knopf.

Tullock, Gordon. 1967. The Welfare Costs of Tariffs, Monopolies, and Theft. *Western Economic Journal* 5: 224–32.

———. 1988. *Wealth, Poverty, and Politics*. New York: Basil Blackwell.

Turner, Henry A. 1958. How Pressure Groups Operate. *Annals of the American Academy of Political and Social Science* 319: 63–72.

Turner, John C. 1982. Towards a Cognitive Redefinition of the Social Group. In *Social Identity and Intergroup Relations*, ed. Henri Tajfel. New York: Cambridge University Press.

Uhlaner, Carole J. 1989. Rational Turnout: The Neglected Role of Groups. *American Journal of Political Science* 33: 390–422.

Verba, Sidney, and Norman H. Nie. 1972. *Participation in America*. New York: Harper and Row.

Verba, Sidney, Kay Lehman Schlozman, and Henry E. Brady. 1995. *Voice and Equality: Civic Voluntarism in American Politics*. Cambridge: Harvard University Press.

Vesenka, Mary H. 1989. Economic Interests and Ideological Conviction: A Note on PACs and Agriculture Acts. *Journal of Economic Behavior and Organization* 12: 259–63.

Vogel, David. 1989. *Fluctuating Fortunes: The Political Power of Business in America*. New York: Basic Books.

Vose, Clement. 1957. National Consumers' League and the Brandeis Brief. *Midwest Journal of Political Science* 1: 178–90.

———. 1959. *Caucasians Only*. Berkeley: University of California Press.

———1972. *Constitutional Change*. Lexington, Mass.: Lexington Books.

Walker, Jack L., Jr. 1966a. A Critique of the Elitist Theory of Democracy. *American Political Science Review* 60: 285–95.

———. 1966b. A Reply to "Further Reflections on 'The Elitist Theory of Democracy.'" *American Political Science Review* 60: 391–2.

———. 1983. The Origins and Maintenance of Interest Groups in America. *American Political Science Review* 77: 390–406.

———. 1991. *Mobilizing Interest Groups in America*. Ann Arbor: University of Michigan Press.

Walsh, Edward J., and Rex H. Warland. 1983. Social Movement Involvement in the Wake of a Nuclear Accident: Activists and Free Riders in the TMI Area. *American Sociological Review* 48: 764–80.

Wayman, Frank Whelon. 1985. Arms Control and Strategic Arms Voting in the U.S. Senate: Patterns of Change, 1967–1983. *Journal of Conflict Resolution* 29: 225–51.

Welch, William P. 1982. Campaign Contributions and Legislative Voting: Milk Money and Dairy Price Supports. *Western Political Quarterly* 35: 478–95.

Wiggins, Charles W., Keith E. Hamm, and Charles G. Bell. 1992. Interest Group and Party Influence Agents in the Legislative Process: A Comparative State Analysis. *Journal of Politics* 54: 82–100.

Wilhite, Allen. 1988. Union PAC Contributions and Legislative Voting. *Journal of Labor Research* 9: 79–90.

Wilhite, Allen, and John Theilman. 1987. Labor PAC Contributions and Labor Legislation: A Simultaneous Logit Approach. *Public Choice* 53: 267–76.

Wilsford, David. 1991. *Doctors and the State: The Politics of Health Care in France and the United States*. Durham, N.C.: Duke University Press.

Wilson, Frank L. 1987. *Interest-Group Politics in France*. New York: Cambridge University Press.

Wilson, James Q. 1973. *Political Organizations*. New York: Basic Books.

Wilson, James Q. 1989. *Bureaucracy: What Government Agencies Do and Why They Do It*. New York: Basic Books.

Wilson, James Q. 1995. *Political Organizations*. 2d ed. Princeton, N.J.: Princeton University Press.

Wittenberg, Ernest, and Elisabeth Wittenberg. 1994. *How to Win in Washington*. 2d ed. Cambridge: Basil Blackwell.

Wolpe, Bruce C. 1990. *Lobbying Congress: How the System Works*. Washington, D.C.: CQ Press.

Wright, C. R., and H. H. Hyman. 1958. Voluntary Association Membership of American Adults. *American Sociological Review* 23: 284–94.

Wright, John R. 1985. PACs, Contributions, and Roll Calls: An Organizational Perspective. *American Political Science Review* 79: 400–414.

Wright, John R. 1990. Contributions, Lobbying, and Committee Voting in the U.S. House of Representatives. *American Political Science Review* 84: 417–38.

Wright, Quincy. 1950. Political Science and World Stabilization. *American Political Science Review* 44: 1–13.

Wuthnow, Robert, 1991. The Voluntary Sector: Legacy of the Past, Hope for the Future. In Robert Wuthnow, ed., *Between States and Markets: The Voluntary Sector in Comparative Perspective*. Princeton, N.J.: Princeton University Press.

Zald, Mayer N., and John D. McCarthy, eds. 1979. *The Dynamics of Social Movements*. Cambridge: Winthrop.

Zald, Mayer N., and John D. McCarthy. 1980. Social Movement Industries: Competition and Cooperation among Movement Organizations. *Research in Social Movements, Conflicts, and Change* 3: 1–20.

———, eds. 1986. *Social Movements in an Organization Society*. New Brunswick, N.J.: Transaction Books.

Zeigler, L. Harmon. 1964. *Interest Groups in American Society*. Englewood Cliffs, N.J.: Prentice-Hall.

Zeigler, L. Harmon, and G. Wayne Peak. 1972. *Interest Groups in American Politics*. 2d ed. Englewood Cliffs, N.J.: Prentice-Hall.

Zeigler, L. Harmon, and Hendrik Van Dalen. 1976. Interest Groups in State Politics. In *Politics in the American States*, ed. Herbert Jacob and Kenneth N. Vines. 3d ed. Boston: Little, Brown.

Zeller, Belle. 1937. *Pressure Politics in New York*. New York: Prentice-Hall.

# Index

Abend-Wein, Marjorie, 130, 135
Aberbach, Joel D., 49
access. *See* political access
agenda setting, 37–41, 59, 108, 123, 141–142, 155–157, 178, 183
agricultural policy, 10, 56, 98, 112, 124, 137, 150, 170, 178, 184–185
Ainsworth, Scott, 37
Almond, Gabriel A., 49, 91
*American Political Science Review*, 45, 64–66, 175–176
American Red Cross, 91
Ames, Ruth E., 72
amicus curiae, 35, 94, 141–144
Anton, Thomas J., 49
*APSR. See American Political Science Review*
Army Corps of Engineers, 61, 122
Arnold, R. Douglas, xvii–xviii, 4–6
Association of American Universities, 31–32
Austen-Smith, David, 37, 136, 141
Axelrod, Robert, 73, 177

Babchuck, Nicholas, 30
Bacheller, John M., 138
Bachrach, Peter, 59–60
Baer, Douglas E., 30, 91
Bailey, Stephen Kemp, 56
Banks, Jeffrey S., 144
Baratz, Morton, 59–60
Barker, Lucius, 142
Bauer, Raymond A., 60–62, 126–128, 149, 155
Baumgartner, Frank R., 4, 11, 16, 29, 30, 40, 48, 49, 74, 90, 91, 97, 108, 110, 112, 114, 116, 122, 127, 137, 170, 183
Becker, Gary S., 23, 66
Bell, Charles G., 104
Bendor, Jonathan, 144
Bentley, Arthur F., 23, 45, 48
Bernstein, Marver H., 121, 126, 144
Berry, Jeffrey M., 4, 9, 48, 70, 93, 101, 113, 114, 121, 124, 148, 149, 152, 153, 156, 162–163, 170
bias in the group system, 3, 7–9, 45, 52–58,

80–82, 85–99, 106, 108–112, 115, 117–119, 166, 169
Bikhchandani, Sushil, 76
Birkby, Robert, 142
Black, Hugo, 84
Blaisdell, Donald. C., 86, 94
Blum, Debra E., 92
Booth, Alan, 30
Bosso, Christopher J., 10, 31, 32, 108, 114, 124, 137
Bradsher, Keith, 98
Brady, Henry E., 8, 30, 58, 79, 87, 90–92, 113–114, 173
Broadbent, Jeffrey, 11
Brown, Bernard E., 49
Brown, Kirk F., 14
Browne, William P., 10, 29, 48, 60, 66, 124, 140, 144, 157, 167, 170, 177, 178
Brudney, Jeffrey L., 145
Brunk, Gregory G., 173
Buchanan, James, 23
Burns, James MacGregor, 86
business advantage in the group system, 9, 61, 67, 84, 92–99, 102, 105–114, 118, 129, 178, 184–185
By-product theory, 9, 75, 158
Byrd, Robert C., 85

Caldeira, Gregory A., 9, 94, 141–142
Cameron, Charles M., 130, 141
Casper, Jonathan, 142
Cater, Douglass, 57, 98, 121–123
Chamberlin, John, 73–74
Chappell, Henry W. Jr., 14, 132
charities, 89, 91–92, 116–117
Chong, Dennis, 8, 9, 76, 140, 178
Chubb, John E., 60, 86, 144
Cigler, Allan J., 4, 7–8, 14–15, 20, 66, 73, 134
civil rights, 42, 73, 76, 88, 96, 105–108, 140, 178
Clark, Peter B., 68, 69
Cleiber, Dennis, 14
Cleveland, Frederick A., 84
Clymer, Adam, 85

About the authors

**Frank R. Baumgartner** is Professor of Political Science at
Texas A&M University. He is the author of *Conflict and Rhetoric in
French Policymaking* and coauthor (with Bryan Jones) of *Agendas and
Instability in American Politics*. **Beth L. Leech** is a Ph.D. candidate
in Political Science at Texas A&M.

DATE DUE

GAYLORD

PRINTED IN U.S.A.